W0246914

PORTFOLIO

# SHE WALKS, SHE LEADS

Gunjan Jain is a bestselling author, investment banker and lifelong student of mindfulness. She is a graduate from the University of Illinois at Urbana–Champaign (USA) in economics and finance, and has earned her master's in wealth management from the Cass Business School, City, University of London (UK).

Gunjan also holds a diploma in image management from the London Image Institute as well as the Academy of Image Mastery in Singapore. She has received a diploma in international etiquette and protocol from the Institut Villa Pierrefeu in Switzerland. She also holds a master practitioner's degree in Neuro-Linguistic Programming from the Society of NLP (USA). She has completed a study abroad session at the London School of Economics and Political Science, studying economics and management as part of her undergraduate studies.

In May 2017, Gunjan was felicitated with the WEF 2017 Award for 'Women of the Decade in Community Leadership' for her inspirational journey and work on *She Walks, She Leads*. She has also been honoured with the Award De Excellencia at the Women Excellence Awards by World Peace and Diplomacy Organization (WPDO) in 2017 and a WCRC Leaders Asia's Pride For Women award for Author of the Year in 2016.

Gunjan is currently working on her first work of fiction, which is a tale of love, loss and redemption. She is also working on a book that aims to help women pursue success without having to compromise on other aspects of their lives, and to establish a deeper connection with their own selves. Gunjan enjoys travelling and has been to thirty-two countries so far; she hopes to strike them all off her list someday. She divides her time between her homes in Mumbai and Kolkata, and enjoys reading when she isn't writing.

# PRAISE FOR THE BOOK

'I have always believed that women possess greater creative power than men. The power to give birth to new life places them on a higher pedestal. However, in modern times, more and more women are also demonstrating that they can excel even in those areas of public life—business, diplomacy, research, philanthropy, national leadership, etc.—that are traditionally regarded as male domains. All the women Gunjan Jain has so marvellously profiled in her book *She Walks, She Leads* are inspiring role models who prove that there is no such thing as a glass ceiling for those with talent and determination to reach higher summits of success. It is society's responsibility to create a supportive environment for every aspiring daughter, sister, wife, mother, friend and colleague, so that women's unleashed creative power can transform mankind as a whole. I wholeheartedly recommend this book to both men and women, in India and all over the world.'

—MUKESH D. AMBANI,
chairman and managing director, Reliance Industries Limited

'*She Walks, She Leads* brings to the fore fascinating profiles of leading Indian women who have carved a niche for themselves in a multitude of sectors. It is an interesting and eclectic mix. Many of these are moving stories of hope, of women achievers in the midst of grappling with life's challenges, given their multiple roles. Sheer guts and grit have seen them through. Quite a few of these brave women have moved out of the shadows of their mentors—men who had stoked their ambitions and helped propel their careers. And indeed done amazingly well. Gunjan Jain has scripted these stories splendidly, capturing the nuances and expressions that have gender agnostic takes.'

—KUMAR MANGALAM BIRLA,
chairman, Aditya Birla Group

'Women make up half of our country's population and if we can unlock their creativity it will create a quantum leap in the economy. Gunjan Jain has used the stories of extremely talented women of India who have mastered not only their own fields but have a much wider impact on the environment. Each story profiled in the book will be an inspiration to others and help the readers in their own growth. A woman has that expression natural to her—a cadence of behaviour, producing the poetry of life. The well-written and inspirational stories are of women who are like the vital health of a nation, not only imparting the bloom of beauty but joy to the mind and perfection to life.'

—AJAY PIRAMAL,
chairman, Piramal Group

'This book is not just about the sixteen women who have shared their stories. It is as much about those who have supported them, encouraged them and stood by them. It is equally about those who have lent their voice to each story through their comments, insights and perspectives. A colossal collection of some of the greatest minds and hearts of our times.'

—ADI GODREJ,
chairman, Godrej Group

'*She Walks, She Leads* is a moving chronicle of the struggle that women have to undertake to achieve their full potential. It will be an inspiration to all women; but its ultimate contribution could well be that it brings home the enormous benefits to be reaped by fully realizing the shining potential of half the human race. This book is a great step forward for gender equality in the Indian corporate world.'

—ANAND MAHINDRA,
chairman and managing director, Mahindra Group

'*She Walks, She Leads: Women Who Inspire India* is a remarkable collection of stories tracing the extra mile that women walk to sustain their leadership in assorted careers—from business to entertainment and sports. The stories, enriched through in-depth interviews with family, friends and professional contacts, I would say, have a universal appeal that should inspire all to walk those extra miles towards an accomplished life and for posterity. Gunjan Jain has a fine ability to express the nuances of one's life to inspire all.'

—DEEPAK PAREKH,
chairman, HDFC Group

'*She Walks, She Leads* is certain to speak to women—those in fledgling careers, those struggling up the ladder, even those nearly at the top. But equally, it is a book for men. A valuable collection that sensitizes them to the many struggles any professional woman inevitably has to face.'

—N.R. NARAYANA MURTHY,
founder, Infosys Limited

'The recent gender changes that are taking place in the leading corporates around the globe are transforming the face of the corporate world across geographies. This is as significant as the paradigm shift that is taking place in technology—both are bound to have a profound impact on the global economic scene and our way of life in future years. Gunjan Jain has done an immense service in trying to capture this change process through the stories of the rise to leadership of the brightest women in the corporate world. The book is significant not only because of the lucid style of narration and the meticulous research which provides authenticity to the narration, but also because of the scope it offers for a more detailed analysis of this change process. The book would be of interest to the present generation who are familiar with the personalities and for the generation next for the inspiration it offers for emulation.'

—NARAYANAN VAGHUL,
former ICICI Bank chairman and philanthropist

'*She Walks, She Leads* is an outstanding book giving us a great perspective of sixteen outstanding achievers. Gunjan Jain does a marvellous job of walking us through these personal stories told from a number of perspectives, and she leads us to a zone of self-discovery about leadership as a practice. This is storytelling and leadership lessons at their very best.'

—D. SHIVAKUMAR,
chairman and CEO, PepsiCo India Holdings Pvt. Ltd

'Gunjan Jain's book is as much a testament relevant to our times as it is to her talent as a biographer and writer. She displays an extraordinarily perceptive ability to capture, so succinctly, the essence of a person she is writing about. It is a refreshing narration of women who have bravely set out to become role models for young India. The book is inspirational; not only for young women but also for corporate leaders and those who aspire to be agents of transformation.'

—R.K. KRISHNA KUMAR,
trustee, Tata Trusts

'Gunjan Jain has written absorbing stories about these super-achievers. *She Walks, She Leads* is distinctive because it focuses not just on the triumphs, but equally on the hazardous paths that lead to them; it looks at the storms weathered by each of these women and provides a compelling understanding of what makes them who they are—legends of their times.'

—RAGHAV BAHL,
founder of Quintillion Media and Network18 Pvt. Ltd

'Gunjan has captured fascinating stories of some of the leading and iconic ladies in today's era with sincerity. Each of the stories is relatable to the individual. *She Walks, She Leads* not only inspires women but also men.'

—CYRIL SHROFF,
managing partner, Cyril Amarchand Mangaldas

'We lack role models in India and more so when it comes to the incredible achievements that women have made in such diverse fields. I hope this book is a beacon for many, many young women driven to make an impact in our country and around the world.'

—RONNIE SCREWVALA,
founder of UTV Group and Unilazer Ventures

'Gunjan has done outstanding research and the product is truly amazing. I would recommend that you go through the book and the inspiring personalities featured.'

—SANJIV GOENKA,
chairman, RP-Sanjiv Goenka Group

'IMF chief Christine Lagarde recently said, "Women's empowerment is not just a fundamentally moral cause, it is also an absolute economic no-brainer." Gunjan's wonderful book that chronicles the stories of sixteen women who have leaned in, defied stereotypes and conventions, and inspired men and women alike with their achievements, is a reinforcement of the moral and economic imperatives for gender equality.'

—BAHRAM VAKIL,
partner, AZB & Partners

'Oprah Winfrey once said, "The key to realizing a dream is to focus not on success but significance—and then even the small steps and little victories along your path will take on greater meaning." With interview-based profiles of a few of India's most successful women, Gunjan Jain does just that.'

—GITA PIRAMAL,
business historian and author

'This book is a must-read for every young man who aspires to be a leader of people and ideas.'

—SUBROTO BAGCHI,
co-founder and chairman, Mindtree

'*She Walks, She Leads* is a powerful collection of stories that captures the journeys and struggles of some of India's most inspiring women. From these narratives emerge the importance of courage, drive and determination, impressing the passion of leadership upon future generations.'

—SHASHI THAROOR,
MP, Lok Sabha

'*She Walks, She Leads* inspires women to create the lives they want to lead, to be leaders at work, to be partners at home, and be motivated towards social change. Gunjan provides pragmatic stories on iconic women who have led these lives and created change. I hope men and women will read the book, to be inspired, and appreciate the journey taken to accomplishment by women across sectors and age groups. The book will help us lead the lives we wish to lead and the world we want to live in.'

—SUBHASH CHANDRA,
chairman, Essel Group and ZEE

# SHE WALKS, SHE LEADS

## WOMEN WHO INSPIRE INDIA

# GUNJAN JAIN

PORTFOLIO
PENGUIN

An imprint of Penguin Random House

PORTFOLIO

USA | Canada | UK | Ireland | Australia
New Zealand | India | South Africa | China | Singapore

Portfolio is part of the Penguin Random House group of companies
whose addresses can be found at global.penguinrandomhouse.com

Published by Penguin Random House India Pvt. Ltd
4th Floor, Capital Tower 1, MG Road,
Gurugram 122 002, Haryana, India

Penguin
Random House
India

First published in Viking by Penguin Random House India 2016
This edition published in Portfolio by Penguin Random House India 2019

Copyright © Gunjan Jain 2016, 2019

All rights reserved

10 9 8 7 6 5 4 3 2

The views and opinions expressed in this book are the author's own and the facts
are as reported by her which have been verified to the extent possible, and the
publishers are not in any way liable for the same.

ISBN 9780143448921

Typeset in Perpetua by Manipal Technologies Limited, Manipal

Printed at Repro India Limited

This book is sold subject to the condition that it shall not, by way of trade
or otherwise, be lent, resold, hired out, or otherwise circulated without the
publisher's prior consent in any form of binding or cover other than that in
which it is published and without a similar condition including this condition
being imposed on the subsequent purchaser.

www.penguin.co.in

MIX
Paper from
responsible sources
FSC® C047271

This is a legitimate digitally printed version of the book and therefore might not
have certain extra finishing on the cover.

*To my parents*

*for making me believe anything was possible*
*and for making everything possible for me*

*I am because of you.*

# CONTENTS

# INTRODUCTION

.

*Let yourself be silently drawn by the strange pull of what you really love*

**RUMI**

.

*A*cts of courage by women often go unnoticed.

The world is awed by an influential woman's positions of power, but it knows little about her journey, her sacrifices, the hurdles she crossed and the constant battles she fights. The primary message she gets from society is that success for a woman—personal or professional—is an exception and not the rule. Even from a place of influence, an Indian woman still inhabits a largely patriarchal workplace where gender discrimination exists. In a world that never expects a man to prove his allegiance to his family in pursuit of his career, a woman has to demonstrate, at every step, that she can balance both without compromising either.

The Indian woman today faces unique challenges at every step within her own home and outside of it. Ours is a country that worships the mother goddess but shuns the girl child. An Indian girl with any trace of ambition has a long, hard road ahead of her and yet, there has never been any lack of incredible Indian women who set out to realize their most audacious dreams—whether in the past or the present. As an ambitious Indian woman myself, I am passionate about and determined to decode their stories. The genesis of this book lies in my admiration for the woman achiever, who has scaled the summits in every field—finance, media, Bollywood, the arts, the corporate world and sports. What I want is to tell the story of how they got there.

## HOW IT ALL STARTED

Before I started researching the lives of successful women, my mother taught me the meaning of feminism and courage—she was a strong and confident woman in a patriarchal set-up. From her, I learnt that achievement does not arrive on its own and sit lightly on the shoulders. Achievement and success have to be sought out and fought for on a daily basis. For all the fights I have seen her pick and win, my mother remains my greatest influence. She ensured that I had every opportunities I wanted, and she pushed me to study all those subjects traditionally seen as 'boys'' subjects.

When I returned from the UK in 2006 with a degree in finance, I was trained for a career in investment banking. Soon, I was consumed by the pace and intensity of my work. Investment banking is a difficult yet exhilarating career. While I loved the rush of the work, I don't think I fully anticipated the long hours, the hard work without much downtime. Hence, I devised a morning routine involving a meditation practice fairly early in my career. Practicing mindfulness helped me see what was really going on inside my mind and cope with thoughts that were dragging me down.

It was during one of these early morning meditation sessions that I realized that I was slowly gripped by a growing feeling of emptiness. I was unconvinced, almost bored, by the idea of numbers and felt a tug towards something 'larger'. Looking around for inspiration, I became engrossed in the success stories of the many Indian women making national and international headlines. I read the interviews they gave and the profiles written about them, but they felt incomplete. These pieces spoke of grand achievements but did not detail the many subtleties that contributed to their success. Of particular interest was one question—what had driven these women to pursue exceptional lives and careers?

Growing up, I loved books. They opened my eyes to the myriad possibilities that life holds for each one of us. To write a book is always a huge decision, but I had no clue just how monumental the task ahead of me would be. In retrospect, this was a blessing in disguise. If I had known the distance I would have to go with it, fear may have stopped me from taking that leap of faith. In that moment, I just knew I had to surrender to my vision and let it guide me to the path—and the people—who would help me bring it to fruition.

As I write this, I realize that it is fitting that all sixteen women profiled in this book had also set out in pursuit of success with determination and faith. In some way, this book's journey—and mine as an author—has echoed theirs. Meeting each of them offered me a rare opportunity and the strength to discover people and territory that were new to me. This was, after all, the raison d'être for the book: to find inspiration and then use it to change lives—my own and those of others.

The sixteen women in this book are pioneers. They are heroes. They are warriors. They are women who set out to transform the ordinary into the extraordinary, who overcame the barriers of patriarchy, who shunned their humdrum lives of ease and comfort to make their existence meaningful for themselves and others, who charted paths that few dared to tread.

## SELECTING THE 16 WOMEN

My first step was to make a list of the women who had inspired me. My first list ran into 200 names. These were all women who stood out in their respective professions: entrepreneurs, writers, artists, bankers, and more. The two questions I asked myself while whittling down the 200 names to the final sixteen were: one, how has she contributed to change in the larger social context of this country? Two, what can a reader learn from this achiever's story that cannot be learnt from anyone else in her field?

I did not restrict myself by age group or profession. Thus, alongside Indu Jain who exhibits the capability to view everything in life through a spiritual prism, there is Saina Nehwal who is unrelenting in her focus to reach and stay at world No. 1. Many will be inspired by Sudha Murty's deep sense of individual identity, and others may aspire to be the next Indra Nooyi, one of the finest examples of how far sheer hard work and grit can take you. My aim was to explore the scale of achievement by Indian women over the past five or six decades: women who did not bow down to personal difficulties and traditional mindsets and stuck to pursuing their life's purpose.

My purpose was a celebration of Indian womanhood.

## GETTING TO WORK

My list in hand, I began establishing contact with all the women and icons that I wanted to interview, making calls and sending out requests for meetings. For someone with no background in journalism or writing, every single step brought home a lesson. There were times I was tempted to give up, because setting up interviews with 150-plus contributors was hard and often discouraging because of how busy my interviewees were. Today, I can see that my career in investment banking honed my perseverance, enabling me to continue on this uncharted journey.

In addition, making the shift to publishing was hard and navigating the world of publishing was a new experience completely. I learnt to trust both my idea and the generosity of the people I met, people who knew the achievers I was profiling and helped me establish connections.

I chose the anthology format as it can be both capacious and concise in our time-starved era. One can read this book from cover to cover or dip in, depending on which achiever one is most drawn to. Some profiles are longer, as it seemed almost criminal to leave out any of the information that I had gathered. As I was reaching out to every woman on my list, I began researching their lives not only via what was reported in the media but also through people who knew them both personally and professionally. This helped me get an academic understanding of each woman's life and a rare window into the more private areas of their lives. As my work evolved, these insights were essential while capturing the breadth and depth of each woman's life and work. In this process, I met and spoke with over a hundred people—all achievers themselves—who were kind enough to speak with me several times and helped me open many doors.

Over the course of three years, I succeeded in getting my top sixteen women to saying yes to being a part of the project; and this book is authorized and supported by each of them.

The first person I met was Swati Piramal, the vice-chairperson and backbone of Piramal Enterprises, and the last was the multitasking, troubleshooting, perfectionist Nita Ambani. My meetings made me realize that almost nothing I had read or heard about them had managed to bring to the fore their personality and character. Each of these women surprised me with their warmth, honesty and compassion. They made time for me, a first-time author, over and over again, and shared their stories with candour and insight. I travelled across the country and abroad to meet my subjects and those who knew them.

What struck me was that, while they remained focused on their goals, these ladies did not forsake their relationships. They drew support from parents, husbands, children, in-laws, friends, colleagues, bosses and mentors. They did not shy away from asking for help or apologizing for their absence to those who mattered to them. This was a key lesson for me. It also became clear that not one of these women had let anything stop her from working towards every goal she set for herself. Each one's journey has been singular, gritty and wholly admirable.

However, what I found common to all of these women was the fact that they all listen carefully to the voice inside them. They build their lives and routines in a manner that allows them to pursue a goal and stay alert and responsive to opportunity. They do not indulge in self-pity. They go where their destiny takes them, surrender to it and revel in it. To let go and trust that things will work out, to not be deterred if the outcome is completely different from what they had envisioned, and then to adapt themselves to the new scenario is to show a rare maturity and an incredible sense of mindfulness.

## SUCCESS VALUES

It is easy to imagine that successful people are helped by a special force; that they have a special line of fortune on their palms, ensuring success from birth. But that's not true and it would be naïve to believe so. When I conceptualized this book, I did so as an admirer; but as I set about giving it form and shape, it became a source of many life lessons.

The conversations that I had in the course of writing this book offered me a rare chance to understand the architecture of success, especially for a woman in India, and this knowledge changed me personally and professionally. I saw myself evolve into a more patient and more empathetic person; these interactions broadened my world view and taught me how to be stronger. As I traced the individual journeys of each of these women, I realized that while each story is unique in its triumphs and obstacles, there are some success values that they have in common.

## SWIMMING AGAINST THE TIDE

Kiran Mazumdar-Shaw was twenty-six when she started Biocon. She had little capital inflow and zero experience at running a business. And she was promoting an unknown sector—biotechnology. But, she was determined to make it big. And she did, shattering every stereotype that came her way. Sudha Murty was a young engineering graduate, about to embark on her career when she challenged age-old norms at an established business house like Tata. She did not let their traditional policies change her path, instead she got Tata to change and employ their first woman engineer. These women make their choices and stick to them, even when it means veering off the beaten track. The courage to push through and achieve their goals has made them icons in their chosen fields.

## GETTING OUT OF YOUR COMFORT ZONE

The women in this book shatter the myth that women are risk-averse. They go with their instincts and take leaps of faith. Take the example of the Piramals: the textile business was familiar territory, an industry they had shaped. But the industry was stagnating and it was imperative to look in a new direction, to explore the unknown. It was Swati Piramal's vision that steered the way for the Piramals to move into the unfamiliar world of pharmaceuticals. 'When I started R&D, people said that Indians didn't know how to innovate, they did not know how to file a patent, and if they filed a patent, anything that they did during a clinical trial would not be accepted by the West,' she remembers. Under her direction, Piramal Enterprises proved all their detractors wrong and scripted the great Indian pharma story.

## STAYING POSITIVE

Some call it endurance or perseverance, I see it as a mental attitude. In these women, I sensed an innate ability to see opportunities in challenges and surface on the bright side of the deepest crises. They adapt, manoeuvre and persist with sheer stamina, never once taking their eyes off their ultimate goals. The unflappable fighter Sania Mirza turned the dusk of her career as a singles tennis player into the dawn of her journey towards the doubles No. 1 position. 'I like to fight back hardest when people think that I am out for good,' she says.

For Shobhana Bhartia, the Home TV debacle was one of the few dark chapters in an otherwise impeccable career. But she doesn't brush it under the carpet. 'You have to bounce back,' she says. 'You can't shy away from failure; instead, you learn from failure and you come back stronger and you take that risk again.'

## NEVER BEING COMPLACENT

Scaling the summit is not the end point; it is the first step of the next phase— staying there. Former PepsiCo CEO Indra Nooyi says, 'It is like climbing Mount Everest—once you reach the summit, staying there is harder than the journey that brought you there. The view is fantastic, but other people are looking to reach that summit.' At the top, with too many critics, few supporters and a lot to get done, standing your ground is not easy. It is, in fact, a journey in itself. For those like Indra, goals are not end points; they are milestones to the next achievement. Sachin Tendulkar tells me, as he analyses badminton ace Saina Nehwal's journey, '. . . staying at No. 1 takes a lot of hard work. It will test one's commitment and one's character. It is important to celebrate victories but not to get carried away.'

## BEING AN ETERNAL STUDENT

Adaptability is perhaps the single most important attribute of these women. They accept their shortcomings and learn from mentors, peers and juniors alike. Good leaders are good students—they listen, absorb and apply. Priyanka Chopra might have reached the highest rung of the ladder, but she says that the 'struggle' still continues: 'It's just that it changes form. Success is a validation but it doesn't mean you are validated for life.' When Anu Aga lost her husband, she found herself responsible for the health and fortune of the Thermax ecosystem. Always ready to learn, Anu appointed international consulting firm Boston Consulting Group to help her turn things around. Then CEO Arun Maira describes Anu's willingness to learn and grow into her new role, 'I would explain everything to her in black and white, and she would pick up whatever she had to.'

## MENTORING, AND BE MENTORED

Successful women don't shy away from having mentors and, as they rise, they are keen to pay it forward. They understand the importance of teamwork and of giving credit where it is due. Equally important is the attitude with which the team is developed. By pulling their teams forward with them, they prove that a great leader is one who is self-motivated and is able to motivate those she leads. Indra Nooyi puts it well: 'Aspiring leaders must raise the bar for themselves all the time. You have to listen a lot, get out of your office, reach people—your employees, partners—and have as much EQ as intelligence.'

## CULTIVATING A SOCIAL CONSCIENCE

All these women also demonstrate an innate capacity for compassion and empathy for the less fortunate. Some of these women were born with the proverbial silver spoon and others had a humble start; but all of them have made it their business to give back to society—whether it is Rajashree Birla's widow remarriage scheme in villages or the Premjis' commitment to the Giving Pledge. To quote Yasmeen Premji, 'What if we can tell the youth that instead of buying more Ferraris, they could build more schools and may be show that off instead?' Then there are those like Nita Ambani, whose 360-degree vision of philanthropy keeps her constantly on her feet; Shabana Azmi, who has been the face of many a cause, and Kiran Mazumdar-Shaw, who has pledged 75 per cent of her wealth to charity.

## STRIKING A BALANCE

For each of the women profiled in this book, their family is the cornerstone of their happiness. When Naina Lal Kidwai started her investment banking career with Morgan Stanley in 1994, she would start work at 5.30 a.m. with a conference call with her Hong Kong team and end with a late-night conference call with the team in the US. Yet, she always managed to find time for her family, especially her young daughter. 'If I had stepped away [from my job], I believed it would have reflected on all women. I was determined to make it work,' she says. Parmeshwar Godrej was a hands-on mother and a doting grandmother who spent a lot of time with her grandchildren in spite of her busy schedule.

My endeavour with every story was to make evident the essence of each woman and share the core nuggets of her success. But as I went about the task of assimilating information, what touched me were not the grand successes, impressive as they were, that these women seemed to have. It was how they seem to succeed every day—winning the daily battles, finding inspiration in the ordinary, and following the arc of growth with focus and intention. Though all the women featured in the book work and operate in different spheres, they have something in common—the pursuit of something better. They looked at a problem, an obstacle, worked on it, and they succeeded and made our world and society better.

I've had the time to reflect on these lessons and my biggest hope for this book is that every reader is compelled to possess three copies—one for their bedside table, one for their desk and one to give as a gift. The lessons in here are inspirational, and they are applicable no matter where one is in their life. These sixteen lives are a testament to the fact that there are as many paths to success as there are people. We just have to discover the path that is right for us, and walk it with courage and conviction.

# NITA AMBANI

*Our mother has boundless energy. She is constantly buzzing and on the move, more often than not on uncharted paths. What makes her extraordinary is the excitement she brings to all that she does. She was working all through our childhood, building some of the country's finest institutions single-handedly, yet she always made us feel like we were her first priority.*

*Our mother took charge of the Mumbai Indians in the third season of the IPL and since then, the team has qualified for the top four positions every year. The one top thing she has done is inspire the team to believe in themselves. It's hard to gain a position of leadership in a group of professional cricketers, with so little experience of the actual sport on the ground. But she did just that! From knowing her, we know that it is, in fact, possible to juggle different roles with ease.*

**—ISHA AND AKASH AMBANI**

*One notable quality of Nita is that she catches on very fast. She trains herself. She is like a sponge; if she gets into something, in whatever available time she has, she is somehow able to educate herself. She is self-reliant in terms of learning about things, whether it is education, healthcare, philanthropy, sports or business. Nita has proven beyond doubt how one can create wonders with a strong commitment to learning.*

**—SHAH RUKH KHAN**

*I*t is one thing to be First Lady of corporate India by title and quite another to become the First Lady in every sense.

Nita Ambani, whose last name has transported her to the upper echelons of the country and the world, truly does own the crown. She is the soft power of Reliance's business and spearheads its philanthropic initiatives; the perfect wife and partner to billionaire business magnate Mukesh Ambani; a devoted and inspiring mother to three children; an educationist par excellence, hands-on patron of sports, a danseuse and a champion of social causes.

Before my first meeting with Nita, I found myself wondering what it must really mean to belong to a family that constantly makes headlines, to perennially be in the spotlight and have every move scrutinized. To get through every day, juggling so much, must need a special brand of courage and confidence. It is interesting to note that Nita—a very private person—took her time to grow into her public role as the wife of the topmost industrialist in the country. And even as she goes from strength to strength, Nita still remains someone we both know and don't know; it is true that media attention rarely shifts from her, but, at the same time, she gives her time and resources thoughtfully.

As I reach the venue for our meeting—Sir H.N. Reliance Foundation Hospital & Research Centre in Mumbai, a dream project of Nita that has won her much praise—I am aware she has a packed schedule, but she's right on time. Dressed in a lace and *chikankari* salwar-kameez with subtle diamonds in her ears and on her fingers, she is the picture of power and grace. I realize that no matter how often you have seen Nita in photographs or on television, nothing really prepares you when you meet her in person. You recognize her, of course, but you're quite sure you've never really met anyone like her before. Her empathy and courteousness hides a steely presence of mind and the ability to cut through clutter and chaos.

'For me, power means to create change, to empower people. I think power cannot be brokered. Power is something that you lend to people and motivate them. The biggest thing is to empower people and give it away,' Nita says to me, starting off the interview in a way that means business.

As we talk and Nita offers me a glimpse into all the responsibilities of her very full life, I can tell that each one requires, and is given, her fullest attention. She has the special ability to focus on several things simultaneously. I cannot label it multitasking because it's more deliberate than that; but it is undeniable that to each of her roles, she brings passion, decisiveness and focus every single day.

Superstar Shah Rukh Khan, a close friend of the Ambanis, says, 'Nita is now a close friend, but initially when I met her, the first thing that struck me was that when you talk to her, she is not just listening to what you are saying; she is actually concerned about you. She is one of the most caring people I have met. Nita does not talk too much, but she has a very clear and simple way of putting things in perspective. When I sit down with her and share a particular thought, she invariably comes up with the simplest solution. And it is not a black-and-white solution. It is a well-thought-out one. We have worked very closely for the last few years and this is something I have observed about her. She sits through a meeting for five hours, she lets every voice be heard, she will be concerned about what each person has to say and then she will distil a five-hour meeting into two simple, effective lines that will put everything into perspective.'

Daughter Isha shares, 'What is amazing is her boundless energy and enthusiasm in her work. Ever since I can remember, she comes back home with great, childlike excitement, as if it has been days since we last saw each other. Huge hugs are followed by enthusiastic storytelling. Even as a five-year-old, I remember her seeking my opinion and consulting me on her work as if I was her most insightful advisor, and I loved it! I felt like I was part of her work. Each day I waited for her to come back—yes, for the hugs, but also to hear about her work.'

## THE WONDER YEARS

Born Nayantara Dalal, she grew up in a large joint family whose lifestyle and values remain Nita's bedrock. 'We were eleven cousins in the same house with uncles and aunts, and growing up in a family like that, you imbibe the culture of being non-judgmental and supportive, of sharing and of love and care. You live so closely that you understand each other and are compassionate about what the other person is thinking or feeling.'

Her grandfather, a professor of French, and her grandmother were Gandhians who believed in the power of education and instilled their values in the children. Nita's father, Ravindrabhai Dalal, who worked with the Birlas, was a sensitive man whose compassion influenced his daughter greatly—every

Sunday morning she would accompany him to distribute food to underprivileged children near their home. He also taught Nita and her siblings to feed birds and stray animals. Nita has fond memories of reading to her visually-impaired uncle, who affectionately called her Florence Nightingale. (In 2012, Nita founded a registered international Braille newspaper in Hindi, called *Reliance Foundation Drishti* in his memory.)

Even as a child, Nita displayed a spirit of fearlessness. She was quite a handful and would climb trees in the compound of the large family home in Santacruz, a suburb in Mumbai. She would often scare her younger sister Mamtha with ghostly pranks and would be pulled up by her mother for this often. That said, she was also a caring elder sibling and when it came to studies, she was a bright and diligent student, and was elected house captain at Rose Manor Garden School. After a degree in commerce from Narsee Monjee College in Mumbai, Nita studied interior design and trained as a teacher.

However, it was dancing that was—and still is—her truest passion. Her mother, Purnimaben, who was trained in Gujarati folk dance herself, would take the five-year-old Nita every day to learn Bharatnatyam under Menaka Thakkar and later at the renowned Sri Rajarajeswari Bharatha Natya Kala Mandir.

At twenty-one, the beautiful, feisty Nita participated in a concert that would go on to change her life. In the audience that evening at the packed Birla Matoshree auditorium in Mumbai was the legendary industrialist, Dhirubhai Ambani and his wife Kokilaben. The next day, Nita got a phone call that changed her life—Dhirubhai Ambani rang her house and asked to see her at his office. With her father's blessing, a 'completely overwhelmed' Nita went to meet the great man in his office at Nariman Point. Little did Nita know that Dhirubhai would go on to become a very important influence in her life; but first, there was the matter of making the match between his elder son, Mukesh, and this bright young girl, who set one important condition—that 'I would like to work after marriage,' and that's what she went on to do. She worked as a teacher for three years under her maiden name—Nita Dalal.

A chemical engineer who had pursued an MBA from Stanford University and had been involved in the family business for four years, Mukesh was a tad uncertain about marriage. In a television interview with Simi Garewal, Mukesh said, 'My father was trying to work from both sides, his usual ploy. On one hand, he was trying to convince me. "Your mother has found somebody who shares our values, upbringing . . . and you should at least meet her," he told me.'

Eventually, Nita and Mukesh met when she and her parents visited the Ambani home in south Mumbai. Mukesh opened the door for them and Nita remembers being struck by the simplicity and humility of that gesture. He remembers being struck by her beauty and grace, and his curiosity to get to know her obviously grew.

As they spent more time together, Mukesh was moved by Nita's unpretentiousness. He appreciated how effortlessly she blended tradition with modern thought and connected with his family. 'He is a great friend to have. For me, it's our friendship, our partnership together. We are friends more than anything else. We just enjoy being together,' she says.

For three weeks Mukesh sent Nita a bunch of red roses every morning and drove down the three-hour distance from Patalganga, where the Ambanis were constructing a polyester plant, to meet her. As she wanted him to experience her mode of transport, they took a ride together once on a double-decker bus—a first for him—and Nita still remembers Mukesh's green Fiat in which they drove around the city. After six meetings, Mukesh proposed marriage, in the middle of a traffic jam on Mumbai's arterial Peddar Road. Nita, who had wanted to finish college before she got married, was hesitant initially, but Mukesh was not willing to wait. Nita recalls, 'I looked at him and said, "Maybe." But he insisted that I say yes or no right then.'

Of course, she said yes. Nita says, 'We met in November, got engaged in December. I wanted to wait for a year to complete my education; but we got married in March. Everything happened in a whirlwind! I was twenty-one years old and unsure of myself.' Her smile as she says all this, however, stands testament to how well everything has turned out and the warmth of the rare camaraderie they have shared over the years.

## A WIFE

For a relationship that began with roses, it seems appropriate that close friend Anuradha Mahindra compares the union to the flower. 'Nita is the rose, Mukesh is the stem. The rose can't blossom without the stem and the stem meets the rose to complete the plant or flower.'

While becoming an intrinsic part of India Inc.'s first family was daunting, Nita was grateful that the values she had grown up with were shared by her in-laws. When I ask her to describe her marriage, she says, 'Mukesh has been an equal partner. He has given me the impetus and the roots to go ahead and achieve what I want to. We have been married for thirty-one years now and I get inspired every time I am with him. He has the floodlights on life. He is shy and a little bit of an introvert, but he talks about the big things, the larger perspective, about change, about taking people with him.'

Her friend Ananya Goenka, former vice-chairperson of the *Indian Express,* says, 'Mukesh is quieter and more reflective, while Nita is exuberant and expressive. Mukesh is a magnanimous host and loves to have people over, while Nita loves to organize it to the smallest detail. They are both pillars for each other. Individually, each one plays a melodious instrument, but together, in harmony, they make a beautiful orchestra.'

Nita says there can never be a formula to make a marriage work. 'There is no single mantra. But there is something that we continue doing—I wait up for him for dinner and he waits for me. When we are in Mumbai, we don't have dinner without each other. That gives us time to bond and share our day's happenings. He still takes me for drives at night twice a week, with my favourite music playing in the car.'

Shah Rukh Khan says, 'In a way they are like pieces of a jigsaw puzzle that fit perfectly together. They are both very different people. It is as if Mukesh is the perfect sketch and Nita fills in the colours. He is the staid, clear-cut, honest, upfront businessman and she brings in all the entertainment in their lives by virtue of the way she is.' Industrialist Sanjiv Goenka echoes Shah Rukh Khan's sentiments, 'I think they are the perfect couple. They epitomize a perfect marriage not only in India but across the world. They complement each other, they work with each other, they love each other, and I think both of them are just outstanding as a couple and as human beings.'

Their abiding partnership has seen them through many a crisis. The first hit was in February 1986, when Nita's father-in-law suffered a paralytic stroke. The family had recently lost Rasikbhai Meswani, Dhirubhai's business partner and cherished nephew. Mukesh was now expected to step up to steer Reliance Industries. As he settled into this new role, Nita was there for the rest of the family and she began to grow into the woman she is today.

Cricket icon Sachin Tendulkar tells me about how she adjusts her schedule to accommodate Mukesh's timetable. 'Everything else becomes secondary for her when it comes to spending time with him. And that is understandable. Mukeshbhai is extremely busy and so she takes whatever time he has, shuffling her schedule around his. I know this because on many occasions when I have been with Nitabhabhi, she has said that Mukeshbhai was on his way home and that she needed to be there with him. Even when we were playing in different parts of India, she would make sure that she was back home to spend time with him. And there, I think, is where the strength of any family lies.'

Scientist and healthcare specialist Swati Piramal, who is close to both Nita and Mukesh, reflects, 'I think she is responsible for his success. Mukesh is a very shy, absolutely brilliant person. But his engagement with the real world is due to her. She has helped him be the one who meets so many people, the one with the knowledge, vision and dreams—and the power to execute them. She is a solid force behind him. She is an amazing wife. Mukesh can't go one second without her. If she is travelling, he will call at least twenty times, asking her to return!'

Son Akash says, 'I think my father has been an absolute rock for my mother, being there for her in every way, and urging her to achieve her goals.'

As a child, Nita often spent Saturday evenings listening to her aunt recite the Bhagvad Gita. That was when her devotion for Lord Krishna took root. 'Something that Mukesh and I do every day is pray together. We don't leave the house without praying.' This deep-rooted belief in the almighty stood her in good stead during the first big crisis that the young couple had to face.

Two years into her marriage, a twenty-three-year-old Nita was told that she may never be able to bear children. She was shattered by the discovery. In conversations and interviews now, Nita remembers how she always desired to have children and cherish the joy of motherhood. It took eight difficult years and the help of Dr Firuza Parikh—who Nita considers a 'soul sister' today—to conceive her twins, who were born two months premature and in a state of medical emergency.

Nita and Mukesh named the baby girl Isha and the boy, Akash. Three years later, their youngest son, Hari Anant, was born. Nita laughs as she tells me, 'Mukesh has raised the kids hands-on. So there was a time when I used to be working late, but he used to be home, looking after the kids.' Motherhood has been a formative experience for her and the most important thing it has taught her is patience. She attributes her calmness to having three kids in three years. 'I count my blessings for being blessed, for being a mother.'

Anuradha Mahindra, who believes that Nita does not get praised enough for being an incredible mother, says to me, 'She has a special relationship with each of the children. They have her drive, motivation and perseverance, and she has inculcated great values in them. She has not lost the ability to be a simple, devoted, normal mother.'

Nita's own upbringing has defined her parenting philosophy. She tells me that when her children were young, she would take them to her parents' home in the suburbs by local train. 'It's very important that we raise our children with the values we think are important in life. If they can give their earnest best and have a sincerity of purpose in all that they do, I will be happy. And do it with honesty and, as my father-in-law said, there is a very fine line between being clever and crooked, and never cross the line.' And, as it happens, every friend and associate of Nita's agrees that Isha, Akash, and Anant are unpretentious and bright children.

Shah Rukh Khan is very close to the children. 'I'm the one they can be naughty with. I think that is why they like me so much!' he says, and believes 'they have turned into fine young men and woman' because of Nita. 'I can sense from the outside that they are all friends and talk to each other like friends. There is no hierarchy within that family. And when you don't have a hierarchy, then you don't have any pressures. There is no artificial show of it—no namaste or touching of feet—they are very cool kids, but they are extremely respectful towards each other and towards everyone else. I also feel that if they do something else, or something different within the space they have, that would be an amazing thing, and I don't think Nita or Mukesh will stop them.'

Sachin Tendulkar has interacted closely with all three of the Ambani kids and says that Nita has a beautiful relationship with her children, 'which I have been lucky enough to see. If parents do not spend enough time with their children, the kids could get out of control, or become brash, but that is not the case with the Ambanis. And I think that is Nitabhabhi's strength—she has spent and continues to spend quality time with her children.'

Akash, who, along with sister Isha, is on the board of directors of Reliance Jio and Reliance Retail, tells me, 'My mother always says that whatever you do, you have to give it your best and do that every day of your life. She lives that way, and is motivated and confident. She has taught me that there are no shortcuts in life and that business is not just about what happens in the corporate world—you need to step outside the boardroom and understand all the details.'

When the kids were growing up, Nita insisted Mukesh stay involved with the kids as well. 'For the kids, at one time he was only their father and now he has become their friend. They look up to him. All three of them hero-worship their father. Their mother they kind of take for granted, but their father they absolutely adore,' says Nita, laughing.

## AN AMBANI

Even as Nita was focused on raising her children, she was preparing to step out into the world and craft her own legacy.

In June 2014, Nita became the first woman on the Reliance board of directors. This was three years after she made her business debut when she was nominated to the board of East India Hotels, operator of the Oberoi chain of hotels. Says Swati Piramal, 'She was actually doing a great deal of work for Reliance Industries. I clearly remember Jamnagar, where the township came up with schools, houses, offices. I don't think there was a building there that did not have her touch. So I think she really deserved to be there. I am glad that she is now a member of the board; her contribution will be recognized better than before. I think it is underestimated how much of a force she is within the company. The compassion, the positive vibes that the company gives out are due to her.'

But her rise was years in the making. She had been entrusted by Mukesh and his father with important projects all along and delivered impeccably on each one of them. Akash, who learnt the ropes of business from his mother, says, 'She knows how business works, who the stakeholders are and how to keep them all happy.' He believes that the ability to take people along, 'with a lot of compassion and trust, while remaining a firm leader,' is one of her most admirable attributes. 'And her eye for the smallest detail. She also has the will to keep learning, and I hope I can maintain that ability too.'

To me, though, it is significant that her first responsibility of creating a home for the family—Sea Wind, the Ambani residence in Mumbai's tony Cuffe Parade—was her first success. Again, in 1992, Nita helped set up a school at the Reliance unit in Patalganga, stepping into projects for the family business, and she did it quietly and efficiently.

The next project truly shone the spotlight on her. Mukesh asked her to develop the arid land in Jamnagar into 'an oasis', and she took it literally. None of this was easy to achieve. The people on the ground assumed Nita would stop visiting after a few weeks. But she was there—with her sleeves rolled up and a hard hat on—twice a week for three years. Her children were young at the time—the twins were five and Anant was two. She would wake up at the crack of dawn to make the one-hour journey by flight to Jamnagar, stay on-site all day in temperatures as high as 42 degrees, and return to Mumbai in time for dinner with the family. Swati Piramal, who remembers Nita 'wearing her heels and delicately stomping over construction sites,' says, 'It is extraordinary how much she has achieved. People think it's all been easy for her, but she works very hard.' More than a decade ago, she planted 3.4 million trees over 2500 acres and changed the landscape from brown to green. The changed landscape has resulted in doubling the rainfall, attracting resident and migratory birds and animals.

She also led the development of Dhirubhai Ambani Lakhibaugh, a mango orchard of world-class standards in Jamnagar. With 1.38 lakh mango trees producing over 130 varieties of mangoes, it stands out as Asia's largest mango plantation in a single location.

The next one, the Dhirubhai Ambani Knowledge City, was almost as complex as the Jamnagar project, and she worked out the nitty-gritty of a high-tech business campus, housing information and communication facilities of Reliance Infocomm. Her passion for building world-class facilities wrought a 125-acre technology-enabled campus within fourteen months and on a limited budget.

Subsequently, Nita played a pivotal role in the design and completion of the ultra-modern and high-tech Reliance Corporate Park in Navi Mumbai. This state-of-the-art facility houses the various offices of Reliance Industries and has emerged as the hub of the company's operations. Nita was also personally involved in the construction of their new home at Altamount Road in Mumbai.

Nita Ambani's position in the Reliance empire has especially stood out as noteworthy with her key contribution in the conception and formal launch of Jio. Undoubtedly, her role in the branding and marketing plan for Jio was evident at the soft launch event of Reliance Jio in December 2017. The opulent ceremony was attended by more than one lakh guests and entirely planned by Nita Ambani.

## AN EDUCATIONIST

Of all the things she has built, the one closest to Nita's heart is the Dhirubhai Ambani International School (DAIS). Education is her passion and she is firm in her conviction that it holds the key to real progress and change. This is why, after she got married, she decided to work as a teacher. 'Just the feeling of entering a classroom, seeing a blackboard and looking into those young eyes seeking knowledge—to see the innocence, to see them enjoy learning—is something that drives me, something I am very passionate about,' she says.

After the Jamnagar project where she also built a school, Nita realized that 'in a city like Mumbai, most parents had to send their children abroad if they wanted them to get an education of international standards.' She says, 'I felt now that I have enough experience in setting up schools, I would like to set up an international school in Mumbai. When I spoke to Mukesh and Papa, they said that if I am committed and have the confidence, they would gladly support me. But they also cautioned me that it would take some time to succeed. And that's how my story with the Dhirubhai Ambani International School started thirteen years ago.'

Shobhana Bhartia, chairperson and editorial director of the Hindustan Times Group, tells me, 'The first public profile of Nita was evident when she pursued her passion for education and started a school, which is today rated as one of the finest, not only in Mumbai but in all of India. Everybody knows that DAIS has been Nita's passion and whatever it is today is largely because of her personal involvement. In my understanding, Nita reflects an iconoclastic journey. It is remarkable because women who aren't professionals right at the beginning or after completing their education and get into it much later—it is much more difficult for them. But Nita has done it after being a homemaker for many years.'

Says Shah Rukh Khan, 'My son is from the very first batch of Dhirubhai Ambani International School and I have no qualms in admitting that most of the credit for my children's upbringing goes to its education system. Now they are studying in London and wherever they go, I have faith that they will be all right because of the education that Nita has imparted to them through her school and through herself.'

DAIS has been ranked the top international school in India in the Education World India School Ranking from 2013 to 2018, and its alumni are accepted in top-ranking universities in the US and elsewhere across the globe. Sachin Tendulkar, whose kids Sara and Arjun have been students of DAIS, says, 'Without doubt, it is India's leading school and probably one of the best in the world, especially given the way they have taken care of our kids. A school forms the foundation for a child's life and Nitabhabhi has played an active role in making this foundation strong. Whenever I meet her in school, I particularly notice that she addresses the children by name . . . each child, not just the children of well-known personalities. It is a clear reflection of her involvement and commitment to the school.' Today through a network of fourteen schools, Nita provides quality education to over 16,000 children.

When I met Nita, in 2015, to interview her for this book, she was working on the planning of the very ambitious Reliance University in the outskirts of Mumbai. 'This is something I want to do—schools for journalism, theatre, performing arts, engineering and medicine. Children need to be given a real choice and all-round development. So hopefully, in a few years from now, that dream will take shape,' she says.

The steadfastness of focusing on the smallest and largest detail, and being fully immersed in the ins and outs of a project are essential to Nita's work ethic. 'She brings amazing passion to everything she does. She has spelt out the causes that she would like to support very clearly. She goes about it with single-minded purpose,' says banking legend K.V. Kamath.

This habit steadies her, even as her next challenge may lie in a completely new and, possibly, daunting field. As it often does.

## A SPORTING WOMAN

At the final game of the Indian Premier League (IPL) in May 2019, the camera panned out from the men in blue celebrating on the field and zoomed in on Nita's face in the stands. Her normally calm features were animated as she whooped in delight. The Mumbai Indians had won the IPL, for the record fourth time in twelve seasons. Within minutes Nita was on the field exchanging high-fives and hugs with the team members.

Sachin Tendulkar has seen Nita evolve with every season of the IPL and he tells me how hard she has worked at it. 'I first met her when the Ambanis bought the Mumbai Indians IPL franchise. To be honest, Nitabhabhi did not know much about cricket at the time, but she took it up as a challenge. She started learning more about the game—educating herself about players, whether they were Indian or foreign; and even those who played county or shield cricket in South Africa, New Zealand, England and Australia. She was soon able to discuss their games and began to be more involved. She would attend meetings, want to know what we were planning and understand the intricacies of the game. So, there was a huge transformation in her involvement in the IPL ever since she took over the reins.'

When Mukesh purchased the Mumbai Indians franchise in 2008, Nita was doubtful and displeased. They had their plates full with business, education, health and philanthropic commitments, but she tells me what made her change her mind: 'We [Mumbai Indians] were at the bottom of the table for the first two years. And then I got involved and quickly realized we needed to bond as a team—the players and us. For one year, before the season started in 2010, I used to watch cricket for two hours every day only to understand the game. Then, I started interacting with the team—sitting and talking to them, trying to understand what makes them tick. I learnt it all on the job. We reached the finals.'

The day she decided to be more than the wife of the owner of the Mumbai Indians, Nita brought to the table her unwavering commitment and enthusiasm that has marked every project she's taken up. Her team was down in the dumps at the tail-end of the second season in South Africa when Nita decided one morning that they needed cheering up and left for South Africa the same evening. Since that day, for her, cricket is part of her work; she travels with the team for up to two months every season, wherever they may be; she regularly visits the shrines she venerates—from Tirumala and Sri Kalahasti to Srisailam and Yellamma temples—to seek blessings. With her innate team spirit and passion for actual fieldwork, perhaps cricket had always been the perfect fit for her. And the hallowed ground of Eden Gardens is a partner in her stupendous success—it is here that the Mumbai Indians lifted their first IPL Cup in 2013 and then again in 2015, with another win in Hyderabad in 2017 and a fourth record win in 2019.

K.V. Kamath tells me how Nita has evolved from being a supportive wife to establishing her own individuality, 'From lending support to Mukesh early on, to someone who is now an anchor to him in all he does, this is a journey Nita has seamlessly traversed over the years. And with her assuming leadership of the Mumbai Indians, she has shown a completely different side of her personality—the ability to plan, drive and execute something completely new and different.'

Son Akash reveals her conflict over her passion for cricket versus her love for the family poignantly. 'The day of my graduation was also the day of the final match of IPL season six. Everyone knows how much Mumbai Indians means to my mother, but she was there at my graduation and I have a wonderful photograph with her. Incidentally, my graduation and the match started at the same time, so she even missed watching it!'

When I ask Nita what she has learnt most from being a part of the Mumbai Indians, she points out that sport teaches you the importance of winning and losing gracefully. From Sachin Tendulkar, she says, she learnt how to respect not just the team but also each individual, because victory is never the work of just one person.

Tendulkar tells me about the transition she made in this journey. 'When someone is new to the sport, watching the match being lost can feel like the end of the world. I used to explain to Nitabhabhi that such losses were bound to happen, now and then. It hurts to lose and takes time to recover, but if we don't recover, we cannot play well in the next game. Hence we have to learn to leave our disappointments behind while starting a new game. I used to speak to her about the importance of pre-match preparations. The post-mortem is important as long as it contributes to improving us for the next game.'

On having the owner of one's team play such an active part in the game, Tendulkar says, 'It does feel nice to have one's owners in the stand, expressing support. Whatever you do on the field is important, but the way you approach a game is equally important and that happens behind the scenes. During the third season of the IPL, which was when we did really well, we had a lot of very interactive meetings with Nitabhabhi. Everyone, from the youngest to the oldest player, was encouraged to speak out, even if only to crack a joke. It kept the team's spirit high. And I believe that if the team is happy, the performance will be good.'

In 2016, Nita was the first Indian woman to be selected as a member on the International Olympics Committee (IOC) and as a part of the prestigious Olympic Channel Commission and Olympic Education Commission. The affinity and skill that Nita discovered she has for sports have come in handy with her work in football now, as the founding chairperson of the Football Sports Development Limited (FSDL), a joint venture of IMG Reliance and Star India. Its first venture has been the Indian Super League (ISL), a football tournament that kicked off in late 2014.

Sanjiv Goenka, who finds Nita 'very focused, very clear and yet understated,' says, 'she leads from the front, she gets into every detail.' Talking about the launch of the ISL championship, he says, 'Nita went through the entire rehearsal of the opening ceremony at 3.00 a.m., every bit; it was raining, she sat through the rain. She didn't have dinner; she was making sure everything was perfect. She just had to get it right. I think that is the Nita you know, focused, driven, yet compassionate and very, very humane.'

Sachin Tendulkar, clearly impressed, tells me, 'Last year, ISL was a huge success and it has grown bigger. The response has been phenomenal. She was again actively involved with the entire ISL team. She tries her best to be at all the venues or once at least at each venue. There has to be a genuine effort in promoting sports and backing what has been initiated. She believes in this and the entire nation has responded.'

Akash tells me that there was an emphasis on sports from the time he was in school. 'My parents encouraged us to be as involved in extra-curricular activities and games as in our studies. My mother's desire is to make playing sports an option for everyone at the national level. Of course, cricket is a passion in India and, hopefully, football will be too. One of my mother's dreams is to have more Indians represent the country in all sports worldwide.'

Reliance Foundation's Jr NBA programme, which has reached out to about two million children across India within just three years of its launch, speaks volumes of Nita's commitment to promote basketball talent. When Satnam Singh Bhamara became the first Indian basketball player to be drafted into the National Basketball Association (NBA) in the US, Nita was extremely proud of Reliance's efforts in developing world-class talent.

The Jr NBA programme entered the Guinness Book of World Record, with the participation of over 3400 Jr NBA students in India

As we chat, Nita tells me, 'We need to be a multi-sporting nation, where every child goes out and plays with ability and agility. India deserves to have many more sports—cricket, football, basketball, volleyball, badminton, kabaddi, hockey, tennis, etc. We are over 1.3 billion people and if I can get kids—lakhs and millions of them—to think of sports as a profession, then I have done my job well. The resounding success of the ISL both in season one and two, proves India's potential as a footballing nation. Today, the ISL stands out as the third most-attended football league in the world.' She is extremely committed to developing sporting talent at the grass-roots level. She ardently believes that for holistic development, children need to enjoy education and sports. She says, 'I think sport is the greatest unifier and leveller.'

When asked why football, Nita says, 'Today, children love football, which is the most played and watched game worldwide. I think the ISL has been able to ignite passion for a beautiful game. Our grass-roots programme is designed to reach out to millions of young footballers and develop their talent to match international standards. This grass-roots movement has already reached out to half a million children and this year we will reach out to another half a million. Going forward, the focus on developing talent at the grass-roots level will be part of the Reliance Foundation's DNA.'

Sanjiv Goenka analyses the reason behind the ISL's success. 'To be able to contribute meaningfully, you need to understand the domain that you operate in and when I see Nita in cricket and I see her in football—she has extraordinary knowledge of both. She is knowledgeable about the nuances of the game, the players and the business of the sport. The ISL is one of the top five most-watched sports leagues in the world today because of her. She has supervised every aspect related to the ISL. She is very calm and she treats the mission like she would treat her own baby. The way she is going about the business of football, the way she is supporting them and the grass-roots training programme that she has launched, she is inspiring the younger generation to take up the sport.'

Nita Ambani, along with Prime Minister Narendra Modi, launched the Reliance Foundation Youth Sports in 2016 with an aim to promote sports as a way of life for Indian children to prepare them for the Olympics. The foundation is present in twelve states in India and reaches an approximate four million children of all socio-economic strata. In 2017, Nita Ambani received the Rashtriya Khel Protsahan Award from President Shri Ramnath Kovind for her work in promoting sports in India.

Shobhana Bhartia says sport in India has received a much-needed fillip because of Nita. 'Sports needs a lot of encouragement and corporate backing in the country and it is quite remarkable for her to have identified that.'

## A PHILANTHROPIST

As the founder-chairperson of the Reliance Foundation, Nita dedicates time, energy and resources to numerous projects, including health and agriculture. The variety in the scope and scale speaks volumes about Nita as a conscientious and committed philanthropist. In our conversation, I am struck by how deeply she has studied each project, and the breadth of her insight on each issue. The foundation has already transformed the lives of over six million people.

'What Nita has done,' Shah Rukh Khan says, 'is taken one wing of being part of the Ambani family, taken those resources and put them to good use. That itself is inspiring. I'm not saying it is easier. When you are at the top you could very easily be someone who is extremely content with what you have and she is—she has got a happy family, a good business, everything is hunky-dory—but to sit down and make a difference in the lives of others because she has got much more than perhaps anyone else does, I think that is very inspiring. And it's not about the charity, it's not about the causes, it's not about the organizations. It's actually a feeling. I read a piece somewhere that mentioned that one needs to get out of the reflective glory and create one's own light. That is worth aspiring for.'

Nita has put her heart and soul into the foundation's Bharat-India Jodo (BIJ) programme because she believes that empowering marginal farmers is a real game-changer in achieving inclusive and sustainable development. Her inspiring narrative of how the Reliance Nutritional Garden initiative has enabled thousands of women to become self-sufficient, says it all. Travelling frequently to the villages, Nita has led from the front and is happy that BIJ has so far benefitted over 3,00,000 people from 60,000 marginal households across 540 villages. Yet, according to her, it is just a beginning and needs significant scaling-up in a vast country like ours.

Nita also plans, supervises and personally leads missions to cyclone, flood-hit or earthquake-ravaged areas (including Gujarat, Uttarakhand, Jammu and Kashmir, Andhra Pradesh, Nepal and Chennai). When flash floods struck Amarnath, for instance, she was there before anyone else, eventually covering some hundred devastated villages, carrying out the foundation's relief work and helping rebuild educational institutions.

The Reliance Foundation was given the India CSR Community Initiative Award in 2017 for supporting flood-affected communities through technology-driven digital platforms during relief operations in Madhya Pradesh. The foundation also reached out to the families of the soldiers who were killed and injured in the Pulwama attack in February 2019, offering health support to the injured soldiers and education facilities to the families.

In August 2017, the Reliance Foundation won The Golden Peacock Award for the reach and on-ground effect of its CSR (corporate social responsibility) initiatives. Akash tells me what differentiates his mother's efforts in philanthropy from everybody else's. 'Today, all companies pay attention to CSR, which is great, but what differentiates our attitude to it from that of others' is that my mother wants to make people's lives easier. We're always among the first to help in disaster-hit areas, whether there has been an earthquake or floods—any kind of devastation. So I believe that for my mother, CSR has an actual goal and is not just a standard compliance initiative.'

In education, the Dhirubhai Ambani Scholarship Programme has funded over 11,781 students so far, of which about 20 per cent are differently-abled and almost 50 per cent are girls. The Education for All initiative supported by the Mumbai Indians has impacted over 2,00,000 children by creating awareness for education using various media and digital platforms, and supporting children's education.

Sachin Tendulkar talks about Education for All, the one organization that is particularly dear to Nita. 'I don't think anyone has done something like this before: providing quality education to underprivileged children and, at the same time, filling up an entire stadium with 25,000 children, so they may enjoy a cricket match. It is not easy to plan and organize an event of such magnitude. There was so much homework and teamwork that went into it, and Nitabhabhi was instrumental in making it happen.'

Nita's Education for All initiative is a beacon of hope and inspiration for these children, giving them access to good education and giving them the opportunity to watch their heroes who put their heart into the game.

She is also committed to the Reliance Foundation Drishti, an initiative run in association with the National Association for the Blind. It is among India's largest corporate no-cost corneal grafting surgery projects for the underprivileged and has successfully completed nearly 16,500 surgeries. Under this initiative, the Reliance Foundation has been organizing art and essay competitions for children, and recently the essay competition has been extended to the visually impaired. The winning entries are used to spread awareness on visual impairment and the importance of eye donation. Drishti has also launched an international Braille newspaper in Hindi, which is circulated in sixteen countries.

One of Nita's most ambitious healthcare projects so far has been the redevelopment of Mumbai's century-old Sir Hurkisondas Nurrotumdas Hospital into the Sir H.N. Reliance Foundation Hospital & Research Centre with a patient-centric focus. The hospital was inaugurated on 25 October 2014 by Prime Minister Narendra Modi, with Mumbai's most accomplished in the audience. It provides world-class tertiary healthcare at affordable rates in collaboration with the world's leading medical institutions. Befitting her passion and commitment towards the healthcare sector, Nita is on the boards of MD Anderson Cancer Center and Massachusetts General Hospital. The hospital has also collaborated with the Johns Hopkins Hospital and the University of Southern California.

The Reliance Foundation, under Nita's direction, has taken on the task of providing primary and preventive care to vulnerable sections through mobile and static medical units, and health camps in areas that have no access to good and affordable medical care.

Sanjiv Goenka believes that 'the overriding, overarching part of her personality is humaneness. She reaches out to people; she touches their lives. She just wants to do good for people all the time. Over the last few years, each time I have met Nita, I have walked away with greater respect for her than the previous time. It is because of her humility; it is because of her compassion. It is because of the way she relates with people. She, of course, is a visionary; she has done extraordinarily well with Mumbai Indians, with the ISL, with the school, with the hospital. Nita has really made a big success of everything that she has done, but, to me, it is the person in her that is fascinating and inspirational. She is certainly among the people I admire the most.'

A trained Bharatnatyam dancer, Nita is well aware of the importance of cultural pursuits in building a rich and fulfilling life. No wonder she has always been passionate about preserving and promoting India's art, culture and heritage. The Reliance Foundation sponsored the 'Gates of the Lord: The Tradition of Krishna Paintings' exhibition at the Art Institute of Chicago, which showcased the traditional Indian art form of Pichvai to global audiences, the first of its kind. And this year, the foundation partnered with the Metropolitan Museum of Art, New York, to showcase the brilliant works of Nasreen Mohamedi at The Met Breuer, the first retrospective of the artist's work on American soil. In an article on Nita based on an interview during the art exhibition, the *Wall Street Journal* wrote, 'Ms Ambani's next move could garner even more attention. Sitting in a silvery sari during a recent interview in the patron's lounge of the Metropolitan Museum of Art, Ms Ambani said her as-yet-unnamed space will go inside a vast convention centre that Reliance is building in Mumbai. Instead of showcasing works from her own collection, her idea is to bring in blockbuster-level travelling shows from museums around the world, she said. It will open in 2018. "I just want the experience of going to see art to be part of people's lives in India," she said.'

Madhuvanti Ghose, the Art Institute's curator of Indian art, said she's grown to marvel at 'the speed at which the Ambanis work; no one else can surpass them.' As for Ms Ambani, she said, 'Art is a new door for her, but now that she's walked through, she sees how desperately we need her.'

In January 2017, Nita Ambani was recognized for her work with rural India and women empowerment, promotion of education and sports in India by The Metropolitan Museum of Art, New York. She is the first South Asian woman to receive this honour. While most may look at it as a daunting task, the fact is that if anyone can do it, it would be her!

## A HOST

At home, just as she does on a sports field or at a board meeting, Nita displays an infectious sense of enthusiasm and an exacting eye for detail. Whether she is hosting ten people for an intimate evening or introducing a world leader to India's most illustrious, Nita is every bit the perfectionist. She is a gregarious and generous host, and loves having people over at her stunning home. Members of the global elite, she and Mukesh ushered in the new millennium with the former US first couple Bill and Hillary Clinton at the White House, and had Sophia Loren, Jack Nicholson and Elizabeth Taylor for company.

Some of Nita's closest friends include Meeta Doshi, whom she went to school with, Firuza Parikh and Anuradha Mahindra. 'I cherish the friendship I have with Nita very much,' says Anuradha. 'We share a great sense of trust and understanding that calls for none of the formalities or rituals associated with friendship, like how often we have to meet or speak on the phone to stay in touch. But whenever we meet, we are instantly connected. We both seem to understand even the smallest nuances of each other's life and I think that's a very special part of our relationship.'

Her skills as a hostess were evident to the entire world when her daughter Isha Ambani married Anand Piramal and the wedding festivities were held in Udaipur and at the Ambani residence in Mumbai on 12 December 2018. Their residence was decorated exquisitely, hosting guests from Bollywood, the business industry, the sports industry, etc. Everyone who attended the wedding spoke about the absolute perfection and meticulousness with which the event had been organized, and Nita had lovingly overseen every single detail. In an interview with *Vogue*, the newly married Isha Ambani spoke about her mother's contribution to the wedding arrangements and said, "During the wedding, my mom was CEO and I was chairperson. She and Dad did all the hard work . . . I didn't go to a single wedding meeting."

Isha shares, 'My mother has a knack of making those around her feel wonderfully special. She cares to know what each and everyone thinks, and cares to help. She sees in others the potential that they don't see in themselves. She sees the good in everyone and everything.' She adds, 'If I have to describe one thing about my mother, then it would have to be the state she is always in—excited! She is excited about the now, she's excited to share her stories from the past and she's always excited about the future!'

Nita is also enthusiastic about marking occasions and achievements of her friends with celebrations. Sachin Tendulkar says, 'When the Indian team became the world's No. 1 test team, they hosted a party for us at their home. Mukeshbhai said that evening that their next big party for us would be to celebrate my hundredth international century. The day I returned after attaining the same, Nitabhabhi called me to say that I should invite anyone I wanted to. It was an event attended by various businessmen, sportspersons and Bollywood stars. Lata *didi* [Mangeshkar] sang a song—*Tu jahan jahan chalega, mera saaya saath hoga*—dedicated to me, which meant a lot to me.'

Sanjiv Goenka says, 'To me, Nita is the closest that you get to a complete woman. She is intelligent, she is supremely confident, she is very caring, she is a disciplinarian and she is dutiful. She cares about Mukesh to the smallest detail; she cares about the children with utmost devotion. She looks after everyone. She just reaches out to people and every action of hers comes from the heart.'

After spending time with Nita and speaking with the people in her life, I am amazed at how much she juggles with such ease and grace. I ask her how she gets through a day and she says, 'When I was at a match in Navi Mumbai during the first ISL season, Ranbir [Kapoor, Bollywood actor] asked me the same question. I told him that every day is different and it depends on a lot of things. To give you an example, that day, I started off by going to school for two to three hours after which I came to the hospital for the next four or five hours and from there, I went to Navi Mumbai for the football league. So, right from education to healthcare to sports—everything was completed in a day and that is something I relish so much because to me, it is an opportunity to make a change, if I can, in various avenues.'

K.V. Kamath believes that Nita has effectively 'marked her stamp on a variety of issues. She did this with her focus on things she truly and dearly believes in, as in matters relating to the foundation. Caring, helpful, attentive to detail, able to dream big and scope appropriately, and to plan and execute at speed make for a good business leader. And Nita has demonstrated all these qualities in ample measure as she evolved to someone with her own personality.'

She tells me that her life runs in meticulously noted bullet points and hence, she can deliver on everything she takes up. Every opportunity that comes her way, which will allow her to contribute meaningfully, is one that she accepts with gratitude. 'Everything I have now gives me more strength to take on multiple things, especially for social impact. I get extremely motivated to do more and I just wish there were twenty-seven hours in a day.'

Shah Rukh Khan, who has seen her in her corporate role, as a sports enthusiast and as an educationist, says, 'I find no difference in the many roles she plays excellently, except, perhaps, in the way she dresses for each occasion! She is equally successful in all these platforms because of her leadership and care.'

'She works for fourteen to sixteen hours a day,' says Ananya Goenka. 'Her passion for work inspires her to take on multiple projects. She has an eye for the minutest detail — a quality that makes her a perfectionist . . . but, mostly, I feel Nita is driven by taking on challenges and by conquering them.'

Anuradha Mahindra elaborates, 'That is something that she has probably had right from the time she was a child, because she was an achiever in school and college as well. So, I think she probably owes this drive to her parents, her upbringing and a very impressive work ethic.'

The iconic Oprah Winfrey once said, 'All of us need a vision for our lives and even as we work to achieve the vision, we must surrender it to the power that is greater than we know. It is one of the defining principles of my life: God can dream a bigger dream for you than you could ever dream for yourself. Success comes when you surrender to that dream and let it lead you to the next best place.'

Halfway across the world, Nita, herself an icon, believes in the same; her deep spiritual core, though, is strengthened by her steely determination and unerring sense of purpose.

After my interactions with her, I have come to know Nita as someone who takes her work very seriously, with inimitable passion and extraordinary commitment. She finishes one project and gets on to another with enormous enthusiasm. For Nita, it's always like that—she constantly seeks new avenues to do good for society and the nation. She loves nurturing talent and believes in empowering team members. The tone and tenor of her thoughts underscore one overriding theme: if you follow your passion with dedication and focus, nothing is impossible. Surely, Nita has many big dreams—dreams to bring about transformative and sustainable change that will make India a happy nation and raise its stature on the world stage. As we come to the close of her interview, Nita shares with me the one thing that encapsulates her life's philosophy: 'Make your best effort, chase excellence every day and don't worry about the results, they will follow.'

# MUKESH AMBANI

*Three decades ago, he wooed her with roses till she said 'I do!' And the ties that bind have only strengthened over time. **Mukesh Ambani**, India's top industrialist, takes time off to talk about his partner for life, the versatile **Nita Ambani**.*

**As the first couple of India's business community, your story appears to be the stuff legends are made of. What was it about the young Nita that won over the Ambani family so effortlessly and enthralled you over three decades ago?**

I clearly remember the first time Nita and I met—there was instant chemistry, we immediately struck a chord of friendship, she is the only person with whom I've ever shared an instant friendship with. I knew from the first second that Nita was the one—it was pure instinct.

Nita's purity of heart and intent is most endearing, and over the years she has only become truer to herself and more selfless. At heart, Nita is the same twenty-one-year-old girl that I had first met with my parents—simple, warm and extremely charming.

We both come from simple families with traditional middle-class values that dominate even today. Our value systems matched from the very beginning and this has only strengthened our bond. Nita not only enthralled me, but my family, too, was floored by her!

She has always been a people person, which explains how she has always found it easy to gel with everyone, whether at home or at work. Building lasting relationships and maintaining them, whether it is with family, friends, business associates or colleagues, comes naturally to Nita.

**Nita has often expressed her indebtedness to Dhirubhai Ambani, for 'educating' her in varied subjects. How have the ideas imbibed by the young Nita determined the way she executes business and philanthropy today?**

Papa was a mentor who always inspired and motivated all of us to widen our horizons. And it was no different with Nita.

Being the elder daughter-in-law of the family, my father had a special relationship with Nita. Our wedding was an arranged marriage and he was proud that he had arranged a perfect match. He took upon the task of grooming Nita very seriously and would spend an hour with her every day. Papa always encouraged Nita to think big and make a positive impact with her actions. His mentoring included global scenarios, Indian politics, family values and purpose of business amongst others. Through their discussions, he nurtured in her persistence and an indomitable will to succeed against all odds. I am sure that even today Nita, with regard to any issue, first thinks, "What would Papa have wanted?" And then she adds value to that thought and executes it flawlessly.

**An avid educator, Nita is all set to extend her expertise and passion for the higher education segment by setting up the Reliance University as a world-class institution. Your thoughts.**

Nita loves children, and is first and foremost a teacher at heart. She has taught me that the most important investment we can make is in shaping the future of our children.

Nita has often told me that most individuals are remembered for about eighty years, except a rare few. Similarly, few corporates last for over a hundred years. However, the best universities have lives of over 500 years.

India does not have any university in the Global Top 100 rankings. It is Nita's ambition to build a world-class institution of higher education that is a societal asset for all of India that pushes forward education in our country. Her dream is to build a university that sets a new standard for higher education in India and, at the same time, allows students to pursue their interests, no matter how varied. I am confident that Nita will build Reliance University as a future-ready world-renowned centre of excellence.

**A hands-on mother, what would you say are Nita's most important parental skills in the context of children growing up in contemporary India?**

Nita, despite her numerous commitments, is a hands-on mother. She has motivated me to be her partner in making our children our priority.

Nita always reminds me of what is important in life. She often tells me that while spending time shaping the future of Reliance is important, this should not be done at the cost of time spent with our children. And she is right; there is nothing more important than imparting our values to our children and that requires time. Nita has made me realize that the greatest responsibility that anyone has is that of being a parent and being able to do that well is ultimately what life boils down to.

She is the anchor for our three children. Our children are truly fortunate to have Nita as their mother, for she is their true guiding light, always supporting and inspiring them through her thoughts and actions. Children learn from what they see, and she has been an exemplary role model for them to grow up with.

**Given your vantage point, please share Nita's lesser-known passions that rejuvenate and sustain her.**

Nita, like our younger son Anant, is very fond of animals—most people think it is Anant who is passionate about animals, but it is actually through Nita's genes that have passed down very strongly that Anant has taken to loving animals!

Nita gains her immense inner strength from her spirituality, it centres her and she is meticulous about following her spiritual paths, be it meditation, yoga or Buddhist chanting. Nita also has always had great faith in the divine—she was brought up in a religious family, and she has brought up our children with great belief in god. She is extremely enthusiastic about following traditions, and constantly seeks to learn and deepen her understanding about Hinduism.

Nita is a voracious reader and is always expanding her knowledge on many topics, from philanthropy to sports to education by reading—she is always well read and informed on the topics that matter to her and one can always rely on her for her expertise.

**Please share the factors that motivate Nita's many cause-based/ philanthropic activities.**

Nita is driven by a purpose. Over the years, I have seen that for her, self is last and benefit to all others is first. Her passion for working with children and youth, shaping their education, making them physically fit through sports, and good citizens through participative events, is infectious.

Her leadership of the Reliance Foundation is inspiring. She is gifted in weaving together talented people to deliver societal values. Nita always ensures that through her dedicated and active involvement, and by learning about the needs of the communities, the Reliance Foundation continues its sustained efforts in positively impacting the lives of people.

**How has Nita transformed philanthropy from a mere cheque-book endeavour into an abiding corporate interest at RIL?**

Nita does not believe in arm-chair philanthropy—she has created a team that executes her vision and initiatives with enthusiasm and in partnership with the communities with which they work. She believes that economic transformation and social well-being can be brought about by partnering with people and communities, and empowering them to be self-reliant.

Fortunately, with Jio we have an all-India presence that her foundation can leverage. She works with her team on the ground in over 10,500 villages and towns in fourteen states across India and this will only grow in the coming years.

Nothing gives her more joy than solving problems and putting a smile on the faces of the people that the foundation touches—Nita exudes positivity, and that's a driving force, as that sets the values of our foundation. Nita's vision to build an institution that serves millions has helped translate Reliance Foundation's initiatives into a social development movement.

**Nita has made significant contribution to Reliance through several initiatives. In what ways has she contributed towards furthering the company mandate through her role as a director?**

Nita's contribution to RIL is invaluable and as my life partner, she has helped me in knitting the talented professionals of RIL into the RIL family.

As a director of RIL, she understands our business, but focuses on the Reliance Foundation, which is her passion. Given her commitment to excellence, which is evident from her professional accomplishments and leadership skills, she adds significant value to the board of RIL.

Nita is also tremendously creative and has a finger on the pulse of India, and in all of our consumer-centric businesses, she is instrumental in setting up and executing the customer-experience strategies.

## Nita has a passion for sports, too. What do you think of her efforts in popularising sports as a tool of empowerment?

For Nita, sports is critical to shaping the future of Indian youth. At present, she is busy rolling out the grass-roots sports programmes across schools and colleges in India through the Reliance Foundation.

In Nita's mind, the focus was always the larger purpose of sports—i.e. empowering our country's youth and instilling in them the right values and building their character. This grass-roots level programme aims to transform India's sporting landscape and enable the youth to compete at the national and international level.

## What mutual qualities have kept you both together over the three decades that you have been together? What about her persona do you consider the most endearing?

A marriage is as strong as the bond between the two people in it; Nita is the anchor of our relationship. She is, and always has been, an equal life partner and a sound life adviser to me. I've been extremely lucky to have a life partner who is my strongest and most unwavering pillar of support. We are both extremely dedicated to each other and our family.

We all enjoy the small and simple pleasures of life, like going for long drives with great music, attending Gujarati plays and being out in nature.

We are fortunate to have close friends with whom we spend time. As our children grow up, they are becoming our best friends, and spending time with them and their friends is fun for both of us.

Nita's zest for life, enthusiasm and can-do attitude, and positivity are truly infectious. She inspires me to reach the next level of excellence in whatever I do. She has helped me grow as an individual and evolve as a person in many ways. She is my true friend and guide.

**Despite her multifarious corporate and philanthropic responsibilities, Nita runs her home with grace and elegance. What makes her so flawless at it?**

Nita, by nature, is a perfectionist and this reflects in everything she does. Sometimes it is hard for us because Akash, Isha, Anant and I cannot be perfect!

I don't know how Nita does it, but she knows exactly what is happening at our home at any time—from when the children get up to what they are eating—all while maintaining the same level of supervision to what is happening at the several projects she is simultaneously involved with at work. She gets into the minutest details of everything with utmost ease.

**Do you agree that Nita has not only proved that even as an Ambani daughter-in-law, one can be powerful on her own steam and actually go about enriching the Ambani legacy?**

Nita undoubtedly has made her own mark with her unique style. She shows exceptional commitment to achieve whatever she sets out to do. She is very hands-on and passionate about her work, always knowing exactly what is going on around her and in all the projects she is involved in.

She has, with her grace and work, continued to set new standards for all of us. She has used the opportunities and resources available for the good of the institutions she established as well as for larger societal needs.

Leading by example in every role, she has evolved as an exemplary person not just at work but equally in the family, always enhancing the Ambani legacy—thinking big, having courage, chasing excellence and working harder with extraordinary commitment.

She always tells our children that they need to earn the Ambani surname and constantly inspires them to face challenges head-on, and live up to the expectations that the family, Reliance and the nation has from them.

**Playing all her different roles every day, Nita has perfected the art of multitasking. In what ways has she been a source of inspiration and sustained support to you? What is it about Nita's journey that stands to inspire the Indian woman today?**

Nita has proved that Indian women can play diverse roles—be it a daughter, wife, daughter-in-law, mother, teacher, educationist or philanthropist—and still pursue their passion to make a mark in society.

Her constant quest for excellence has earned her much recognition, which stands testimony to her unwavering commitment and focus to make a lasting impact on our nation's progress and inclusive development.

She strongly believes that supporting women is neither CSR nor philanthropy. She says it is our moral responsibility to support the idea of a better world—a world with equal opportunities and a world where women inspire all of humanity. Nita believes that we must all create the world where women can make their own choices and where India is at the forefront of that change.

# RAJASHREE BIRLA

•

*Mummy has been a symbol of grace and quiet dignity ever since I have known. She has moved from being a complete homemaker to someone who goes to the office and looks after the CSR activities of the group. Everyone in the family really looks up to her and my grandparents-in-law and aunts-in-law consider her word as final. Have rarely seen her get ruffled or in a hurry! Something quite alien for us Mumbaikars! The trusteeship concept combined with the giving person that she is, serves as a driving force for her philanthropy.*

**—NEERJA BIRLA**

•

Rajkumari Fomra was ten years old when her engagement to Aditya Birla was fixed. The little girl from Madurai was thrilled to be the centre of attraction—it felt like a celebration! Rajkumari had heard about Birla schools and temples, but did not know much more than that about the family into which she was to marry. The enormous sense of responsibility that came with being part of the hallowed Birla clan sank in only when she grew older—and that did give her the occasional jitters.

Her grooming began immediately after her engagement. In Kolkata, Rajkumari would stay with an aunt, but would often visit the Birla family home, Basant Vihar, in Birla Park. Aditya's mother, Sarala Birla, closely monitored her studies and acquisition of poise. She would even take Rajkumari swimming to the Calcutta Club in the hope that it would help add a few inches to her height!

Seven years later, in 1965, Rajkumari was married to Aditya and her new family renamed her Rajashree, after the deity who safeguards a kingdom and looks after its welfare.

The beautiful young bride was unaware of the many challenges that destiny held for her, or the implications of the role for which she'd been chosen at such a young age. When I hear this story from Rajashree, at one of our meetings in Mumbai, it moves me to imagine this elegant matriarch as that bright, cheerful little girl, who bravely faced the ups and downs of her life, remaining a portrait of resolute courage through it all. 'I take life as it comes. I have no complaints and hold no grudges. I am essentially content and God is very gracious,' she says to me, with absolute conviction.

The Birla legacy can be traced back to Shiv Narain Birla, a Marwari businessman from Rajasthan, who moved to Mumbai in 1857 to start a cotton trading house. Pioneering India's industrialization, the Birlas were noted for their nationalist spirit, especially as supporters of Mahatma Gandhi. Now, the Birla name is recognized and respected across the globe. The significance of this history comes home to me as I make my way to the impeccably designed headquarters of the Aditya Birla Group in Worli, Mumbai.

In the sprawling waiting area, questions are racing through my head. Many weeks of research have gone into preparing for this interview with Rajashree. A few minutes later, I am led to her office in the most private area of the building; and, as I walk in, I get a sense of the honour of being welcomed into the inner sanctum of the group. Her son, Kumar Mangalam's office is next to hers: this mother–son bond is a particularly close one.

Rajashree's office is elegant, simple and minimalist; and its occupant is immaculately turned out—every strand of her coiffure in place, her sari pleats in a perfect line at her shoulder—as she acknowledges me with a smile. The wall behind her showcases a majestic portrait of her late husband, Aditya Birla. It is from here that she spearheads the group's CSR activities across forty companies.

Gazing in admiration at the woman who has made such a stupendous success of a job that was thrust on her by circumstances and for which she was totally unprepared, I recall her sister-in-law, Shobhana Bhartia, chairperson of the Hindustan Times Group, telling me, 'It is really amazing to see how she transformed from being a homemaker to someone who is treated with a lot of respect in the professional world, a person who is known for her philanthropy.'

## THE PRECIOUS YEARS

Rajashree was born in Bikaner to Parvati and Radha Krishna Fomra, and was named Rajkumari; her family had lived in Madurai for generations, and her father owned several petrol pumps in the city. Her mother was a homemaker, devoted to raising Rajkumari and her three sisters. Talking about her childhood, her eyes light up: 'Our family was conservative and we were never allowed picnics, or going out often. But we accepted that and were still very happy.' Her early years were mainly influenced by her mother—'I was shy, and she was very sociable. I used to watch her with friends, and tried to learn from her.'

Rajkumari's match with Aditya at the age of ten was proposed by a family friend, and seeing the question in my eyes, she elaborates, 'Arranged marriages were the custom then. At my engagement, I felt like I was going to a grand party and did not really understand it.' Her visits to Calcutta, now Kolkata, began soon after, and Rajkumari began to learn what it meant to be a Birla.

When she was fifteen, her fiancé of five years went to the Massachusetts Institute of Technology (MIT) in Boston to study chemical engineering. They had met only a few times on Rajkumari's visits to Calcutta, and she was aware that he would be going off to America to study while she continued her education in Madurai. However, her visits to Basant Vihar became more frequent as the wedding date drew closer. When Aditya returned a graduate in 1964, he was the most educated member of the Birla family, and much was expected of him.

'He was sporty, fun-loving but conservative when it came to matters of the heart. I remember phoning him a couple of times after he returned from MIT but because the elders may not have approved, he did not speak to me,' Rajashree says.

Aditya turned twenty-one on 14 November 1964 and his parents were keen that he get married and start a family. On 19 January 1965, their marriage reception was held in the garden of the sprawling Birla family home, with friends and family gathered from all over the world.

Making an unusual choice, Aditya and Rajashree picked Ranchi as their honeymoon destination and, even more unusually, took close friends with them. 'My husband enjoyed having people around,' smiles Rajashree. 'So the more the merrier, even on our honeymoon, though people were amused.' She was a shy teenaged bride and Aditya's extended circle of friends helped in a curious way to ease the early relationship between the couple.

On their return, the young couple settled into Basant Vihar and Aditya immersed himself in the affairs of Eastern Spinning and Hindustan Gas. He had been taking an active interest in his bride's studies—she was a student of science at Madurai's Fatima College—and suggested she switch over to arts. Aditya's father was very keen that she graduated, but her son, Kumar Mangalam, was born in 1967, before Rajashree could take the final examination. With the family's stellar support, she did manage to graduate, later, in English and political science from Calcutta's Loreto College, becoming the first Birla *bahu* to earn a degree; she credits her in-laws for this.

In April 1967, a fire broke out in the Birlas' rayon plant, and employees went on strike soon after. Both Aditya and his father, B.K. Birla, were forced to work from home, and Rajashree has wonderful memories of those days. Every spare moment the young father had, he would spend with their baby son, playing with him, bathing him, and changing diapers!

By 1967, Calcutta had become a difficult place to do business; Communist-inspired labour strikes and Naxalite attacks had become common. B.K. Birla felt that it was time for his son and his young family to move to Mumbai. In keeping with the Birla tradition of seeking opportunity wherever possible,

Aditya and Rajashree moved to Mumbai in February 1971; their home was a sixteenth-floor apartment in the city's posh Malabar Hill neighbourhood.

For Rajashree, it was like moving into a different world. While she missed the protective cocoon of her joint family, her in-laws and friends, the safe haven of Mumbai enveloped her after the tense years of political turmoil of Calcutta. And she gradually grew to enjoy her new independence as a nuclear family.

Aditya set to work, and kept a very busy schedule with great discipline. Rajashree recalls his routine to the minute—wake up at 7 a.m., leave for office at 9.30 a.m. sharp and return around 8 p.m. for a sit-down dinner with the family. On leaving the office at 6.30 p.m., Aditya would play badminton at the CCI Club before returning home and after dinner, a couple of nights a week, the couple would go to the theatre or the movies.

In June 1976, when Kumar Mangalam was nine, Vasavadatta was born—at the peak of the Emergency in India; the couple had longed for a little girl and cherished their family. Given the difference in the siblings' ages, Rajashree was able to focus on both her children equally, which worked especially well given Aditya's long hours at work. Whatever time she got away from home, Rajashree spent on philanthropic activities. However, when Kumar Mangalam and Vasavadatta were older, she accompanied her husband on his business trips, which gave them precious moments away from the diverse pressures of Mumbai.

I am keen to know what Aditya and Rajashree were like as a couple, and Vasavadatta fills me in—'Papa was the stronger personality. He brought life into the house with his spirit, expressive love and laughter. Mamma complemented him beautifully with her inner strength, selflessness, love and cheerfulness.' She was a much-loved member of the family, who was even bullied by some of them, Vasavadatta adds in jest, painting in for me a few more vivid strokes to her personality. 'I often joke with her that she was so patient as a [young] mother that either it was an inherent quality or she just got lucky with kids like Bhaiya and me!'

## DARK CLOUDS

In July 1993, when Aditya and Rajashree were on their way to Washington, a hoarding advocating the need to check for prostate cancer caught his eye.

It compelled him to take a test once they were back in Mumbai. He tested positive. Rajashree remembers the struggle to cope with the news, steady the family and hold on to hope. The strength to do that came from Aditya himself who did not want rumours of his illness to have an adverse impact on his company. He underwent treatment at the Johns Hopkins Institute, Baltimore, but after two terrible years, he passed away on 1 October 1995.

Rajashree was outwardly composed even as the wonderful family she had created with such love and care came apart before her eyes. But she was devastated within at the thought of life without her husband and was deeply dejected after his death. Her children, friends and family rallied round her and when her daughter got engaged soon after, planning the wedding helped her overcome her grief and loneliness.

Scientist and public health specialist Swati Piramal, who is a great admirer of Rajashree, says, 'If there is one woman I think I would love to emulate or who I really look up to as being the perfect woman—it would be Rajashree Birla.' Swati tells me that when her mother, a cordon bleu chef, ran a patisserie, Rajashree would order Aditya's favourite sweet treats during his illness. 'It was a terribly trying time for her, yet she would call to thank my mother and convey her husband's appreciation, which showed her grace under extreme pressure. That is something I learnt from her.'

Vasavadatta is all admiration for her mother's courage during the most difficult phase of their lives. 'Sometimes I wonder what Mamma is made of and where she derives all her strength from. My brother was grappling not only with the emotional loss but also with issues on the work front, I was still young, and often, my mother consoled me rather than the other way round. I remember waking up from dreams in which my father was still alive and crying inconsolably and Mamma saying that she wished I could go back to the dream and be with him. She held us through it all.'

Even as she was piecing life together for everyone, destiny had other plans for Rajashree. She had never thought of joining the family business, but Aditya's death took its toll on their son, Kumar Mangalam, then twenty-eight, who had to take control of the company while still learning the ropes. The responsibility of a large multinational corporation, with interests spread across the region between Thailand and Ethiopia, now rested on his shoulders. Business writer Gita Piramal recalls how after Aditya Birla's death, global investors, joint venture partners and the business community were getting impatient with Kumar Mangalam. 'She became an oasis of calm for the family,' she says. Rajashree knew that she had to steer him through this difficult phase, even though she knew little or nothing about the business.

It's his mother's unflappability when faced with a crisis that Kumar Mangalam has inherited, according to Ranjit Shahani, managing director, Novartis. 'She has given him a quality of mind, *sthira-buddhi*. He is young and modern but there is still this calm in him.'

Swati Piramal adds, 'It was, undoubtedly, the worst phase of her life. First, she was focused on being the source of strength for her broken-hearted children and grief-stricken in-laws. Where she derived that mountain of strength, I can't say but what might have helped partly was that she started working. Being who she is, she gave herself completely to it and remains the same until today—regular, punctual and dedicated to the job.'

Others remark on her emergence as though out of a chrysalis, sure and unapologetic. 'Rajashree is truly understated in spite of having gone on to accomplish so much. She is obviously very media-shy, but if you start chatting with her, she really flowers and is able to communicate and share what she thinks and talk about what she is doing,' says Shahani.

There were other dimensions to this transformation, too, to which Gita Piramal alludes astutely. 'All mothers have to change as their children grow up . . . Rajashree grew into the matriarch's role elegantly, without fuss.' Her daughter Vasavadatta is married to Kushagra Bajaj, sugar baron and vice chairman of the Bajaj Group. Earlier, Bajaj Auto was the flagship company of the family-run concern but the businesses were divided following differences among siblings. Piramal says, 'When the Bajaj family split, the situation inevitably became tense. The Birlas and the Bajajs have been friends for over 125 years. Rajashree walked the fine line throughout with immense poise, supporting her daughter, yet never interfering.'

## THE CHAMPION OF CAUSES

Philanthropy has always been a passion for Rajashree and, as she stepped into the company formally, she began to shape CSR at the Aditya Birla Group with a simple mantra—*integration of social vision into business vision*. Social welfare is deep-rooted in the group's value system.

As with most things in Rajashree's life, the roots of this are firmly grounded in the Birla family history. From the first Birla who left his village to seek his fortune, to his descendants, whenever they made some money they went back to their village to build a water tank or a school or temple. Rajashree's grandfather-in-law, G.D. Birla, was an active participant in the freedom movement and, post-Independence, in national service. She says that Aditya's philosophy was not just giving handouts, but empowering the underprivileged to stand on their own feet, thereby engendering self-respect.

In 1976, Aditya and Rajashree started their first CSR project at a time when no one had even thought of anything similar. It had been her dream to found an orphanage, and it came true with the Aditya Birla Centre for the Welfare of Children, a home for destitute children, in Chembur, Mumbai.

After Aditya's tragic death, Rajashree and Kumar Mangalam took it upon themselves to take forward his social vision. Spending most of her workdays in the office, she has worked with her son to organize all of the companies' existing initiatives_ into a professionalized structure and is primarily responsible for the company's CSR activities.

Swati Piramal is overawed by 'her work in polio—just the scale of it—which is path-breaking. Not too many people know about it, but her contribution to the public health of India has been huge. To put your hand to the wheel and say, "This is what I am going to do," and then to do it, is phenomenal. This was the time that I saw the biggest change in her. She would personally get involved to remain aware of the vast challenges, the nationwide support that was needed and the effort required in maintaining a cold chain in rural India. And she would do all this without trying to garner credit from society—her work was silent, but its social impact was like that of a sledgehammer.'

'I admire her strength, her patience, her purity, her selfless nature, her effortless desire to give, her ability to forgive and forget, her ability to focus on constructive and positive work, her natural ability to stay equanimous, her ability to adapt—the list is endless,' says Vasavadatta.

She is a great source of inspiration, not only for her leadership team but down to the 200 CSR professionals and 1500 fieldworkers who constitute the framework for one of the largest CSR initiatives in the country through which they have touched seven million lives. As the chairperson of the Aditya

Birla Centre for Community Initiatives and Rural Development, Rajashree understands the importance of the corporatisation of social responsibility.

'Over the last decade, philanthropy has become a management science,' says Gita Piramal. 'Today's charities need MBA skills. More so when the charity spends over Rs 150 crore annually. Add the new rules that listed companies must spend 2 per cent of their profits on CSR initiatives, the total spend of the Aditya Birla group will jump from FY 2015 onwards. Ironically, because of the highly skilled nature of the job, charities have started poaching from each other. Rajashree's CSR team is a favourite hunting ground. Initially upset by the trend, she quickly realized the Aditya Birla group's invisible contribution to raising standards and then she was okay with it.'

Rajashree is justifiably proud of the high standards in her CSR activities similar to those in their business, for she believes that it is this that makes her team members take pride in their work. The centre focuses its CSR programmes on education, health, sustainable livelihoods, infrastructure support and social reform. But there's no room for complacency—she knows there's a lot more to be done and her team is working to cover many more of India's six lakh villages in the programmes.

The group also works with water conservation, awareness building being a major part of it. As the newly appointed chairperson of Habitat India's indiaBUILDS campaign, Rajashree also has her eyes on her next milestone—100,000 houses by 2015. She interacts with a host of Indian companies and MNCs to solicit money and other resources.

Many companies have a CSR agenda that offers them scope for self-congratulation. But, as Bhartia explains, 'Her philanthropy really stands out the most because when you look across the spectra, there aren't many people who actually are trying to support other [non-traditional] causes. People say that she has a very large heart because when you go to her for a good cause, she won't turn you away.'

As a daughter who has seen her mother grow into an important corporate role, with philanthropy becoming a way of life for the longest time now, Vasavadatta says, 'Her work speaks for itself. If *soft* influence can be taken to be *strong* influence, then that's so true in her case for she leads by example. Her work is her worship—she does it with the attitude of an ego-free person, letting a higher purpose and higher energy work through her.'

In 1998, during one of her visits to villages, Rajashree was shocked to learn how many girls were still married early, widowed when they were young, and then condemned to face hardship and social exploitation for the rest of their lives. She wanted to give them a second chance, but realized that this was a sensitive issue, and so took the panchayats into confidence to initiate the widow remarriage scheme. She says she was extremely moved when she witnessed the remarriage ceremony of 100 widows who ultimately received the respect they deserved.

Perhaps this is where Rajashree becomes something of an icon for women everywhere, inspiring them not to give up hope. 'She lost her husband at a very young age but she recovered from that and became a perfect head of the family. I am sure that she inspires and builds confidence in these women who might otherwise have wilted away. With her example before them, they have been able to push themselves back into the game,' says Shahani.

Turning into a source of strength for others does not come easy for most; it calls for plenty of maturity, as Bhartia points out. 'Rajashreebhabhi has gone through many turbulent times and has always been able to hold herself together. I admire that and the fact that she is able to give of her own inner resources to others. I think the many awards she has received are recognition of the determination of a woman to step out of the normal mould and get into a more public profile, with the required maturity and dignity.'

## FAMILY FEELINGS

Her sister-in-law's inspiring words highlight how profound Rajashree's role in the Birla family is. She spent most of her formative years with her parents-in-law and learnt everything she knows today from them. I am both touched and awestruck by the fact that for fifty years, she has been a part of the family she married into—she had first stepped into the family as a ten-year-old and her in-laws are as much mother and father to her as her real parents. Even now, despite living in different cities, Rajashree is in touch with them every single day, not out of obligation, but love.

The young Rajashree also developed a special relationship with Dadoji, her grandfather-in-law, G.D. Birla, who was very affectionately disposed towards her, and concerned about every single member of the family. She laughs when she remembers his quirky sense of humour, 'One morning, he was sitting in his room reading the newspaper. I stopped by to say hello and he told me he was checking to see if his name was in the obituary section.' She regrets that she did not get to see him much and learn more from him but feels lucky for the time she did spend with him.

In September 2017, Rajashree celebrated her seventieth birthday with a set of intimate events that were attended by all of her family, some of whom flew down specially for the occasion.

## THE SPIRITUAL SIDE

Rajashree has been a student of the Bhagvad Gita for many years and as a student myself, I can relate to its impact on her day-to-day existence. Rajashree reads the Gita twice a week with a guru, Shri Nandlal Pathak, a professor at Sophia College (Mumbai) and Hindi scholar, and much of her personal philosophy and understanding of spirituality is inspired by it. She also learns from contemporary experts on the matter, such as Deepak Chopra, whose work she credits with helping her understand the mind-body connection, and the importance of approaching life positively.

Rajashree was also influenced by her parents-in-law's unshakeable belief and faith in God. She saw them play host to spiritual leaders like Swami Chinmayanand, Swami Akhandanand, Swami Girishanand, and perform yagnas in various parts of the country. Over the years, she was also witness to their service towards thousands of poor at their dharamshalas and the Birla temples. The Chinmaya Mission is a cause that has been close to the Birlas and they have been supporting it for more than four decades. Rajashree herself strongly identifies with their goals and has been working closely with them.

I understand that this facet of Rajashree's personality is tempered by her greater understanding of looking beyond rituals as well. She chants the Gayatri Mantra daily, as it gives her peace and sets the mood for the tasks ahead. She does not believe that mere performance of daily rituals amounts to spirituality, but weaving it intrinsically into one's daily existence is what counts. Spirituality, for her, is a principled way of life and correctness in attitude. She places integrity, acceptance, largeness of heart and humility as the cornerstones to a well-rounded spiritual self. She believes that spirituality encompasses both: service to others with compassion and service to self through inner reflection. Talking with her, it is clear to me that these are qualities she has endeavoured to seamlessly weave into her life.

## OF MUSIC AND FOOD

The work she does outside the house has been one facet I discover. But she has other interests outside work that bring joy to her life. Music, which her late husband was passionate about, is one of them; it is her most effective stress buster. Her favourites remain bhajans and songs from old Hindi films. She tells me that at the end of a day, there is nothing that soothes her more than falling asleep to music.

She has also channelled her love for music into initiatives that she began with Aditya, such as the Sangeet Kala Kendra, designed to nurture talent in the field of music, drama and other art forms. Preserving the heritage of Indian music is important to her and her role in that sphere has grown as president of the Kendra, which has 1500 members. She works hard to keep its annual calendar lively and of interest to all age groups. In 1996, she launched the Aditya Birla Kala Shikhar Puraskar, which is presented each year to a performing artiste of excellence.

'Rajashree and Aditya both loved classical music. He used to sing and paint,' says Swati Piramal. 'I have attended many music concerts and theatre performances at Sangeet Kala Kendra. Unlike health or education, it is always difficult to measure the impact of efforts in promoting culture and the arts. But culture is at the heart of a nation and must be carefully nurtured for future generations.'

Food is another passion and I find it very endearing that she has a sparkle in her eyes when she talks about it. Her favourite, she says to my greatest surprise, is chaat, the spicier, the better. And she has a sweet tooth. It is difficult for me to imagine her having any weakness at all, but I take her word for it. Her love for travel has led her to try different cuisines globally, and Ethiopian food is a favourite. Once a year she takes off on a three-week holiday with a group of very close friends, visiting different continents and countries. Likewise, she takes short breaks with daughter Vasavadatta and her grandchildren. She is also very close to her three sisters and their families, and travels with them when she can.

All of this, though, is evened out by her commitment to staying fit and healthy. She has a gym in her house where her daily two-hour workout is integral to her routine, something that she has practised for fifteen years now. She uses the treadmill or the cross trainer for her workout and also works with a yoga teacher, having graduated to dynamic yoga with more complex postures.

As I piece together her life to find the most essential lessons, it is clear that Rajashree has taught herself to keep evolving. At every stage in her life, new challenges were thrown at her and instead of succumbing she made the most of them. Be it adjusting to a new city and new family in her early teens, or shouldering her family's responsibilities after her husband's untimely death, or taking on the CSR activities of the Birla group, or even something as basic as learning to use WhatsApp to stay in touch with her grandchildren.

Her awareness of the spiritual dimension to life helped her through difficult days when she and Aditya unconditionally accepted his illness as 'God's will'. Most people map their lives from their childhood and envisage their dreams and their hopes, but Rajashree does not believe in doing so. She tells me she lives life as it comes and has never had a particular desire, so nothing in her life is unfulfilled.

From a distance, I have always admired this incredible lady's grace, dignity, compassion and calm. Talking with her, I discovered her tremendous spirit, which has helped her not only identify her purpose in life but also live it, while coming to terms with tragedy, loss and disappointment. She makes the most of every single day and I feel privileged to know her personal *mantra*—'This, too, shall pass. This phrase gives me tremendous energy, resilience and a lot of hope.'

# KUMAR MANGALAM BIRLA

*Critics wrote off the Aditya Birla Group when the twenty-eight-year-old **Kumar Mangalam Birla** took over its reins following the sudden death of his father, Aditya Birla, in 1995. This was when his mother, the unassuming **Rajashree Birla**, relegated her personal tragedy to the background to stand rock solid by her son, a greenhorn in business at the time. Kumar Mangalam talks about his mother's amazing transformation from a homemaker to a respected public figure and her role in his life.*

**Rajashree is the epitome of fortitude and old-world grace. How has her incredible life influenced you?**

My father used to travel extensively on work. It was my mother who brought me up, largely, in Calcutta, and was a major influence in my life. Of all the people I know, she is the most equanimous—I have not seen her angry, ever. She is also the most giving person; at times, more giving than she needs to be, and that is often a bone of contention between us. I realize now that this is a part of who she is—it is not that she does not understand, or is being duped. It is just who she is.

Speaking of her humility and mildness of manner, suffice it to say that she's as polite with her driver as she would be with the President of India. Also, my mother has a unique power of adaptability; she has flowed with life. Her life revolved around my father when he was alive. A couple of years after his passing away, she reinvented herself—which can be very difficult to do— giving her all to philanthropy. She took on the task of heading the various CSR projects of the Aditya Birla Group. And the way she has gone about it is simply astounding, building it not just in terms of scale but also in terms of the significance of the work.

**What memories do you have of the way she raised you?**

Every time I was agitated, my mother would explain things to me calmly. She would say, 'This, too, shall pass. It's just a phase, don't get worked up. Remember to look on the bright side.' Not being able to grasp the truth of her words and feeling invariably irritated, I would exasperatedly say, 'Mom, come on!' But in hindsight,

47

her words always rang true and I would realize that it really had been a passing phase and I should not have been so affected. She is someone who has always been very quiet and gentle, yet very strong.

**Rajashree went from shy wife to outspoken matriarch and philanthropist. How did this happen?**

She just grew into that role; I think she probably felt that it was her calling and that this was the way in which she could contribute the most, not just to the group but to keeping the memory of my father alive. My mother was aware that at the end of his life, this is what my father would have wished to do — work for the marginalized sections and give back to society. She travelled, ran centres for destitute boys and conducted many other programmes that he would have wished to. So I think my father's unfinished agenda was what drove her towards philanthropy.

**Your mother oversees the group's social and welfare activities. How has her helming the group's CSR initiatives made a difference?**

My mother has brought about an unprecedented expansion of the group's welfare activities. While she has put a lot of heart into the work that was being done, she has also institutionalized the various operations. These processes have helped make the activities a lot more impactful.

**The loss of your father was a terrible blow to the family, and your mother stood very tall through it all. Could you return to that difficult time?**

Shortly before my father passed away, I was in a state of denial, and imagined he would somehow be saved miraculously. Two days before his death, my mother said to me, 'You have to stop thinking like that and accept that he will pass away.' That's when reality hit me. She was making her peace with the fact that my father's death was inevitable and that he would never want to see her cry or get upset.

I remember that she was the one looking after the family, rather than the other way round. Given that it was her life that was so profoundly and painfully impacted, I never saw her sad or depressed. She remained very positive for the sake of everyone around her.

**You met with a great deal of criticism when taking over the business after your father's death, but your mother was a pillar of strength. In what way did she help you?**

Sometimes, one tends to run away from situations in one's life, but my mother not only accepted the loss of my father, but helped me come to terms with it. She is a very strong person, and I think I just absorbed strength from her, never thinking of breaking down. She was a quiet, never intrusive, but immense source of support. She explains herself without pushing it, or forcing you to do something. She is a straightforward person who says things upfront and in a frank manner. Parents can tend to use every trick in the book to get their child to do something, but that is not like my mother. Her inputs have been invaluable to me at every stage.

**Your family has known much adversity and faced it with singular courage. That spirit seems to be part of the Birla DNA. So what leadership traits do you think come to you from your mother?**

I think my ability to deal well with both success and failure is something I have imbibed from my mother. I don't get too carried away with success and, similarly, failure fails to pull me down too much. Also, the fact that one should try and be the bigger person and not get caught in petty issues – these values, attitudes and principles are universal and they apply to every aspect of life. Whether you are a housewife, a student or a professional, the earlier you can inculcate them, the better. They not only make you a better person, but also a happier one. All of this, I have learnt from her and I feel proud because it makes me feel lighter as a person.

**Observing your mother both at home and at work, what have been the learnings for you?**

My mother believes in going with the flow and not getting overly affected by any situation, in a positive or negative manner. For someone who suffered such a deep loss and had to manage both home and work, she had the enormous strength to stay composed, and focused on her duties. I have learnt a lot from her about maintaining equanimity, and the need to reinvent oneself at different points in life.

I have never seen her not do her duty and she always does it enthusiastically. She draws from the simple things around her and is very meticulous in her approach. My mother is always striving to do something different and contribute to society. When one sees someone consistently striving to bring about a change for good, it is bound to inspire and impact those around her.

**What does the future look like for your mother?**

Just as she would want it—my mother really sets her own goals now. I am sure she will continue with what she is doing besides finding newer avenues for welfare activities, depending on the emerging needs of society. Her effort at the introduction of vocational training is one such example. To summarize, giving back is what my mother is all about.

# SUDHA MURTY

•

*Mrs Murty is many things . . . She is a great seeker, incurable dreamer, tireless doer,
passionate teacher, eternal student, storyteller, story lover, selfless giver, childlike life
enthusiast, engineer, homemaker . . . and so very human. But above all, she is an inventor . . .
a leader—because she is inventing the future of those at the fringes of survival in India, slowly
changing their what is, to what could be.*

**—VISHAL SIKKA**

•

On a warm April afternoon in 1974, at the Indian Institute of Science, Bengaluru, a student was strolling in the shade of the lush gulmohar trees on campus when she chanced upon an advertisement by TELCO (Tata Engineering and Locomotive Company; today Tata Motors) for the job of an engineer. Her attention, however, was drawn to the disclaimer: Lady candidates need not apply.

Sudha Kulkarni felt the advertisement seemed to mock her achievements as an engineering graduate and gold medallist from Hubli and her history of being the only woman on two all-male campuses. That it came from as reputed a company as the Tatas' fuelled her ire and she shot off a postcard to J.R.D. Tata, lecturing him on gender equality.

Days later she received an interview call from TELCO. With a confirmed research position at a foreign university in hand, Sudha had no interest in the job but decided to visit Poona at telco's expense and buy colourful cheap saris there. Certain that she wouldn't be offered the job, Sudha confidently shared her feminist concerns with the interviewers, who were aware that she was 'the girl who wrote to J.R.D.' Sudha was even more surprised to be offered the position of TELCO's first female engineer, which she accepted as her father advised that she must take the offer if she truly believed in her letter to J.R.D.

Sudha's is a unique life lived on her own terms: she funded her husband, N.R. Narayana Murthy's dream tech start-up, Infosys, and gave him three years to realize his dream while she ran the household and raised their children; and later, when Infosys was established, she chose to teach computer science. A philanthropist who works at the grass roots, she is chairperson of the Infosys Foundation and a member of the Gates Foundation. The prolific author of several bestsellers, Sudha champions the culture of Karnataka, and, with her family, symbolizes a new India, which thrives on knowledge and innovation.

Mindtree co-founder and chairman Subroto Bagchi's words encapsulate her multifaceted persona: 'If one has a half-hour conversation with her on any subject, be it rural poverty, sanitation, restoration of heritage, one finds that she is one of the five most knowledgeable people on that subject. It is mind-blowing. This level of knowledge can come from an intensity of engagement that only happens when someone is emotionally invested in the matter.'

As I negotiate the Bengaluru traffic en route to Infosys Foundation, I ponder over the rare quality that distinguishes this pioneer—her intentions are as peerless as her actions. Sudha is a visionary who has taken tough decisions and set both benchmarks and an example throughout her life: not only does she do, but she thinks very carefully about why, and then articulates that philosophy to the world.

Walking into Sudha's third-floor office, a framed photograph of J.R.D. Tata catches my eye. I smile as I remember that it was on just such a warm afternoon thirty years ago that Sudha had dashed off an indignant letter to this godfather of Indian entrepreneurship. A spark of that spunky young woman still glows in the warm smile of the charming lady in a pretty cotton sari who greets me. Sudha's office is functional but welcoming, stationery stacked neatly on the desk. Tata Group founder Jamsetji Nusserwanji Tata looks out from another frame beside J.R.D. Sudha's only accessories are a small bindi and simple *mangalsutra*; her grey hair is tied back neatly, adorned with a solitary fresh flower. She looks exactly as she does in every photograph and reminds me of what fashion designer Coco Chanel said—'Simplicity is the keynote of all true elegance.'

As Sudha offers me tea, she says, 'When we are expecting guests, we order a litre of milk instead of the usual half-litre.' That statement disarms me—one reads so much about the Murthy family's prudence and thrift but to see it first-hand is humbling. When I say that, she responds, 'My father brought us up on age-old Indian values of truth, simplicity, love and respect.'

Even as we speak, I watch her circle stories in the newspaper that highlight issues or people that could use her help. Early into our meeting, I realize that Sudha is curious and astute, albeit polite. Aware of her reputation of being thorough with her research, I am not surprised when she asks me everything about my book before she begins the interview. After my answers to her frank questions satisfy her, she settles back and speaks with the skill of a practised raconteur. Just as after a good book one feels like the author is an old friend, listening to Sudha narrate her life makes me fight the urge to give her a hug.

## THE ETERNAL TEACHER

Sudha, the second of four siblings, was born in Shiggaon, Karnataka, to Dr R.H. Kulkarni, a professor of gynaecology, and Vimla, a homemaker. Both her parents have now passed away. Hers is a family that respects education and erudition over all else: 'My father didn't buy a refrigerator for years, but our library was vast. For us, academics were not only a priority but a way of life.' As a young girl, her maternal grandparents were an important influence on her, especially her mother's father, H.R. Kadim Diwan, a Sanskrit scholar and Gandhian. From him, Sudha imbibed the spirit of independence, a strong sense of self-worth and nationalism, and her love for literature, history and mathematics.

But it was through her grandmother, who was unlettered, that Sudha learnt one of the most important lessons of her life. 'My grandmother loved Triveni, a famous Kannada writer, but had to depend on me to read out the weekly excerpt of her novel, *Kashi Yatre*, from a magazine. One week, I was at a wedding and when I came home, I found my grandmother crying, frustrated and helpless. The magazine lay in front of her but she could not read it.' From the very next day, twelve-year-old Sudha began teaching her sixty-two-year-old grandmother how to read. A year later, the elder was able to read *Kashi Yatre* on her own.

This incident taught Sudha that education changes lives and it is never too late to learn. It is a conviction she has passed on to her children. Son Rohan remembers learning mathematics, and computer code programming from his mother—'I started writing code when I was about eight or so and whenever I had questions, I would discuss them with my mother. One of the best traits I have inherited from her is a deep respect for education, for knowledge. My parents always encouraged us to do something on our own. They told us our identity cannot be entirely inherited.'

Bagchi believes that Sudha is the quintessential teacher. They met twenty years ago, when she invited him to address her students at Bengaluru's Christ College; understandably nervous of meeting the iconic Narayana Murthy's wife, he found her to be 'just a computer science teacher—completely no-nonsense and genuinely invested in the welfare of her students.'

It was Sudha's parents' commitment to education that built a strong foundation for their children's future success. 'My father believed that education is essential for women. Even his assets were evenly divided among all of us. He had the same rules for all of us.' Sunanda, Sudha's elder sister, is a gynaecologist; her younger sister, Jaishree, is a physicist and computer scientist married to tech entrepreneur Gururaj Deshpande; and her brother,

Shrinivas, is a professor of astronomy and planetary science at the California Institute of Technology.

As for Sudha, she studied engineering in the late-60s, when it was an unheard-of vocation for women. When I ask her what her life at college was like, she accepts that it was 'certainly unusual for a girl from a middle-class Kannadiga family.' Apart from being stared at constantly, she had to walk a mile just to find a washroom she could use. With characteristic cheerfulness and scrappiness, she crossed those hurdles and now chooses to remember that time as idyllic. It was hard work, however. Driven by her desire to prove her mettle and silence the patriarchal voices that dogged her, Sudha graduated top of her class.

Buoyed by that success, she decided to pursue a postgraduate degree in computer science at a time when India was barely familiar with what a computer was. Again, at the Indian Institute of Science, she was the only girl in class; Sudha eventually graduated as a topper, the recipient of a gold medal from the Institute of Engineers and a silver medal from the Karnataka government.

One can understand why such a brilliant and industrious young woman was angered enough by an advertisement to write to J.R.D. Tata. In awe of her steeliness, I ask Sudha whether she had been apprehensive about the consequences. She looks at me—unfazed and nonchalant—and says it had been only the right thing to do. The gravity of her action only occurred to Sudha when she was at TELCO in Pune; she remembers remorsefully that she had been 'rather impolite' even to the panel interviewing her. They told her that while her academic record was impressive, she may be better suited to a research job, rather than one on a factory floor. 'I replied that they had to start somewhere, else no woman would ever work in their factories,' she tells me.

Sudha got the job and moved from Bengaluru to Pune. At the telco factory, she had to work in shifts and learn to drive a jeep. Her inspiration was her grandmother, who had chosen to change her life at sixty-two. All of Sudha's experiences reached a crescendo when she met J.R.D. Tata while at TELCO: 'I was very nervous. But all that he said was, "It's nice that girls are getting into engineering in our country."'

This balance of courage, candour and humility is intrinsic to Sudha. Always respectful and friendly, she speaks with authenticity and profundity, both to academic audiences and friends at a party. Sociable and devoid of pretence, she has an inherent poise and dignity. 'She's a very deep, giving and lovely person; very open as an individual and is an amazing human being,' says Kiran Mazumdar-Shaw, chairman of Biocon, who has known the Murthys for decades and is Rohan's godmother.

## THE UNCONVENTIONAL BRIDE

The job that Sudha had never coveted led her to the man she eventually married. When I ask Sudha about Murthy, she blushes at the memory of how they met. They had a common friend who worked in TELCO, from whom Sudha often borrowed books; several of these bore the signature of N.R. Narayana Murthy. 'In my mind's eye I pictured Murthy as someone bold and confident, but when we eventually met he turned out to be a shy, soft-spoken introvert. We started meeting regularly as part of a group and much later alone.'

An alumnus of the University of Mysore and the Indian Institute of Technology (IIT) Kanpur, Murthy had just returned from working in Paris when he met Sudha. Perpetually broke as a research assistant with a computer systems firm in Pune, the bespectacled young man was not the knight most young women dream of. 'He never had money and always said to me, "Will you pay my share? I'll repay you later,"' laughs Sudha, who had maintained a tab of all the expenses funded by her but tore it up when they married.

The proposal when it came was as unusual and original as the couple. One day, when the two were in a autorickshaw rattling through the streets of Pune, Murthy turned to Sudha and solemnly declared, 'I am 5 feet 4 inches tall. I come from a lower-middle-class family. I can never be rich. You are beautiful and intelligent. You can get anyone you want. But will you marry me?'

'He proposed to me by highlighting the negatives in his life!' says Sudha, and admits that it made her appreciate Murthy's genuineness and honesty; she had, in her own way, come to love his simple charm.

Convincing her parents, however, was not easy; they were reluctant but finally agreed to meet him. Sudha still laughs when she talks of that meeting. Running late and dressed in a bright red shirt, Murthy spoke to an already unimpressed father-in-law-to-be about his plans to start an orphanage and join the Communist Party of India to overhaul the political system. Sudha's father, though progressive, was horrified that this was the man his lovely, bright daughter wanted to marry, but her mother was won over by Murthy's Kannadiga lineage and erudition.

Bolstered by her mother's support, Sudha gave her father an ultimatum—she would not marry Murthy without his blessings, but neither would she marry anyone else. 'After three years, at the end of 1977, Murthy began working at Patni Computers in Mumbai. That broke down my father's resistance, and we got married in a simple ceremony at Murthy's house in Bengaluru on 10 February 1978, in the presence of our families,' she says. The bride and groom split the cost of the wedding, which was Rs 800. And Sudha became the proud owner of her first silk sari!

Directly after, the couple moved to the US, where Murthy had a training programme to undergo. With him at work, Sudha backpacked across the country alone for three months—and what an adventurous time it turned out to be! Once she was arrested in New York as a suspected drug trafficker, thanks to her *dabba* filled with curd rice, and another time she was stranded for the night at the bottom of the Grand Canyon with no means to inform Murthy, who was panic-stricken.

Sudha and Murthy have dissimilar personalities, with a common passion for books. Sudha is an extrovert who loves travelling and Indian classical music; Murthy prefers being home and enjoys Western classical music. So is it a classic case of opposites attracted to one another, I ask Sudha, who replies with a smile, 'We are opposites that complement each other. The inscriptions in the books that he presents me with, always say *"From Me to You"* or *"To the person I most admire".*'

However, the true secret of their abiding relationship, jests Sudha, is something very different. 'Early in our relationship I made peace with the fact that my partner is a man of few words. Our marriage has worked because we have no unrealistic expectations of each other. It's a simple arrangement—I talk, he listens.'

Sudha worked at TELCO for eight years before quitting in 1981 to help Murthy found Infosys. When she told J.R.D. that she was leaving to support her husband—even though she was not sure the new venture would do well—he said, 'Never start anything with diffidence, always start with confidence. And when you are successful you must give back to society.' The

Murthys continue to live by those words and, as Mazumdar-Shaw tells me, 'Sudha and Murthy's life is about simplicity, being grounded, not flaunting your wealth, integrity and honesty.' Says Sudha, 'I value money but feel God gave me this much for a reason. That realization has never let me be at ease. It inspires me to always do more.'

## THE SEED INVESTOR

Infosys was birthed on a cold January in 1981 by Murthy and six of his software engineer colleagues in the Murthys' house in Mumbai. Six months later, it was registered as a private limited company, with start-up capital provided by Sudha.

She says, 'I was apprehensive because not one of these seven people had a business background or capital reserves; they were driven solely by a passion to create quality software. It was typical of Murthy to dream but have no money to support the dream. I gave him my savings of Rs 10,000 and said that for three years, I would take care of our financial needs while he chased his dream.' The couple had had their daughter Akshata by then—Infosys is affectionately called their second child—so it was a courageous step by any measure. But Sudha's commitment to supporting her husband was greater than her fears.

Working with the Walchand Group to pay the bills, Sudha also chipped in at Infosys, writing software. Her modest house in Pune was the start-up's headquarters and she was, variously, cook, programmer, clerk, secretary and office assistant. 'We had no car or phone but all of us juggled our lives, working hard and having fun. It was like a joint family. Rohini Nilekani helped, Sudha Gopalakrishnan looked after Akshata with great love, while Kumari Shibulal cooked.'

Infosys grew prodigiously and co-founder Nandan Nilekani suggested that Sudha join the board of directors. As its seed investor and someone who had worked and made huge sacrifices for its growth, Sudha agreed. Murthy did not, which shocked and deeply hurt her. He was adamant that both of them could not work together but, to emphasize that he was not being selfish or patriarchal, he offered to step down if Sudha wanted to work full-time.

It was a tough call for Sudha, who was more qualified than all the founders, and driven enough to do the job. She had trouble overcoming her sense of rejection even as she tried to understand her husband's stand. She admits that the episode rankled for years, though Murthy consistently acknowledges his wife's sacrifice at that juncture and he often attributes his success to her. But to Sudha, 'It was Murthy's dream at the end of the day. I just made what I thought was the right choice.'

While she is modest, Rohan underscores his mother's immense contribution: 'Without my mother's support I am quite confident that my father would not be very successful. I have seen in transaction after transaction, in event after event, that my mother is the backbone for my father, Infosys, our family. The lesson that I have learnt is that without such support it is impossible for anybody to build anything.'

When I compare the couple to Pierre and Marie Curie, who, too, worked together to build something enduring, Sudha is embarrassed; but my observation is based on fact. Infosys had a market capitalization of $39 billion in mid-November 2014; it is the second-largest IT company in India, and the first one listed on an American stock exchange. Three decades after she funded his first venture, Sudha sold shares in Infosys worth approximately Rs 430 crore (nearly 70 per cent of the seed capital) to finance her husband's second, Catamaran Ventures. Little wonder then that she is considered one of the most successful investment managers in the world.

Given her own brilliance, I ask how Sudha feels about being known as Narayana Murthy's wife; her cheerful reply is: 'I would rather be remembered as an author and social worker than the wife of a billionaire business tycoon.' In fact, she spells the family name differently because she was told that the 'h' is unnecessary; and over the years, Sudha has been very clear that she is her own person—a woman who plays various roles but who refuses to be told who she ought to be.

## THE COMMITTED MOTHER

Both Rohan and his sister Akshata stand testimony to the immense significance of Sudha's sacrifice. She has been a devoted mother, drawing from her own wonderful childhood and anchored by her parents' values. 'Children need their mother more when they are young and less as they grow,' she tells me. 'Those early years are crucial to teach them values. When your husband is building a company like Infosys, all of his concentration is on work. Today,

I have no regrets. I am very happy I was there for my children when they needed me most.' She made sure, though, that the children understood the reasons for their father's absence. Rohan remembers that she 'clearly explained to my sister and me that we were all in this together and my father had to work overtime to build this institution. We saw him working very, very hard, and her taking on a lot of responsibility.'

Mazumdar-Shaw, who has known Akshata and Rohan all their lives, says, 'The children are a great blend of both parents and have imbibed their warmth and sensitivity. Sudha has inculcated in them her simplicity and very strong values—a caring outlook, strong pride for background and culture, respect for elders.'

Passing on values of frugality and thrift were not easy in the post-liberal India that Akshata and Rohan grew up in. The dichotomies were compounded by the family's growing wealth, as Infosys expanded globally. Sudha persisted, teaching the children to respect money by being accountable for it—'If Akshata bought five dresses, she had to give away five old ones. I didn't want her to think of herself as a rich kid.' Similarly, Rohan ate out with friends, but never at a five-star hotel. Both took the school bus and, on birthdays, donated money to a cause instead of hosting lavish parties. Akshata had only one birthday party ever, and Rohan none, though neither regrets it.

Sudha says, 'When you have money, teaching your children its value is difficult. Even today, I think twice about spending on an autorickshaw if I can walk instead. My children have seen wealth from a young age, so I don't have the same expectations of them, but as parents, we lead by example.'

And that example has been a beacon. Akshata, who has an MBA from Stanford University, engages with artisans for her eponymous fashion line. Rohan's interest in philosophy, history and the classics—he has degrees in computer science from Harvard and Cornell—prompted him to donate $5.2 million to establish the Murty Classical Library at Harvard University.

## SIMPLE LIVING, HIGH THINKING

My next meeting with Sudha is at her home of over two decades. If people's houses are a reflection of their philosophies, the Murthys really do walk their talk. The Murthy family home is beautiful in its simplicity, and is maintained by Sudha with loving care. Indeed, for many years, she ran her home without any staff, doing household chores herself. The core of minimalism epitomizes the Murthys' lives. Even when Infosys went public in 1993, earning them great wealth, they chose to continue living in the same house instead of moving into bigger, more luxurious premises as is the norm, and use their expanded resources to make the world better.

Once again, barring a watch and a *shakha-pola,* Sudha wears no jewellery. She tells me she wears her *mangalsutra* occasionally, like 'if I have to attend a family function or visit my elders. In fact, there are no lockers in my house because I have no jewels to keep safe. At most times, I wear inexpensive stone earrings.' Her energy is radiant and, at home, with few material possessions around her, her philosophy becomes clearer.

What has sudden wealth meant for her personally, I ask. 'I don't feel guilty about having money because it is the result of hard work, but I don't flaunt it, either. Our only extravagances are books and CDs,' she says. In fact, on a trip to Varanasi twenty years ago, where tradition demands that one should renounce something, Sudha gave up shopping.

Given her leaning towards austerity and service, it was inevitable that Sudha would become a respected philanthropist. The seeds of it were sown by her father but it was fifteen-year-old Akshata, however, who was responsible for her mother's greatest epiphany. Her daughter used to read to a blind student and when she asked Sudha to help, the latter—busy with her job and home—suggested they make a donation instead. Akshata was furious and told her mother she had no right to talk about philanthropy if she did no social work herself. 'Her words set me thinking. I questioned myself on what I had done for others in my forty-five years and found no substantial answer. Thus, the Infosys Foundation was born in 1996.'

This foundation is at the core of Infosys' CSR programme and is anchored by Sudha, whom Bagchi prefers to call a humanist, not a philanthropist— 'She is an instrument of change and development, deeply concerned with humanity. If she didn't have Narayana Murthy's money, she would still be doing this, the scale might have been different.'

Talking about Sudha's gruelling fourteen–eighteen-hour days and travel for twenty days a month, and the physical discomfort of it, he adds, 'She is not just a thought leader, sitting in a glasshouse or an ivory tower and trying to create change. She is out there in the middle of it.' Sudha truly believes that her life is enriched by her travels. 'I have learnt the best lessons of life from meeting people in villages across the country, no matter how remote or rural.'

Infosys CEO and MD Vishal Sikka says that her 'compassion, idealism and sheer awesomeness' has inspired large numbers to walk in her footsteps. His wife, Vandana, is engaged in setting up the Infosys Foundation, USA, under Sudha's mentorship. 'She is open to new ideas, which is crucial to invention. And while a large majority of us look to our peers for direction, she is one of the select few who looks inwards and doesn't pay too much attention to the social matrix.'

Describing the difference in her approach, he says that while CSR in Indian corporate circles of the 1990s had come to signify mostly making donations or funding welfare projects, Sudha was 'unstinting in contributing not just financial resources but her passion, deep involvement and often radical ideas—as a full-time career philanthropist—to truly make a difference. She brought, and continues to bring to this day, a great combination of energy, knowledge, values and conviction to continually rethink philanthropy. She thought of this all-important question – should I revise my agenda based on this new idea? From changing the way she dressed to blend more seamlessly into the cultural folds of conservative, rural India, to changing her career path and life direction, she stopped at absolutely nothing to respond to the idea, of supporting the poorest of the poor in India, when it first emerged.'

Mazumdar-Shaw tells me of the foundation's support to the devadasis—temple dancers who are treated almost like prostitutes—'Sudha helped the devadasis come out of their despair. She's given them hope and better lives through education and employment.'

Sudha chooses causes that may not be on anyone else's radar because she has been somewhere and seen what is needed. Former Infosys chairman K.V. Kamath believes Sudha is 'extraordinarily brilliant . . . with a clear focus and vision.'

Under the foundation's aegis, Sudha has set up libraries, schools, hospitals, science centres and midday meal and sanitation programmes. It provides grants for rural livelihood and education projects, health programmes and rehabilitation for people with disabilities. It also equips government schools in Karnataka with computers and libraries. Given her family's love for books, Sudha has personally supervised the inventories of these libraries.

As chairperson of Infosys Foundation, too, Sudha has founded many orphanages, which was what Murthy had wanted to do as a young man though that dream could have cost him a wife. Sudha laughs when I point that out and says that his sense of purpose has never waned either. 'We have an understanding. He earns and I spend, mostly on philanthropy.'

Bagchi lists Sudha among the twenty-five 'most striking' people he has met, from among heads of state and captains of global industry—'Here is a computer science teacher, who was an engineer on TELCO's shop floor, and is a champion of causes from building toilets in villages to education to restoration of art, literature and heritage.'

For their part, the Murthys are averse to showing off their philanthropic pursuits: 'Philanthropy is a personal and private matter.' This quiet commitment to social causes, which they quietly take up and make their own, is perhaps what propelled ET Awards to felicitate Sudha as the Corporate Citizen of the Year on behalf of the Infosys Foundation in 2016; similarly, the Indian Chamber of Commerce Lifetime Achievement Award for her work in 2017.

In 2018, the Infosys Foundation committed to accelerating social impact and development with the launch of the Aarohan Social Impact Awards, instituted to recognize individuals, teams and NGOs that are developing unique solutions for the social sector, with the potential to positively impact the underprivileged in India. The prize amount is set at INR 1.5 crores. The Infosys Foundation has always been at the forefront of social development in India since its inception, and this award will help achieve better living standards for everyone through research and development.

## THE STORYTELLER

Storytelling has been a lifelong passion. She began writing while in college, published her first Kannada book circa 1980, and is now a feted author with thirty published titles and 200 translations in every major Indian language. 'I don't need to create fictitious situations. Travelling for twenty days a month, all over India for my philanthropic work, gets me plenty of material,' she says. 'I just need to be convinced of a thought. For instance, it took me seven years to convince myself that I had to write *House of Cards* but only forty-five days to complete it.' Sudha writes between 5 a.m. and 7 a.m. 'I shut myself away from everything else. This talkative person retreats into total silence.'

Says Mazumdar-Shaw, 'I really admire her for the amount of passion and dedication she has for everything she does. At the drop of a hat, she'll be off on a train or a bus to a village somewhere, doing something with children or women or the elderly. She sits with people like weavers and always comes back with some great stories.'

While Rohan refuses to comment on his mother's writing, he is very proud of his experience at the Jaipur Literature Festival in 2015. 'We were all speaking on very different topics—me on the classical library, my father on the Indian economy, and my mother was there in her own right. What was amazing was the number of people who came to listen to her. I was thrilled that so many children had read her books and wanted to talk to her.'

For Sudha, writing is akin to breathing, and it shows in the sheer number of titles she puts out every year, even while balancing all of the other hats she dons regularly. It is a testament to her steadfast belief in the value of telling meaningful stories in every language that she was chosen as the Bengaluru Press Club Person of the Year for her immense contribution to Kannada literature, language, and social service as well as the Lifetime Achievement Award at the Crossword-Raymond Book Awards in 2018.

It was also her writing that led Sudha into cinema and television when her Kannada novel, *Dollar Sose*, was serialized on Zee TV as *Dollar Bahu,* and *Pitruroon* was adapted for a Marathi film. With her delightful sense of adventure and curiosity, Sudha also tried her hand at acting but with the caveat that she would not change her hair or wear garish saris. She played a judge in a popular Kannada TV show, *Preethi Illada Mele*, and also starred in a film, *Prarthane,* which highlighted how Kannada language and culture are getting a raw deal in the time of economic reform. 'I don't like applying make-up and I was very uncomfortable doing so even for a film. But I am fascinated by all art forms and, to me, acting is an extension of that.'

I set out to meet Sudha Murty because I wanted to understand what compels her to lead the extraordinary life she does. I get my answer when she says to me, 'It was destiny that Murthy and I were chosen to be successful and wealthy. We are trustees of this wealth and it is meant to be used in a fruitful manner.' Sudha's personal and professional life—as also that of her family— are guided by a spiritual compass, and reflect the thoughts of Lao Tzu, the Chinese philosopher-poet who said, 'I have just three things to teach: simplicity, patience, compassion. These three are your greatest treasures.'

# N.R. NARAYANA MURTHY

*When one talks of the Murthys, more than thinking about the iconic company that they have founded, one thinks of the simplicity that they have come to represent in a world given to excess.* **Nagavara Ramarao Narayana Murthy,** *was founder-chairman of Infosys when India found its place on the global information technology map. His north star is* **Sudha Murty,** *a trailblazer in her own career, which she gave up to help her husband found his company; raise their two accomplished children; become a bestselling author; and a committed grass-roots philanthropist. Narayana Murthy talks about his wife and lifelong friend whose independent spirit, cultural rootedness and excellent people skills still have him just as enthralled as he was when they met four decades ago.*

**Sudha cherishes her eight years in TELCO Pune, which was when she met the two most important men in her life—J.R.D. Tata and you. What are your early memories of her?**

She was an extremely cheerful, talkative, happy-go-lucky and enthusiastic young lady. Sudha always brought out laughter in people, including me. Full of energy, she would be ready to head out on a trek at 6 a.m. and remain enthusiastic even at 11 p.m. Even back then, Sudha enjoyed being with and related to people of all ages and classes. She would be as happy talking with the cleaning lady from her hostel as she was with a business tycoon. She was as good friends with young people—say eight-to-ten-year-old children of our friends—as she was with sixty- or seventy-year-olds. Sudha always had something relevant to share with the people she was talking to.

**When you proposed to Sudha, you had a temporary job as a research assistant and were said to have little ambition. Perhaps you were not the most eligible suitor, but she agreed to marry you anyway.**

Well, I can only say that she was very kind to take a liking to me! Frankly, I didn't consider that a possibility at all. I was sure that her parents, especially her father, would not be happy. Which father would be happy if his daughter were to come home and say, 'I'm getting married, but he doesn't know what he's going to do and he doesn't have a job. He might start an orphanage!'

Sudha, however, seemed very clear and determined. For her, I think, life meant a lot more than just money, clothes and material comforts; it was about sharing pleasant conversations, pleasant memories—maybe going for a movie or dining at an inexpensive little restaurant. It was way beyond how rich you were or how powerful or handsome. So, she just took the decision.

**Sudha was both the only woman among 250 men at her engineering college and the sole woman engineer at TELCO. What are the lessons that young women can learn from her?**

Like me, Sudha walks the talk and believes that leadership is best demonstrated through example. While teaching at college, she would exhort every young girl to be independent, confident and aspire for the very best. Addressing women engineers at Infosys, she said that the only barrier women face is that which is self-imposed—it's all in the mind. Overcome the inhibitions in your mind and the rest will automatically fall in place. Citing instances from her own life—bringing up her daughter the way she has, helping her younger sister get into IIT Madras and take up jobs in Canada and the US—Sudha motivated numerous women to realize their potential.

**Sudha is known to possess an incredible sense of adventure and independence. Have there been particular instances of it that you still remember?**

In almost everything she does Sudha's adventurous. Because of her work, she needs to travel across India and for a long time, I would insist on her being accompanied by security personnel. She always refused saying, 'No, people are generally good. If people know that I have good intentions, they'll have good intentions too!'

Once when we were in Mumbai, she said, 'Look, I want to spend my weekends usefully.' When I would ask, she simply replied, 'Let me try and write.' For someone who had not written anything ever before, Sudha wrote her first work, a novel—so simply and quickly, so well—it seemed incredible.

**Could you tell us what she is like, as a mother to your two children, Akshata and Rohan?**

Sudha has always led by example, conducted herself simply and inculcated in our children the virtue of contentment and enjoying the small things. The best thing she did was to bring them up uninfluenced by money. She has never said that we must have this or that car, or encouraged spending for the sake of social status. She never gave the children more than she thought necessary. For Sudha, going to the temple or a movie was a big thing, and the house we still live in has been our home for twenty-five years.

**Can you tell me a particularly evocative story about her as a mother?**

Before our first child was born, we discussed that we would bring up our children in a way that they embrace progress without losing sense of their tradition. Sudha recommended speaking to them in Kannada at home while I would converse with them solely in English. Both Akshata and Rohan chose Kannada as their second language right up to high school, and I think that was excellent.

Even today, whenever we wish to speak in confidence when out in public, Akshata and Rohan speak to me in Kannada. While they are, of course, modern in their thought and lifestyle, they can read as well as write Kannada, enjoy Kannada literature and movies. In short, the children have worked out a fine balance between the need to operate in the modern world using English while conserving our tradition and discovering the beauty of our mother tongue, thanks to Sudha.

Also, she and the children use 'ty' and not 'thy' when they spell our last name, because Sudha felt the right spelling for Murty as written in Kannada should not include the 'h.'

**Sudha's brand of philanthropy is about reaching out to those in need, personally. What drives her towards grass-roots work?**

First of all, she comes from a doctor's family. Both her father and sister were professors in hospitals. When you are associated closely with government hospitals, you see a lot of suffering first-hand. What Sudha saw at that impressionable age stayed with her. Besides, her parents sent their children to government schools and instilled in them the virtue of caring for people from diverse backgrounds. Sudha's upbringing established in her this commitment towards uplift of the downtrodden.

**She has excelled as a teacher, technocrat, social worker and author, and you have had your own incredibly successful journey. How does she inspire you?**

I think we operate more as friends than anything else. She is an extremely balanced person. If I was in distress, she would reassure me saying, 'Don't worry, we have learnt to live simply. So, it doesn't matter, we'll continue to lead simple lives.' When our second child was born, she willingly gave up her job as a college teacher to devote herself to our children's care. She taught me the very important lesson that it is possible to live within your means, even if they are little. Whenever one of us at home is not keeping well, the first person we all turn to is Sudha. She will not just take the person to the doctor but be there for her/him twenty-four hours. She inspires us with her empathy and caring ways. When I view all this together, I realize just how extraordinary her contribution to my life has been.

**What would you say her contribution has been to Infosys?**

When I was planning Infosys, she knew we would need to move out of Mumbai and she would have to quit her job. And this, when she was the only one among all the co-founders with a significant job and was earning twice as much as all my six colleagues put together. Yet, she did not once express concern about forgoing it all.

When we founded Infosys, she was perhaps the best educated among us all. A first ranker in all semesters, she alone had obtained a scholarship to do her PhD in the US. But, when we sat down and discussed that there has to be just one boss in the office and it was to be either of us, she didn't think twice. She simply said, 'Don't worry, you do it because you are so passionate about it.'

Yet, Sudha's always been there for me, with the attitude that she did not have to be a part of it to support me fully. Once, she even pawned her jewellery so we could pay salaries to my six colleagues in the US. And she did it with a smile. Whenever a situation demanded sacrifice, she made it willingly without claiming any credit. She has contributed immensely to Infosys while remaining very much in the background.

**What are the hallmarks of Sudha's success and how does she remain an inspirational role model for women?**

First and foremost, Sudha does everything with complete attention and interest. Second, nothing is too small for her. Third, she derives joy from everything. Once you realize the importance of each thing, no matter what it is; once you derive happiness from whatever you do, and realize that nothing is too small, you will do it well. In short, it's very important to be giving, smiling and full of confidence. These attributes of Sudha have inspired me and I'm sure can inspire women in India and across the globe.

# YASMEEN
# PREMJI

*Yasmeen is a wonderful friend to have; she cares and values her friendships. She is very grounded and, of course, extremely intelligent and modest. I always find her interesting to talk to because she can engage on different issues with her own point of view. She writes beautifully as you can see from her recently published novel and is perceptive, picking up nuances that you wouldn't generally think about . . . Yasmeen is very much her own person.*

**—KIRAN MAZUMDAR-SHAW**

When Yasmeen was writing her debut novel, the acclaimed rags-to-riches saga, *Days of Gold & Sepia*, she had to extensively research to convincingly portray to her readers how a poor man could acquire such enormous wealth in one lifetime. Not remarkable, until you stop to think who this writer is. Yasmeen Premji is the wife of billionaire industrialist and philanthropist, Azim Premji, whose life followed not a very different trajectory. A woman who, as part of a pioneering business family, stands at the centre of a world that is driven by the creation and sharing of wealth. Yet, it is part of her ingenuous charm that money and material success are not central to her life. They are instruments of opportunity, not indulgence.

The unassuming wife of a reclusive tycoon, Yasmeen is never overshadowed by her husband's wealth or influence; her life focuses as much on being herself—wife, mother, friend, writer, self-taught architect and an integral part of the family's philanthropic initiatives—as on representing the Premji name. Yasmeen refused to sacrifice her own and her family's privacy by deliberately maintaining a low profile and holding on to her core values and valued personal space. It was only to promote her debut novel that she finally stepped out of her fiercely guarded life to give interviews and play the role of an author, before retreating gracefully back into her world.

I meet Yasmeen at the Bengaluru office of the Azim Premji Foundation designed and built by her—obviously much thought has gone into this building, and much heart. It is a structure in exposed natural stone and brick—there is not a false stone here, a tribute to her genuine architectural acumen. Dressed in a classic green cotton Kanjeevaram sari with simple accoutrements, she greets me warmly. I had been drawn by an old photograph of hers in a newspaper, and seeing her in person affirms that Yasmeen's charm is rooted in an inner temple of grace. Her disarming manner and warm smile puts me at ease instantly. She leads me into a simple sun-drenched reception and a brick-walled meeting room beyond, where we settle in for our chat, which stretches from the scheduled half-hour to two-and-a-half hours. There are no hangers-on and no fuss.

As her elder son, Rishad Premji says, 'I am amazed at how little my mother has been affected by my father's success. She remains the same grounded person she was when I was a child. One of the most important lessons I have learnt from her is—be who you are unapologetically.'

Talking to Yasmeen, I understand that she lives by her own standards without pretensions.

'Sometimes, when our lives change, we get caught up in trying to live up to others' expectations of us, occasionally even moulding ourselves to fit into their image of us. I try to stay away from all that. In the end, you need to figure out who you are, what gives you joy, where your core lies and how to stay true to it,' she tells me.

## GROWING DEEP ROOTS

Yasmeen Chinoy grew up in erstwhile Bombay, now Mumbai, where her family owned, among other interests, what was once one of Asia's largest garage-cum-car showrooms when it opened almost a century ago. As part of a joint family, the youngest of three children and the only daughter, Yasmeen's childhood was filled with warmth and laughter. Yasmeen's older brother Zahir says, 'As a little girl she was very bubbly and would overwhelm you with her exuberance. Everyone was very fond of her because she was sweet and helpful.'

Her level-headed, unflappable personality, Yasmeen believes, comes from growing up in a conventional but not conservative family and a city like Mumbai, before it became 'maximum city'. She says, 'For me it was a very special place . . . It was cosmopolitan and broad-minded and generous. Women could walk freely without fear. It was safe and nobody got unduly offended and tried strong-arm tactics to tell law-abiding citizens how to live their lives. It was, in short, a civilized city—a city that allowed its citizens the freedom to grow . . . and I loved growing up in it.'

Her close relationships with her mother and later, her mother-in-law, deeply influenced Yasmeen's life, shaping her confidence, beliefs and principles. Her mother was married off at sixteen, three months before she could finish school, which she made up for by reading voraciously. Despite being a high school dropout, 'Shah, my mother was one of the most educated women I knew, because she read widely on philosophy, religion, history, biography, literature. Whatever excited her she shared with me.' Fascinated by her mother's stories and conversations, Yasmeen, too, became a lover of books and secretly longed to become a writer. 'On my eighth birthday, my mother gave me a dictionary and index book. "Anytime you read a word you don't understand, look it up and write down its meaning," she said,' and Yasmeen did.

Zahir agrees that it was their mother who influenced Yasmeen most during her growing years. 'She had our mother's sunny temperament, and was non-judgemental and open-minded and yet a very private person. You knew if you confided in her, it would never go beyond.'

The summer she was fifteen, when a visiting cousin, with whom Yasmeen had shared her secret ambition to be a writer, said in a matter-of-fact way, 'If you want to write, write,' it was like a door opening. And she did. At seventeen, her first short story was published under the pseudonym 'Wye' (after the initial 'y' for her name) in the *Indian Express*'s weekend supplement. 'I was young and thought using a nom de plume was the stylish thing to do!' Subsequent stories were published under her own name.

Yasmeen was brought up on par with her two brothers and had her freedom. It was an upbringing based on love, values and mutual trust. In college when out with friends she was not given a deadline like many other girls. 'We were not smothered with overprotection. Absence of strict rules did not mean one ran wild, it meant learning to set one's own limits, take responsibility for one's own life.'

Yasmeen's relationship with her father was more formal but he encouraged her to study and never curbed her dreams. Her ability to balance her independence and individuality without unduly flouting convention is rooted in the manner in which she was raised. She shrugs off my suggestion that, from a young age, she was determined to live life on her own terms: 'It was not such a big deal actually. I was just fortunate to have had an enlightened broad-minded family,' she says. 'I could do the things that I found exciting because I could convince them of my passion for what I wanted to do. But I wasn't doing anything that extraordinary. Nothing about me is extraordinary.' But there are those who would beg to differ!

Writer Bhaichand Patel in one of his breezy columns remembers her as one of 'the prettiest girls in town, very bright, with an enchanting smile. We were all in love with her,' he writes, which of course Yasmeen waves away with an embarrassed smile as 'just so much fluff!' Launching Yasmeen's book, *Days of Gold & Sepia*, in Mumbai, actor Shabana Azmi remembered her from their schooldays at Queen Mary's as an immensely popular student in school and also as their games captain. 'Like many others,' confessed Shabana with a smile, 'I, too, had a huge crush on her!'

Even today, close friends of more recent years like Kiran Mazumdar-Shaw, chairperson and managing director of Biocon Limited, says, 'To the general public, Yasmeen might seem to be reclusive and reticent, but, in fact, she's very gregarious, especially among friends. She is extremely engaging, and a lot of fun. At a shaadi, you will invariably find her on the dance floor. It's a side of her very few people see.'

## TAKING FLIGHT

At St Xavier's College, Mumbai, Yasmeen majored in psychology and topped her class. An avid sportswoman, she represented the college in athletics, basketball, chess, captained the hockey team, and was a member of the winning Mumbai University hockey team. She also played for Mumbai and was captain of the junior team. Zahir tells me an interesting anecdote from their childhood, when he and his friends—all boys of fourteen–fifteen—played hockey on their terrace on weekends. Yasmeen, then eight or nine, would insist on playing, much to his embarrassment. But she enjoyed it so much that his good-natured friends accepted her 'as one of the boys'. That was the beginning of her passion for the game!

With characteristic modesty, Yasmeen adds, 'Whatever I did, I did for the sheer joy of it, whether sports or studies or design, and if along the way I occasionally achieved something, it was icing on the cake! No surprise then that in college, the coveted trophy for the sportsman of the year, awarded to person with the 'best sporting spirit', fell into her lap.

When Yasmeen wanted to go overseas for advanced studies like her brothers, her parents told her that they couldn't really afford it. But she was determined. While in her final year at St Xavier's, entirely on her own she researched and wrote off to several colleges in the US, fine-tuning the list and eventually zeroing in on a full scholarship for a master's degree offered by Smith College. 'Not only was she independent and self-sufficient,' says Zahir, 'but persevering too. She knew she could do it, and she did!'

Yasmeen's two years in the US, especially at Smith, will always be special. 'They opened my mind and taught me to expand my thinking. At home I rarely questioned the written word, but there students were encouraged to think independently and express themselves. It was an exposure to a whole new world.'

After her graduation in the late 1960s, Yasmeen decided to travel through Europe on her way home. Yasmeen backpacked across Europe on her own, keen to see as much as she could on her limited budget before returning home, for she was not sure if she would ever have a chance to travel abroad again.

'In hindsight,' says Yasmeen, 'I realize how generous it was of my parents to have encouraged me and given me that space within the conventional middle-class framework. Travel makes you grow. You learn to fend for yourself in different situations, to land on your feet. Remember this was at a time when even calling home, let alone getting help, was not a viable option. You learnt to make choices: whether to eat three whole meals a day, or to spend instead three more days in Paris and get by on peanuts for lunch!'

On her return to Mumbai, Yasmeen was selected by Esso (now Hindustan Petroleum) as a management trainee and was posted as personnel supervisor. Enthusiastic and full of ideas, Yasmeen enjoyed her first job and was a valued recruit. Her boss suggested that if she got a degree in management, she had the potential to someday head the HR (then ERD) department. Yasmeen seriously considered it, but realized that climbing up the corporate ladder was not for her. She stayed on the job for over two years but quit as soon as she got an opportunity to travel again.

'She had this travel bug in her,' reminiscences Zahir. 'In those days it was extremely difficult to travel abroad. It was very expensive, besides which one was allowed almost zero foreign exchange. But Yasmeen was so determined to go that she somehow managed to get herself a brief stint at a carpet exhibition in Germany, which came, believe it or not, with a return air ticket in hand!'

'I worked for five months and saved enough from the pittance I earned to travel for ten! I think that was a great deal whichever way you look at it,' says Yasmeen with a laugh, 'I would not have exchanged it for anything!'

## FAMILY MATTERS

In 1974, Yasmeen Chinoy married Azim Premji. Their families had known each other for many years and Yasmeen's father was on the board of Western India Products Limited, the company owned by Azim's family.

The wedding, though hosted by two reputed business families, was a simple affair. Both families were sticklers for rules, which at that time did not permit feeding more than a hundred guests at any function. In fact, it was so casual that they even forgot to arrange for a photographer at the small lunch reception in their garden following the wedding! Decades later, Azim and Yasmeen's elder son Rishad married Aditi Mehta in a quiet civil ceremony and the wedding celebrations, though not quite as simple as his parents' were, at the children's insistence, a relatively modest, intimate affair.

Yasmeen's new family shared the same kind of values that she had grown up with. Azim's widowed mother, Dr Gulbanoo Premji, a strong, intelligent and generous lady, ran a charitable hospital in Mumbai for children with polio and cerebral palsy, which she had helped found. 'Like my mother, she was an extremely sensible and straightforward person. There was nothing artificial about either of them. What you saw is what you got,' says Yasmeen. 'I knew that if she [Gulbanoo] ever had an issue, she would come to me directly and there would never be any backbiting. She was a wonderful person—generous of purse, heart and mind.'

Azim was twenty-one when his father died. He had dropped out of Stanford barely three months before graduation to return home and shoulder the responsibility of the small family business which would one day grow into IT major Wipro. Interestingly, much like his mother-in-law—the high school dropout, Azim—the college dropout—worked hard at educating himself. He read prodigiously. A workaholic and dreamer, Azim realized that to achieve the kind of growth he envisioned, he would have to recruit professionals from outside the family, an idea rare in small family-run businesses in the 1960s and certainly ahead of its time.

As he told Yasmeen, 'If you want to command the respect of those who work with you, you've got to know as much, if not more, than them.' He would spend all his spare time reading. Often, he would give me notes to write. He built his career on hard work, clear-cut goals and focus. My mother-in-law often said, 'It's not hard work that kills you, as much as lack of focus that stresses you out.'

With a workaholic husband, Yasmeen had to find ways to keep herself busy. She laughs as she recalls, 'I think the only reason he insisted that I design his first office was to keep me occupied, as he was too busy to spend much time with his new wife!' Though she had already completed a certificate course in interior design earlier, the entire exercise turned out to be such an exciting learning experience that it motivated her to go on and complete her diploma in design.

Yasmeen's two sons, Rishad and Tariq, arrived in quick succession. Yasmeen and Azim raised them to be good human beings, with basic family values of right and wrong. They grew up in middle-class comfort but were grounded in the family's level-headed attitude to money. They went to good schools but travelled by school bus, and if they missed that, had to take public transport.

Rishad says, 'My mother was never a hard taskmaster. She did not believe in imposing on us any agendas. She focused rather on a democratic upbringing, in the hope of rearing independent, balanced children, with good values who would be able to think for themselves, and less on instilling driving ambition.'

Asked about her role as a wife and the relationship the Premjis share, Yasmeen smiles, 'I enjoyed Azim's quirky sense of humour, his liberal view of life, his basic decency. He is a man of principles and someone you can look up to and respect.' Friends of the couple comment on how Azim and Yasmeen both complement one another—both appear reticent, but open up with friends. They share common interests and a mutual understanding which enables them to maintain their individual, richly textured personalities. 'The fact that Yasmeen is a supportive wife and at the same time her own person, is something to emulate,' says author Susmita Bagchi, who is a good friend.

'She's absolutely been the bedrock of support to my father—as a wife, the mother of his sons, and a partner. Being the pillar of strength in his personal life was a very important contribution to his professional life,' says Rishad. 'My mother, though very modern in her thinking, retains the values of a traditional wife whose first focus is the family.'

Having children shifted Yasmeen's focus, but her love for writing and design persisted and once the kids started school, Yasmeen began working at *Inside Outside*, then India's leading design magazine, as assistant editor. She worked for close to fifteen years, quitting shortly before the family moved to Bengaluru. She enjoyed her job. 'Those were good years,' she recalls with a smile. 'They gave me the opportunity to do what I enjoyed the most: writing; and it gave me an exposure to the best in Indian architecture and design.'

It was her time at the magazine which taught Yasmeen that you did not have to be a formally qualified architect to design a building, which gave her the confidence to build the family's first country home—a small stone cottage outside Mumbai. It was very challenging and exciting and every phase was a learning experience! We both laugh when she confesses that only when the house was almost complete, did she discover to her consternation that she had forgotten to design in the staircase!

Business historian and writer Gita Piramal has fond memories of Yasmeen from those years—'We first came to know each other as young writers. Yasmeen was working part-time at *Inside Outside* and I was trying to establish myself as a freelance business writer. Whenever we bumped into each other, we would swap notes on our writing. Yasmeen has a charming yet dry sense of fun. Most design writers don't get the opportunity to convert dreams into concrete reality. I'm glad that Yasmeen could go on to design and construct the Azim Premji Foundation as well as the Premji Investment office buildings in Bengaluru. Both have her signature style, the use of exposed stone and brick, fireclay tiles and terracotta *jaali*s, with plenty of light and cross ventilation.'

It was while designing these buildings that Yasmeen had the chance to exercise her creative freedom. 'I always wanted to design spaces like that, flooded with natural light and air. A place which, when it was built ten years ago and even today, has only one air-conditioned conference room, as you can still sit in most areas without one and not feel too hot,' she says. Her love for exposed earthy materials is evident and when I visited, I was struck by how every element had been chosen with care and had a meaning within the larger design.

## A NEW HOME

The Premjis moved to Bengaluru in 1998, as Azim thought it best to shift his headquarters to the IT capital of the country. Yasmeen quit *Inside Outside*, and though leaving her beloved Mumbai must have been wrenching, she knew it was important and necessary. 'One has to take things as they come and move on,' she says matter-of-factly. 'But I was very fortunate in my new home, and I have come to love Bengaluru and its people just as much.'

Life in her adopted city soon became busy and enriching. Her modest circle of friends ranges from thespian and litterateur Girish Karnad to dynamic entrepreneur Kiran Mazumdar-Shaw. They describe Yasmeen as 'a large-hearted hostess' who is humble and caring; someone who makes time for theatre, art and culture but never uses her name and position to secure favours. 'People take to Yasmeen as she is naturally unassuming and doesn't throw her weight around. I have never heard her say anything mean or malicious about anyone,' says one of her friends who has come to know her well.

## THE ALPHABET OF LIFE

It was in Bengaluru that Yasmeen's dream of writing a book finally found fruition. A long-postponed novel had long been simmering on the backburner. When her father died and more old stories came tumbling out of the family closet, Yasmeen was struck anew by the extraordinary richness of ordinary lives, and an outline for her novel began to take shape in her mind. A rags-to-riches story set in old Mumbai . . . an intricately woven saga, which would encompass not only many of the fascinating family stories she had grown up with, but also the story of old Mumbai, the vibrant city she loved.

*Days of Gold & Sepia*, published in 2012, tells the story of Lalljee Lakha, a penniless orphan who leaves his native land of Kutch, like Yasmeen's own grandfather, and goes on to find fortune and fame in Mumbai, city of gold, becoming the city's 'Cotton King'. The book, which tells a riveting tale, is set in the fascinating period between 1857 and 1947 and is peopled with the colourful characters of the time—merchant princes and maharajas, courtesans and soothsayers, pirates, freedom fighters and soldiers of the British Raj, and peppered with historical titbits.

'I was writing not just to have a book published in my name or for financial success. I was writing for the sheer joy of writing,' says Yasmeen. She wrote the old-fashioned way—putting pencil to paper. 'Many pencils were sharpened,' she comments wryly. 'Many scraps of paper piled up.' Sometimes she would write for weeks, sometimes not for a couple of years. No wonder it took twenty years! Yasmeen's writing was a private enterprise, rather like writing a diary. She didn't tell anyone, and because nobody knew, nobody pressured her to complete it. She only told her family when she had a signed publishing contract in hand! 'Needless to say, they were proud and pleased when I broke the news to them, and much more importantly, they really liked the book!'

Rishad tells me, 'I believe that my mother really wanted to prove to herself, more than to anyone else, that she could do it. I read the manuscript before it was printed and loved it. I read it twice—and I don't usually read anything twice—that was how much I enjoyed it. The storytelling is crisp and efficient, and my mother has a fantastic command over the English language.'

## AN INSTRUMENT OF GIVING

The move to Bengaluru was crucial for Wipro as the company had expanded its it services. Few had heard of the low-key Azim Premji until the IT boom of the late 1990s and even post that, he preferred to maintain a low profile, never feeling the need to become a public figure. This suited Yasmeen—herself a private person—very well. 'I don't think Wipro's trajectory changed my life in any meaningful way,' Yasmeen tells me. 'I felt completely detached from the financial gains of Wipro and preferred to keep away from the glare of publicity.' This is echoed by son Rishad who, in an interview to *Forbes*, quipped, 'I am not trying to be cool about this, but the truth is our lives are relatively untouched by the much vaunted wealth.' As is Azim's own life for that matter. He is famously known to fly economy and stay in three-star hotels on work trips abroad. Those tempted to label him as parsimonious were stumped when they discovered that he has committed a significant part of his wealth, a staggering Rs 50,000 crore, to charity, the largest donation by any Indian in modern times.

Money is not something that Yasmeen likes to talk about. While conceding that it is very important, she holds that for her, success in life is not about how much money you have or the symbols of wealth you acquire, but about personal fulfilment and inner contentment. 'I am a person who is moved by what I need, rather than by others' notion of what I ought to be or how I ought to live. I am not in a circle that pressurizes me to want more . . . and personally I am brand blind.'

I certainly didn't see any visible signs to the contrary. There was no Prada or Louis Vuitton handbag on her arm, no fancy watch flashing on her wrist, no latest gadget.

Bagchi tells me, 'Yasmeen is always well dressed, in an understated way that I like. She has her own style. Her biggest adornment is her humility.'

It is her brother Zahir who explains that money was never given overriding importance in their family while they were growing up. It was education and a sense of moderation in all things that was emphasized. Besides, Yasmeen was always an easily content person. If she topped the class or won a match, she was naturally jubilant, and if she didn't, it was all par for the course. 'I'm glad that wealth has not changed her,' he adds with quiet pride.

Influenced by Mahatma Gandhi's philosophy of the trusteeship of wealth, Azim firmly believes in the concept of 'fiduciary responsibility.' For her part, Yasmeen holds that it is for those to whom much is given to share with those to whom much less is given. 'Whether you give with your heart or with your mind or with your time, there is a great need for every kind of giving.'

In 2001, Azim set up the Azim Premji Foundation (APF) with a singular focus on education. It engages primarily with the government school system in rural areas in several districts and states, which caters to the most deprived segments of our society. The idea behind initially choosing education as an area of focus, Yasmeen explains, was that it was felt that education, specially of the girl child, would over time create more empowered women and families, who would be better equipped to make educated life choices, whether in matters of health, livelihood or education, thereby improving not only the quality of their own and their families' lives, but in the long term, of the fabric of society for the better.

Though APF is professionally managed by a committed team, all members of the family play some part in the foundation. Azim, Yasmeen, Rishad and Tariq are on the board, while Tariq works full-time in the foundation's critical endowment function. Yasmeen explains with characteristic humility— 'Professionals do the hands-on work, I am just a member of the board and we meet regularly to assess what is going on.' While giving Azim all the credit for starting the foundation, she does concede that it had to have the unstinting support of the family. 'And naturally that support was always there.' After all, the tradition of giving runs in the family.

As Dileep Ranjekar, CEO of the Premji Foundation, said in an interview with Bengaluru's *Talk* magazine, 'Yasmeen Premji does not talk big but has strong views. She believes Indian society must change and equality is the need of the hour. All people should have access to food, clothing, shelter and education, the basics of life.' Those, like Mazumdar-Shaw, who know her well, point out that at heart Yasmeen is 'as much a philanthropist as her husband. She's a big support to him, quiet, but a very solid anchor.'

In 2010, in an attempt to address the glaring shortage of qualified professionals in the social service sector, Azim started the Azim Premji University in Bengaluru, offering postgraduate degrees in education and development with the intent of creating a pool of well-qualified, dedicated young people committed to the social sector. This year a new undergraduate stream has been added.

Recently, looking at the enormous needs in every sphere of society, the Azim Premji Philanthropic Initiatives was started to extend support to different philanthropic endeavours.

## ROUNDING OFF

Yasmeen is one of those people who have been given to introspection early in life and are, therefore, among those who can more easily come to terms with it. She is so transparently comfortable with herself. As Piramal puts it, 'Self-knowledge distils life through a different prism, making it happier.'

Yasmeen's authenticity and concern about others remind me of American writer Maya Angelou's observation: 'People will forget what you said, people will forget what you did, but people will never forget how you made them feel.' Through all of my interactions with Yasmeen, there is a sense of ease——I never had to put on a front, because it was plain that she wasn't putting on one; she was always just herself. And I will never forget how she made me feel, which I can see was not just to create an impression, for, as she explains at the end of our chat, 'I don't feel the need to be remembered.' For her, playing the game rather than winning is what matters, living life rather than being applauded for the living is what finally counts.

# AZIM PREMJI

*Padma Vibhushan **Azim Premji**, pioneering IT tycoon and listed as one of the world's greatest entrepreneurs, is also among India's richest people. In this rare interview, Premji waxes eloquently about his partner of forty years, **Yasmeen Premji**, the woman behind his stupendous success, and their long companionship, their shared interest in education and social work, her groundedness and artistic inclinations.*

### Can you please tell us your first recollection of Yasmeen?

The first thing that struck me about her was her smile . . . the sparkle in her eyes that lit up her entire face . . .

### What are the characteristics of her persona that you have appreciated the most?

She has been a solid, sensible partner to me, mature enough to have tolerated my whims and idiosyncrasies with remarkable humour. My sons assure me I am not the easiest person to live with and that not too many modern wives would have endured me for four decades!

She took great care of my widowed mother whom she was exceedingly fond of, and who lived with us throughout. The two of them became close friends and companions. In fact through her, Yasmeen more than anyone else, became the repository of family stories.

### Please share your thoughts on Yasmeen as a mother to your two sons.

I am grateful she is the mother of my children. She was always there for them while I was engrossed with my work. I'm afraid I was a workaholic and didn't have as much time for the family as I would have liked, so that she often had to play both our roles for the boys. But she was there to instil in them basic values, guide them as they grew. I believe an important aspect of parenting is being a role model. Yasmeen is an intrinsically down-to-earth, grounded human being with an innate 'sense of humour' by which I mean an ability to take life as it comes, and I think growing up with her the children have imbibed her simplicity and her understated-ness, values which I personally appreciate.

**Yasmeen tells me that she wrote her critically acclaimed, bestselling debut novel *Days of Gold & Sepia*, inspired by fascinating stories she'd heard from her mother and mother-in-law, over twenty years on scraps of paper. Don't you think that's tad ironic for the wife of an IT czar?**

Absolutely! But that's Yasmeen for you! It was probably her way of keeping it a secret! Long hours on the typewriter or computer would have invited curiosity, and she wanted no one to know she was writing a novel until it had been not only completed, but accepted for publication by a reputable publisher. She is wary of raising expectations she might not be able to fulfil . . . She doesn't like letting people down.

**Over the past ten years, you are known to have committed a staggering Rs 30,000 crore to endow the Azim Premji Foundation. What do you see as Yasmeen's role in the foundation?**

Yasmeen is a trustee and a member on the board of the foundation, which supports not only our educational endeavour, but also the Azim Premji Philanthropic Initiatives. She brings a different point of view and an alternative perspective on various issues, which is very useful when making important directional decisions. And she is the architect of our foundation building, which she designed entirely both externally and internally and had erected under her personal supervision. She loves natural materials and eco-friendly designs, and the stone and brick edifice, with its natural light and ventilation, is much appreciated by all who work there.

**Yasmeen prefers to keep a low public profile. Your thoughts.**

That's the way she is, a discreet, self-contained woman, a private person who does not need to be seen and heard in public to know who and what she is!

# INDRA
# NOOYI

•

*Indra had a road map and she took PepsiCo on that road map even before she became CEO—she did this when she was doing strategy, when she was the CFO, and later when she became the CEO. So I think she has had a long-term vision of not just what PepsiCo ought to be, but a long-term vision of the kind of marketplace context companies like PepsiCo would have operated in and, therefore, getting the organization ready both strategically as well as operationally to be competitive in the markets of tomorrow.*

**—VINITA BALI**

•

*I*n a modest household in Chennai in the 1950s, two young girls were asked one question by their mother at the dinner table every night—'What will you do to change the world?' Their answers were taken seriously, and the exercise continued with similar questions, until both girls began to believe that they have the power to do something extraordinary.

The younger of those two sisters is Indra Nooyi, former chairperson and chief executive officer at PepsiCo, the second-largest food and beverage business in the world. The older, Chandrika Krishnamurthy Tandon, is an ex-McKinsey partner, bank turnaround consultant and now a Grammy Award-nominated musician. And Indra still talks to their mother, Shantha Krishnamurthy, two or three times a day, crediting her as the motivator and early architect of her phenomenal success—she figures on virtually every list of powerful women in business; in 2015, she was ranked as the second most powerful woman in business by *Fortune* magazine, making her the highest ranked India-born figure.

Indra's climb up the corporate ladder—and the numerous influential positions she holds outside her job, too—are a beacon of hope for everyone, of course, but especially seminal for women who are often conditioned to believe that they can only advance so much before they are stopped by that imperceptible glass ceiling.

'It is glass because we can see through it and it can be broken,' Indra tells me, with the confidence and calm of someone who has reduced it to shards on the strength of her own work. Her response to dealing with all manner of ceilings is simple, unequivocal, powerful—all that counts is one's performance and commitment and keeping the focus on the task at hand, not on breaking the glass. 'Do not start off saying that you want to be a CEO. If you do that, you will be disappointed by the tricks and turns of your life. If you do your current job phenomenally well, people will automatically take you for your next job and the next one. People, too often, are focused on the destination and not the task that will take you to that destination.'

Indra's life and background fostered such focus in no uncertain terms. Her success has been made up of the small steps she took every day and the many beliefs, big and small, that she lives by. Her journey at PepsiCo started in 1994, when she joined as its senior vice president, strategic planning. In 2000 Indra was appointed senior vice president and chief financial officer and, by the beginning of 2001, she had become its president and CFO, and was named as part of its board of directors. She was appointed CEO in 2006, becoming the first woman in the company's history to take over that role and, under her leadership, PepsiCo earned a total shareholder return of 162 per cent between 31 December 2006, when Indra assumed office, through December 31, 2017, before she resigned from the post of CEO in 2018. Total cash returned to shareholders through dividends and share repurchases amounted to $79.4 billion from the beginning of 2006 through the end of 2017, and dividends per share nearly tripled from $1.16 in 2006 to $3.17 in 2017 at a compound annual growth rate of nearly 10 per cent. Her crowning glory, however, remains a growth in net revenue from $35 billion in 2006 to $63.5 billion in 2017 at a compound annual growth rate of 5.5 per cent.

Indra wields an influence far beyond the company's corridors as she is also a member of the boards of the US-China Business Council and US-India Business Council, besides being appointed by the Obama administration to the US-India CEO Forum as well as the Trump administration to the Government Business Forum to assist in preparing an economic agenda for the USA. At the beginning of 2019, Ivanka Trump alluded to favouring Indra as a frontrunner to lead the World Bank. Yet, none of these honours distract her from her work at PepsiCo—she has crafted the firm's global strategy for over a decade, steering it to adapt to the changing market successfully while reshaping its core values. She was the force behind the divestiture of its restaurants, the buying back of its bottling operations, the acquisition of Tropicana and its merger with Quaker Oats. Her prescience, and emphasis on diversification and innovation, are paying off. PepsiCo has consistently outperformed competitors in recent years and the company appears well-positioned to deliver sustained long-term growth. For example, nutrition businesses now account for approximately 20 per cent of global net revenue. And investment in research and development is up 35 per cent since 2011, translating into a series of highly successful new product innovations that are driving PepsiCo's top-line growth. Innovation, defined as products launched from 2011–14 comprised 9 per cent of PepsiCo's revenue in 2014.

How did Indra get here, and what motivates her every day to stay at the top? D. Shivakumar, CEO, PepsiCo India, attempts to decode Indra's success for me. 'The obvious ones are her talent, the position she holds and the influence she wields over her network,' he says. 'But the not-so-obvious one is that she is a big giver. Indra gives a lot more than she gets. Not just to the job, but to society at large. As president of the US-India Business Council, she gave her heart to that role to really ensure the development of US-India ties. Indra has a very positive influence on all the people she works with and talks often about working hard; being focused; keeping in mind the right thing to do; teamwork; being candid; learning all the time and acquiring a unique skill set that others don't have. She is also extremely responsive and very approachable as a leader.'

When Indra retraces her rise for me, she does so in a manner that pays homage to the trust that the company has reposed in her—'The point about PepsiCo is that as long as you perform well, make meaningful contributions to the company and put the firm before yourself, they do everything possible to move you ahead.'

As I prepare for our meeting, I am most curious about understanding Indra's life mantras and the impact they can have on others, including me. She is a delight to interview—gregarious, generous and startlingly honest as she shares the story of her life for me.

## SHOULDER TO THE WHEEL

To Indra, nothing can replace plain, old-fashioned hard work—'That has been my rule over the past twenty years.' This ethic was drilled into her from a young age by her Tamil Brahmin parents; the world that she spent her formative years in placed a high premium on academic excellence. Indra was born in Chennai in 1955. Her father worked in the State Bank of Hyderabad and her mother was a homemaker—both taught Indra, Chandrika and their brother, Narayanan, to always aim for the highest marks. It was customary in their extended family and social circle for parents to compare the academic performances of their children, and Indra was always motivated to do extremely well at Holy Angel's Convent.

In 1974, Indra enrolled at the prestigious Madras Christian College for a bachelor's degree in chemistry, physics and mathematics; her teachers still remember her enthusiasm with warmth. 'When others shied away from a task, she would come forward to complete it. Indra grabbed with both hands all the opportunities that came her way,' college principal V.J. Philip told a newspaper soon after Indra's appointment as CEO of PepsiCo. She went on to study management at the premier Indian Institute of Management, Calcutta.

While her academic doggedness may make her seem like a dull Jane, who was all about work and no play, this was far from the truth. As a young girl, Indra had a healthy bit of rebellion in her. She played the guitar in an all-girls' rock band and was also an avid cricketer—'I was a happy-go-lucky, athletic, shiny young girl. I played cricket and volleyball, climbed trees, participated in every debating competition possible and was always pushing myself to do things that were seemingly impossible to do; I worked very hard.'

'Very energetic—bubbling with energy,' is how Madhukar Kamath, group CEO and MD of the DBB Mudra Group, describes Indra, whom he has known since the early-70s. They met as debating competitors—he from Loyola College, Madras, and she from MCC—and became lifelong friends. 'I guess which is why she did what she did. We joked around often at that time. She would be behind the mic because when she was debating, she was forceful, very aggressive. And at the end of it, she was always ready for a conversation, which is wonderful, you just don't remain competitors.' Their friendship continued when they were part of the debating fraternity when Indra was at IIM Calcutta and Kamath at XLRI Jamshedpur.

At home, while academic success was the Holy Grail, and dinner-table conversations forced the two girls, especially, to aim as high as possible in their life goals, their mother also threatened to marry off Indra and Chandrika at eighteen. I ask Indra if she ever felt insecure, receiving these conflicting cues that swung between lofty ambitions and the trappings of tradition, and she says, 'If my mother had truly decided that she did not want me to get ahead at all, she could have put her foot down and kept me home. But she let me go to Kolkata to study. When I wanted to move to the US, and my dad said it was okay to, she supported me, every step of the way. She is a brilliant lady who never got a chance to go to college and so, in many ways, I think she has lived her life vicariously through her children.'

## A LIFELONG STUDENT

Indra remains a student at heart, every day, and in every aspect of life, bringing the focus and purity of a beginner's mind to her career, as well—'[I have a] constant desire to learn; to re-conceptualize situations and not be happy with the status quo. Aspiring leaders have got to raise the bar for themselves all the time. They have to embrace learning and be a student all their lives. You have to listen a lot, get out of your office, reach people—your employees, partners – and have as much emotional quotient (EQ) as intelligence.'

Indra has lived this philosophy from her first job onwards—after she graduated from IIM C, she joined Mettur Beardsell, a textile firm, as brand manager. She reported to work on the first day to be told that she would be in charge of printed fabrics (the company made plain dyed fabrics, too). It had no training programme for new recruits and Indra realized that she would have to learn everything on her own. Did they have any files left behind by the predecessor, she asked, more out of curiosity than dismay. Her colleagues pointed her to a cupboard, which, when opened, regurgitated files, books and swatches of fabric in a pell-mell fashion.

'So for the first week, I decided I was not going to be product manager, but staff assistant, cleaner, organizer, file keeper,' she has said in an interview with Tom Gilligan, dean of the McCombs School of Business, University of Texas, Austin. 'Because lesson number one is that if you don't sweat the details, and if you don't organize yourself, it's not going to work.' And that's precisely what she did at Mettur Beardsell; she organized every printed fabric the company had produced in a methodical way so that people after her, too, could follow the same system.

Indra tells me that the second lesson she learnt was to 'go deep before you go wide. Being open and willing to learn, and to be able to say, "I don't know," really made a big difference.' If one does not understand everything about the job from the very basics one cannot be a credible leader, she points out. Indra spent about ten days at the mill, chatting with employees in every department until she understood every aspect of the business. This from-the-ground-up approach is of critical importance, she stresses, and it was important to depend on the people she worked with to teach her the job. True to herself, Indra still credits all that she learnt to the time and largesse of the millworkers, wholesalers and retailers to whom she had spoken at length—'But I had to ask to be taught, or the opportunity to learn would have been lost.'

What also singled her out for greater responsibility was her obsessive pursuit of flawless execution; once the designs of the printed fabric were approved, Indra would oversee the printing when it was being done in batches at night, making sure it matched what had been specified in the swatch. 'I was so obsessed with everything having to be perfect as there was so much riding on these printed fabrics,' she recalls. (As the CEO of PepsiCo, she was known for her incredible eye for detail, and tremendous work ethic. Nothing escapes her attention.)

S.L. Rao, the director who recruited her into Mettur Beardsell, wrote in a letter to the *Economic Times* after Indra became CEO of PepsiCo – 'She did not tolerate chauvinism or bullying and in conservative Chennai and the south India of those days we had many seniors (male) who could not take her quick responses, sharp mind, ability to concentrate and unwillingness to bow down before anyone just because it was a senior or a man.'

At her second job as product manager for Stayfree sanitary napkins at consumer giant Johnson & Johnson in Mumbai—Indra got a chance, again, to make a mark. The product range was new to India, and shopkeepers were uncomfortable stocking women's hygiene products, which could not even be advertised. She decided to use direct marketing, an old-school method, and travelled to schools and colleges to introduce girls to Stayfree.

Indra had bigger goals to accomplish, however, and with this solid work experience backing her, she applied for admission to Yale University's School of Management for a master's degree in public and private management where she was granted financial aid. Yale University in the early-80s was not as diverse a campus as it is today nor as well-equipped in terms of a support system for foreign students, and Indra has spoken in an interview of the hard time she had making ends meet. 'We were always broke,' she says, laughing about how everyone was friendly with the one dormmate who had a car. However, Indra remained grateful to Yale for the skills that the course helped her inculcate and improve. In 2016, the Yale School of Management named a deanship in honour of Indra after she donated an undisclosed amount to the college, making her the first woman to endow a deanship at a popular B-school. She is now Yale's biggest alumni donor.

## 'DO THE BEST JOB YOU CAN'

On graduating from Yale, Indra joined the prestigious Boston Consulting Group (BCG) as a strategist. Over six years, she worked with clients from a wide range of industries—textiles, consumer goods, chemicals and retail, and learnt on the job every day. At Motorola, where she subsequently worked between 1986 and 1990, Indra rose to become vice president and director of corporate strategy and planning. Next, she was senior vice president of strategy and strategic marketing for ASEA Brown Boveri.

I am curious to understand what she gained from each of these diverse jobs and Indra says, 'In every job, I worked extremely hard. I didn't care what the job was, I just wanted to learn and contribute.' This attitude is rooted in her childhood, and her conversations with her grandfather, who would tell her—'If you are given a job, do it the best [way] you can so that your boss says to you, "I don't ever have to check your work,"' Indra told Tim Gilligan in an interview.

Clearly, however, a lot of Indra's success is due to her ability to work very, very hard, as Shivakumar says, 'Indra works more than 24x7, maybe she works 48x7. [Her thoroughness and meticulousness] are difficult to find. She has a good sense of the detail while being focused on the big picture.'

What I find really interesting is how Indra harvests this incredible work ethic and energy to not just master her job—all aspects of any job—but to also think more about the linkages that the job has with every other function in the office. Consequently, she joins the dots to understand the impact of her work on the rest of the company, and how that could be used to work better as a whole. When I ask if this attitude did not engender suspicion or reluctance on the part of others to collaborate, Indra explains that co-workers responded instantly to her attempts to do the best and most composite job possible because they understood that she was driven by a desire to make the company better, and not gain personally.

And if she changed jobs, it was because she thrived on new experiences, evolving with each one—'The biggest advantage of being in different industries, having different experiences and working in all parts of the world is that you get a very broad perspective of business: I learnt about everything—from technology to heavy engineering to banks.' It was this wealth of learning that she brought to PepsiCo when she came in as the company's chief strategist in 1994.

Indra's broad perspective soon led to PepsiCo's transformation into a more focused food and beverage company and an early mover in the health and wellness space. In 1997, PepsiCo spun off its restaurant division, which included Taco Bell, KFC and Pizza Hut. Indra joined others who believed that changing demographics and consumer demands would lead to greater growth in nutrition. In 1998, PepsiCo purchased Tropicana from Seagram for $3.3 billion, bringing into its portfolio a product seen by consumers as naturally nutritious. Soon thereafter came the acquisition of Quaker, which also included Gatorade. In 2018, PepsiCo acquired SodaStream International, which is an at-home sparkling water brand that transforms tap water into flavoured carbonated water, for $3.2 billion, putting PepsiCo at the forefront of plastic waste reduction as well as product diversification. These moves laid the foundation for the PepsiCo of the future—a complementary portfolio of brands that could offer consumers a range of products to meet many needs from morning to night.

These moves quickly started to show promise. In the US, PepsiCo products became the number one source of supermarket profits. 'We're in the sweet spot of the food and beverage business,' she said then. These early moves also demonstrated Indra's vision and understanding of the need for businesses to constantly be looking to adapt and change.

## BECOMING A CHANGE AGENT

Being a changemaker is inherent to Indra's personality. Chanda Kochhar, managing director, ICICI Bank, points out the virtues of such adaptability when she says that even in the developed world, large companies don't have too many brilliant leaders—'It is really to Indra's credit that she, having studied science, started with a textile company and then got into consumer-oriented businesses. This is to do with her adaptability, not keeping any barriers in the mind, and accepting change and new environments all the time.' Former CEO of Britannia Industries, Vinita Bali, commends the fact that over the years, 'What hasn't changed about [Indra] is her adaptability.'

She is now a naturalized American, having spent nearly four decades in the US, but when she first moved there, Indra had to adjust to cultural issues not unlike most expatriates. For her first interview, she could not afford to buy an appropriate outfit and ended up wearing a suit that was uncomfortable and ill-fitting. Upset when she did not get the job, she asked her professor for feedback and he advised her to wear what she would wear in India for her next job interview. She wore a sari and did get the job. There was an important lesson in there for Indra, who learnt that she had to be herself, but never

96
•

be rigid about who that was. While she still sports a sari on rare occasions, over time, her approach to change has acquired balance and nuance. She does not deny her Indian-ness but embraces the environment in which she has to function in order to be at home in both cultures—'The most important thing when you come to a foreign country and decide to participate in mainstream business is that you can preserve your individuality, even as you embrace the local culture. And I balance that very carefully.'

Kamath adds, 'Indra is a person who is very driven, and very clear about what she wants. You could notice that she had embraced what it took to succeed in the US, and she was very clear about her own career and everything else.'

To me, Indra admits that she had to change in many ways to fit in—'I had to learn to be more clear, and write in a much more logical and simple way.' Her decisions on what to change and what to retain are all based on what keeps her functioning optimally—'Coming to work was not just about putting my background and individuality on display, it was more about getting the job done. I focused on how to position myself as a better executive, get people to pay attention to what I was saying and not how I looked or what I was wearing.'

One way Indra found to fit in was to develop an affinity for baseball, a story I personally enjoy because it demonstrates how she was able to skilfully adapt to the environment around her. When she moved to the US, she missed playing cricket, but found a substitute—baseball. She realized that at work, people analysed the game the morning after and she would feel left out unless she could join in their conversations. As it happened, the Yankees team were having a great season in 1978 and she fell in love with them.

Indra's understanding of the need to adapt extends to how she sees the world and makes decisions. 'In today's volatile world, if you are not a change agent, you should not be a leader. The world is not standing still, something is changing every day and, as a leader, you have got to make sure you are always growing the company in spite of all the volatility.' What is interesting to observe is that Indra applies this philosophy in a holistic manner and not just in advancing her career path. Having grown up in water-starved Madras, when Indra became CEO, she was firm that big companies have an obligation to contribute to the greater good, and PepsiCo's focus began to include more nutritious products and the firm started to address issues of sustainability.

R.K. Krishna Kumar, director of Tata Sons who has known Indra for some years adds, 'You must have a mind that is global in nature, that is open to new ideas, that is not weighed down by any legacy issues, bold and fresh enough to see the world as it unfolds—Indra has that quality. She also possesses an uncanny ability to be at the cutting edge of what managing a big national or international enterprise should be. You have to maintain an intrinsically exotic state of mind, to be able to assimilate, at one level, the western environment and yet hold on to your own cultural foundations. That is the challenge.'

PepsiCo's operating philosophy became 'Performance with Purpose' and its mission was to 'deliver sustainable growth by investing in a healthier future for our consumers, our planet, our associates, and external partners and the communities we serve.' Shivakumar points out that Indra, through this mission, made it clear 'why this company was a great one to work in. Equally, by calling it 'Performance with Purpose', she put a very clear standard on it. It was like saying, "This is what I want the world to measure PepsiCo and me by."'

'Indra is someone who is not afraid to go ahead and do something if she believes in it. She has diversified the portfolio and, most importantly, she has diversified the mindset and thinking of the organization, which I think is very important. She has been bold enough to share that vision and to retain it in a manner which is still within the DNA of Pepsi while driving towards a more diversified portfolio,' says Bali.

The 'purpose' in her 'Performance with Purpose' includes a commitment to doing business the right way by seeking ways to offer consumers a wider range of foods and beverages, from treats to healthy eats, increase environmental sustainability and develop and support employees. Indra tells me 'Performance with Purpose' is more than 'just giving away money for charitable causes—we are conducting business in a much more responsible manner.' Her plan for the company upholds the interests of external stakeholders, including global experts in the nutrition, science and global health policy communities and environmentally focused groups such as Ceres and the Carbon Trust.

As part of PepsiCo's commitment to environment sustainability, the company is committed to reducing its carbon footprint and water usage. Since 2009, PepsiCo India has been water-positive, meaning, the business conserves more water than it uses each year. Indra's and PepsiCo's commitment to water stewardship extends around the world. For example, PepsiCo's facility in Chongqing, China, is designed to use 22 per cent less water and 23 per cent less energy than the existing facilities within the country. Globally, PepsiCo has reduced water use per unit of production by 23 per cent since 2006, exceeding its public target of a 20 per cent reduction by the end of 2015. In recognition of these and other efforts, PepsiCo received the prestigious Stockholm Industry Water Award in 2012. Up to 2019, PepsiCo has received numerous awards as one of the world's most powerful and respected brands from Fortune World, Fortune 500, Barron's World, NYSE, etc.

Indra continued to transition the company to a more balanced portfolio with the acquisition of the Russian dairy company, Wimm-Bill-Dann—which afforded it the opportunity to be a major presence within Russia. Peter Golder, professor of marketing at Tuck School of Business, says, 'It provided the platform for them to roll out dairy into other markets.' Historically, dairy products have been 'under-branded, so when PepsiCo brings its marketing power to bear on milk, it opens up a giant opportunity to make milk and yogurt-based drinks a component of its wider portfolio.'

Bali says that the strategic acquisitions Indra has made over the years point to her keen intellect—'They are indication of an underlying belief that there is a commercial purpose to business that we can't run away from, but that commercial purpose can be served even more convincingly and truthfully when you look at how you can embed socially responsible behaviour and practices into the business itself.'

## A GLOBAL LEADER

Shivakumar believes that these forays into new products and geographies have made Indra's approach that of 'somebody who has the bandwidth but is equally extremely sensitive to local nuances. She can look at a drink in China or India and go into why that local flavour is doing well. She can go into details and salute the local consumer for his/her choice while still having a global view.'

By the same token, he sees her as a global, and not an Indian, leader. Even though she may be thoroughly committed to investing in India, Indra is able to zoom out for a universal perspective, which makes her one of the tallest leaders of her ilk. 'She is able to see the world from both macro and micro perspectives, with a clear eye. She also has a very good connect with key stakeholders in a global world,' he adds. 'She understands issues and concerns, she is tough, but in a caring way. That's what I think is unique about her compared to all the other CEOs that I have worked with.'

'I have taken on very difficult problems and been courageous in proposing the right solution, which is not necessarily the popular solution,' Indra says. 'This means that people know that if something came from me and my office, I have studied it, analysed it and the conclusion I have reached may not be politically correct, but is the right one for the company.'

Kochhar applauds Indra's openness and straightforwardness when speaking at public forums. 'She says what she has to with passion and without fear,' she observes, having also witnessed her capacity for great personal warmth. 'Most of the inhibitions are in our own minds. It's only when you seize an opportunity that you can actually show what you are capable of—and Indra has probably done that all the time. She puts in hard work, determination, focus, but I think that, as a leader, it is also her style of attaching equity to the changing environment which people draw strength from and enables them to excel whether they are in the local environment or one that looks out of reach.'

Once asked by *Fortune* magazine about the best advice she had received, Indra said, 'Embrace tough assignments. Nobody notices when you do an easy job well. It's far better to challenge yourself by raising your hand for the toughest assignments and work to solve problems that no one else has been able to solve. By demonstrating that resolve, you start to signal to the higher-ups that you can be brought into the centre of the company. That's how you truly become a trusted leader inside an organization.'

Kamath adds, 'I don't think she is defining success as position. Success for her has been doing what she wants to do. She does not come through as a powerful icon; I would rate her more as a human icon seriously. She has been able to communicate her beliefs and follow through.'

When she resigned as CEO to make way for Ramon Laguarta in 2018, such was the shock of her announcement that PepsiCo share prices went south before stabilizing at a slightly lower level. Globally, business leaders acknowledged Indra's stupendous efforts in making Pepsi a more health-conscious and environmentally-conscious brand. By then, she had already started serving parallelly to the ICC Board as the organization's first independent female director. Indra Nooyi has consistently proved that she is someone who will break every glass ceiling that ever existed.

## HUMANIZING THE CEO

Indra's 'Performance with Purpose' philosophy has to do with people, talent sustainability or figuring out how to have employees of PepsiCo bring their 'whole selves' to work. To build a connection with her employees and their families, Indra often does something unconventional—even surprising: she writes to parents of high-performing employees. Once, when she was pitching for a talented recruit to join the company, she called up the candidate's mother. She also encourages associates to embrace their role in the company and implement the changes they would like to see at PepsiCo.

Closer to home, Indra's 'Performance with Purpose' mission deeply influenced a change in the company's HR approach, enabling employees to work towards an emotional goal, as well as an intellectual one. She points out that doing business the right way, making money the right way, and operating with integrity and ethics make for a better company and one that generates pride in those who work there. Indra has said she expected resistance, but she got cooperation instead, with people feeling connected to the company, their families and society.

This emphasis on interpersonal communication is owed, at least in part, to her father. He taught her to always assume positive intent in whatever a person said or did. 'Growing up in India, you are surrounded by warmth, big families, lots of people and a society that embraces you. So I think, in many ways, I have brought that with me to PepsiCo—I view it as my big family. The warmth of Indian families, the all-encompassing way we embrace second, third, fourth, fifth cousins, is something I have carried with me,' Indra says.

'Her initial years influenced her to be competitive; in the next phase, she had to balance being a wife and mother, and take on senior management roles. There was also phenomenal transformation in Indra when she started going up the ladder—first as CFO and then as the CEO. So she has actually effortlessly moved from orbit to orbit, while remembering and respecting the past, but not living in it,' says Kamath.

## STAYING LOYAL

The observation that stays with me from our meetings is that Indra uses the words 'us' and 'we' frequently when talking about PepsiCo. Her interest in the company overrides all other considerations and her dreams and aspirations are inextricably linked to the prospects of the organization she is leading. This passion and dedication are, to my mind, those rare aspects that distinguish real leaders from the amateur ones, that is, those who suspend their egos and put the cause of the company before their own. She confirms my faith as she tells me, 'The biggest decision I have made during my time at PepsiCo was that even when other very attractive offers came to me from other companies, I was so committed to this one that I said an absolute no to them. Whatever the problems might have been at that time at PepsiCo, I stayed because I feel that when one is a very senior executive in a company, one is responsible for solving problems. I have an incredible sense of ownership and simply love my time here. When I leave PepsiCo, I want to leave a company that people consider amazing. I want people to think of PepsiCo as a defining corporation. That's one hope and dream that I have.'

Mentoring—both the receiving and sharing of it—are important to Indra, who is a great believer in the force mentors play in helping leaders succeed and the responsibility that women have to help other women in their professional ascent.

'If Indra has had people mentoring her, it is because they saw something exceptional in her, or maybe glimpses of what they themselves had done or could go on to do,' Shivakumar says.

Kiran Mazumdar-Shaw, chairman and managing director of Biocon, says, 'Indra didn't let gender come in the way. And such women become great leaders. If a woman starts believing that being a woman does not deter her in any way and that she is going to play to her strengths, then she can lead, she can aspire to greatness.'

Indra has also shown a deep commitment to running an ethical organization that takes responsibility for its actions.

Shivakumar corroborates this—'We have a very strong governance culture, which is far more important than anything else. If the ecosystem calls for us to do something that is not in line with the governance code, we don't enter into it at all.'

Despite the transformation and growth she has brought to the company, Indra's regime has not been without its challenges and critics. She tells me, 'It is like climbing Mount Everest—once you reach the summit, staying there is harder than the journey that brought you there. Because the view is fantastic and other people are looking to reach that summit, you are being hit by the winds, it's very cold and the platform is really very, very small. Being a leader is very much like that. Once you get to the top, too many people are looking at you, there are too many critics and very few supporters, and you have a lot to get done. You are always in some sort of a fish bowl.'

Indra is constantly aware of the fact that to do justice to her position, she has to do the job better than anybody else, and sometimes that means functioning on four hours of sleep a night, if need be. She obviously never intends to rest on her laurels. 'Nobody is going to push you—you have to push yourself. You have to stay motivated. The worst thing is to be motivated for a few days and then dump it—it does not work that way. If you approach your job as just another job, it will be difficult and terrible. Every morning, I approach my work, I ask myself—what can I do to make the company a better place, and the world better? I come to work every day saying I wish I could be a better leader, I wish I could show the human side of being a CEO.'

Krishna Kumar adds, 'On the one hand, Indra is a classic example of a conventional south Indian Brahmin girl—someone who dressed conventionally, wore her hair in two pigtails, learnt classical music and was expected to be married young and have many children! She has fulfilled an outstanding destiny and I would not have expected her to maintain such a fantastic balance between her professional career in the US and the charm of her cultural legacy, and the traditions she has inherited from her wonderful mother. Indra is brilliant in her analysis of global business situations, but at heart she remains quintessentially Indian and that too south Indian!'

## IN THE SPIRIT OF SACRIFICE

Most of the rules Indra plays by in her life are those that other successful women and men follow. But there is one aspect, she has repeatedly pointed out, that puts women at a disadvantage. Because of the inherent bias, social and professional, women have to work twice as hard and sacrifice a lot more than men. 'There is no question that women who reach the top have to perform at a higher level,' she says.

In 2014, in a now-famous talk at the Aspen Institute, Indra raised many hackles when she admitted that 'women can't have it all.' While many feminists would consider it unfair to ask a woman how she balances personal and professional commitments when a man is rarely asked the same question, Indra set aside such political correctness to do what she is good at: telling it like it is. She says women could pretend all they wanted, but they had to make decisions on a daily basis to pick either work or family.

Married to Raj Nooyi for over thirty-five years and the mother of two daughters, she works with the knowledge that expectations remain unchanged no matter how well a woman does. She has been known to say, 'Stay-at-home mothering is a full-time job. Being a CEO for a company is three full-time jobs rolled into one. How can you do justice to it all? You can't.' Krishna Kumar tells me that Raj 'is a wise and understanding man, who himself is an accomplished manager; to be able to give her that space is commendable.'

Indra has pointed out that a woman's bio-clock and her career clock are in complete conflict. 'When you have to have kids you have to build your career. Just as you're rising to middle management your kids need you because they're teenagers . . . And that's the time your husband becomes a teenager, too, so he needs you . . . And as you grow even more, your parents need you because they're aging.'

She tells me, 'My decision to be a wife and a mother, while also being a good daughter and daughter-in-law, has been very difficult. There are only so many hours in a day and juggling all of these roles was very hard. Maybe I have not done as well as someone who was focused on them may have. I have tried to be a mom when I could, a wife when I could, and so on. I wish I had seventy-two hours in a day, and not twenty-four.'

She has often talked about how she feels guilty and inadequate as a mother because of her professional commitments. Years ago, at her daughter's school, she couldn't attend the weekly class coffee with the mothers because it was held at 9 a.m. on Wednesdays. Her daughter would come home and list the mothers who were there and remind her she wasn't. Over time, to counter this, she started calling the school to find out who attended the session and who didn't. That way, when her daughter accused her of not being there, she quickly reeled off to her the names of the other mothers who were also not there. 'You just die with guilt,' she says, though, with touching candour.

Indra confesses that PepsiCo's place on her priority list is above her husband, Raj. She once recounted how Raj said to her—'Your list is PepsiCo, PepsiCo, PepsiCo, our two kids, your mom, and then at the bottom of the list is me.' Indra had retorted in jest, 'You should be happy you're on the list!'

And then there is the famous story of how, on the night that she was told that she was going to be president of PepsiCo, she went straight home to tell her family and was greeted by her mother, at the door, asking her to go out again and buy milk. Indra wanted to know why her mother had not asked Raj to run the errand, but went anyway and on her return, gave her mother the news of her promotion and pointed out that she'd had to run an errand before getting a chance to share such an incredible achievement with her family. Her mother, however, would have none of it and reminded Indra that at home, she is a daughter, wife and mother above all else. Given the challenges of this balancing act Indra has to maintain, she enlists all the support she can get. She says her success rests on three important pillars: family, friends and faith.

Mazumdar-Shaw tells me about the pivotal roles that husbands like Raj play in such marriages. 'She comes from a background very similar to mine in that her husband is a great source of support, a pillar of strength. I admire him the way I admire my husband because they are kind of overshadowed by our dominance, and our visible kind of prominence – we are the ones who are talked about, we're the ones who are famous, always in the news, we're the ones being profiled. Yet, our husbands are such confident secure human beings that they lend all the support they can to us. Indra's husband does a lot of charity work and spends a lot of time in India on these programmes.'

Kamath adds, 'As a personal friend, she is exceedingly grounded. I mean you could be talking about her to prominent world leaders; but when I visit her in New York, we would just put our feet up on the sofas and sit in the same room where all the luminaries have been hosted . . . And she got up to make dosas when my wife and I visited her last time.'

Indra is clear in her belief that, 'If you want to have a family, their support is very important. There are those who will say, I don't want to have a family and am just going to be single. But I am a very family-oriented person and there was no way that I was not going to have one, and have kids. Raj has been a great support and I do not know where I would have been without him. He has been a sounding board and friend.'

She is also grateful that her mother has been around through the tough times, helping with the children and being there whenever needed: 'She has been the biggest force in my life.'

Indra has learnt to adapt processes and get help wherever possible. Working mothers occupy all manner of conflict zones, and Indra grants that the glass ceiling does still exist, but things are looking up and women should seize the day.

'Many of us have already walked the trail and I think the time has come for women to commit and rise up to big positions. I don't think companies have a choice. In many ways, I think that if a company does not attract, retain and develop women employees, it cannot be successful because women are getting most of the degrees today—college, advanced and professional. So the next two decades, especially, are decades of women. The question that we all have to answer for ourselves is: are we willing to put in what it takes to move ahead?'

If Indra Nooyi has, I don't believe that the rest of us have an option, except to say yes and follow.

# AJAY BANGA

*They are global citizens who both took a similar route to success. **Indra Nooyi**, chairperson and CEO, PepsiCo, and **Ajay Banga**, president and CEO, MasterCard, are eminent Indians who today hold top positions in corporate America. They are examples of what hard work and perseverance can bring about irrespective of the circumstances of one's birth or country of origin. Both also today have an important presence on the US-India Business Council. Indra preceded Banga in carving out a place for herself, overcoming every kind of prejudice and privation that an immigrant in early-80s America could expect and, in many ways, paving the way for future generations of aspirants with the spunk, drive and vision to reach the top. Banga offers his insights about Indra and all that it would have taken her to reach the pinnacle she has.*

**Fortune magazine has, in recent years, named you 'Best Businessperson' while Indra has been ranked 'Second-Most Powerful Businesswoman' in 2015. What makes her so important globally?**

She deserves the ranking. 'Powerful' is a complicated word. But if one were to rank businesswomen around the world on their ability to lead their company through good and bad times, and provide a working environment for people, Indra ranks among the top. She has performed against all odds. There are a lot of challenges in her company, in her industry, but she is doing a great job. She definitely deserves the ranking, not only as 'powerful', but as 'able' and 'capable'. To me that is more important than 'powerful'.

**What are the challenges, the advantages of not being citizens of the countries in which the companies you head are headquartered?**

We are both naturalized American citizens even though we were born in India and were Indian citizens. It is a very big advantage to have been born elsewhere—Indra and I are global citizens. I have lived and worked in many countries around the world. She has lived and travelled and worked everywhere. This gives one a global perspective, it leads to better decision-making, it makes one more sensitive to cultural differences, and how one needs to adapt one's management style accordingly when dealing with the governments of other countries, their regulators and managers.

**How would you describe Indra's journey within PepsiCo? What leadership qualities have helped her stand out?**

When I was in PepsiCo, I didn't know Indra. We were in different businesses—she was in the Frito Lay and beverage business. But what makes her a really interesting leader in the global business arena is that she is very strategically oriented. She also has a very high level of maturity in terms of EQ, not just IQ. All this stands her in very good stead when she has to compete on the global business stage.

**Were there other factors that helped her shatter the glass ceiling?**

Nobody succeeds without the right guidance, development or mentor. It is not possible to break through the glass ceiling without senior people willing to support or provide one the opportunity to grow, people who have a hand on one's back and not in one's face. She must have had people above her who were supportive, senior managers at PepsiCo and BCG, who cared for her future, who saw in her the ability to be the senior-most person in the company one day and nurtured, developed and created a pathway for her to succeed.

**Indra has steered PepsiCo towards being socially responsible and embracing the ethos of 'Performance with Purpose'. How has she achieved this?**

Indra is committed to social responsibility. She has focused mostly on healthier food. And she has put her money into the effort. She has a great strategic mind, buying into Tropicana juices, Gatorade sports drinks and yogurt companies. She is trying to diversify the company's product portfolio into a healthier group of food and drink items, which is a very socially responsible thing to do. It is easier to keep doing what you are already doing. Change is always tough, but she is embracing it and persisting with it. I tell people in my company, you can do well and do good at the same time. That's what Indra is trying to do.

**The first few years in the US were tough on Indra. Student by day, she worked as a receptionist at night. She was Indian and a woman. How much of one's nationality can one wear on one's sleeve and still fit in when society then did tend to be wary of the foreigner while also endorsing the melting pot?**

I came to the US much after Indra did—only in 2000. There were others who came before me from India and different parts of the world— people who came here as professors, those like Indra who came to study management, and management gurus like the late Prof. C.K. Prahalad, who must have faced very different circumstances from what I did. They made the path easier for me because they had already demonstrated that people of Indian origin were good, reliable, excellent at their work. So I didn't find it tough being an Indian in the US. I also came here after having worked for fifteen-seventeen years at Nestlé and Citibank, not completely fresh out of college. So my experience was a little different from those who came here to study and then started at the bottom of the rung, particularly those who came some years ago.

**Indra worked with BCG, followed by Stinson Motor. What must have been the challenges she faced in making it to the top, being new to the country and being a woman?**

Everybody faces a great deal of challenges when starting out. One can also assume that whoever gets recruited by the BCG is a really smart person. The sheer process of getting interviewed and selected for a high-quality company means that one has joined very smart, competitive people. One is competing with people in one's own batch and with those a year or two senior, who are all doing well.

Indra must certainly have had to shine among really smart people to be able to go far. So, the fact that she grew fast in that environment tells you how good she must have been at her work because she had to stand out among peers who would have been among the best.

As for gender issues, it's still not easy for women to succeed in American business, they just are not visible at the senior-most levels of management. But it's easier than it was twenty-five years ago, when she must have had to work doubly hard not only to get noticed, but to overcome that initial barrier that existed in those days vis-à-vis women at the workplace.

## What was the impression you had of Indra before you actually met her? And after your first few meetings?

I first met Indra in 2001–02. We had a mutual friend, named Jassi, who was her classmate at IIM Calcutta, and used to play golf with me when I lived in Delhi. So we were very good friends, and he came to New York on a holiday, when we all got together. Indra was then CFO of PepsiCo. And my impression of her was of a high-achieving woman. All I knew about her was from articles I'd read: that she was actually very informal, that she engaged very easily with people, that she wore a sari to work, and so was not conscious of her background. I didn't know Indra as a person. And then when she came over for a drink, and later invited us over to dinner at her place, I found her very down-to-earth; she was deeply involved with everything, including serving the dinner herself. She was completely relaxed. We have had other opportunities to spend time together and talked about everything. I found her an easy-going person.

I have since got to know her very well both through the business community and also through the US-India Business Council and the US-India CEO Forum. I now consider Indra a friend more than anything else.

## Indra stands as an inspiration, not only to the younger generation, but to aspiring leaders all over the world, doesn't she?

She shows you that you can be born in India to relatively modest circumstances, be educated there, come to the US and acquire more education, and then stand shoulder to shoulder with anybody in the world, whether businessman or politician or leader. That's a great example for people in India and elsewhere. One makes one's life by what one does and how one does it. It's one's education and conduct that count, not how one looks or where one has come from. And that's the ideal that Indra is living up to.

# KIRAN MAZUMDAR-SHAW

*Kiran always used to bully me as a child, but growing up, she was a lot more serious and focused about what she wanted to do in life. She's always been very interested in knowledge, in attempting complicated stuff—her application of mind and her interests were unlike that of others. Her creativity, combined with her passion and her sense of perfection, have brought her to where she is. She's a very affectionate friend.*

**—VIJAY MALLYA**

*A* little more than five decades ago, two schoolboys frantically searched for a young Kiran when their game of hide-and-seek took a scary turn in the sprawling campus of United Breweries (UB) in Bengaluru, where her father worked as brew master. They finally found her hiding behind a huge mash tun—an insulated vessel in which beer is brewed—enjoying the happy aroma of boiling wort.

While the boys were relieved to find Kiran, their beloved big sister was a tad annoyed that her brother and his playmate—her 'adopted' brother, Vijay Mallya—had discovered her secret hiding place. For some time, Kiran had been sneaking into the cellars of the fermentation wing at the crack of dawn when mash was stirred to relish the enchanting smell of malted barley. This fascination slowly turned into a keen interest in brewing as a technology and a profound appreciation of life science. And years later, Kiran set up her pioneering biotechnology company, which today is among the top twenty globally, and paved the way for the growth of India's biotech industry.

Today, Kiran Mazumdar-Shaw is chairman and managing director of Biocon; scientist par excellence and innovator; among the most powerful women globally; India's richest self-made woman; philanthropist; proud Bengaluruan; vociferous civic activist; recipient of a litany of awards and accolades; and much more. At sixty, Kiran remains as unconventional as her rebellious younger self, whose confidence helped her turn failures into successes and challenges into opportunities. Perseverance and determination have been her greatest strengths; she wakes up every day with fresh resolve that guarantees success.

My morning with Kiran inspires and informs me; her deep reserves of confidence and faith still resonate. Meticulous and a morning person, Kiran is at work when I enter her offices at 10.30 a.m. Immaculate in a chic business suit, with simple jewellery and a watch as accessories, the warmth with which she receives me touches me deeply. Her office is redolent with the fragrance of flowers, and a large window overlooks the sprawling green campus.

What keeps her going, I ask. 'Life can be difficult, but if it were not, it would be boring. Tackling challenges gives you confidence, and when you pick yourself up after you fail, it makes you stronger. My failures have made me the woman I am today.'

Her answer reminds me of Theodore Roosevelt's words: 'Courage is not having the strength to go on; it is going on when you don't have the strength.'

## THREE HARD KNOCKS, AND A TURNING POINT

As a young girl, Kiran was intelligent and diligent, but a diffident person. In fact, her phenomenal success later in life left those who knew her then pleasantly surprised. One of her teachers, Anne Warrier, has said, 'Kiran was an obedient, bright student but I would never have thought she had it in her to be so independent, confident and entrepreneurial.'

Kiran and her two brothers grew up in the United Breweries' gated community in Bengaluru. She owes her strong will and confidence to her secure, fun-filled childhood. Her face lights up as she talks about her father, Rasendra Mazumdar, who was the head brewer and general manager at United Breweries, and her homemaker mother, Yamini; their unstinting support and encouragement gave Kiran the confidence to dream big.

Liquor baron Vijay Mallya, who was Kiran's neighbour at the mini-colony of people working at UB, has fond memories of being a part of the Mazumdar family – 'Kiran and I go back a long time. I was friends with her younger brothers, and she was the big sister who would always bully me! We still crack jokes and pull each other's leg, like we did as children.'

Resurrecting herself after being bottomed out has been a way of life for Kiran. The first instance of growth happened when Kiran was still at school. The fact that her father was a brewer and worked in the liquor business embarrassed her as she thought it was a 'tainted profession'. One day, she picked up the courage to talk to him about it and he made it clear 'that brewing was a science; it was not about getting drunk.' He taught his daughter a valuable lesson—'to never judge a person or situation without understanding the entire truth.' And he continued to play a pivotal role in Kiran's life; she had wanted to study medicine, but did not qualify for a place on merit in medical college. She asked her father if he would pay the capitation fee to secure her admission, but he refused. Kiran was affronted at being 'let down' in this manner. She railed at him, 'If I were a son, you would have coughed up the fee. Don't save for my wedding, give me the money now.' He did not relent.

She was acutely disappointed, but quickly turned her focus to earning a bachelor's degree in zoology, graduating in 1973 from Central College,

Bengaluru University. Soon after, she was offered a chance to earn a doctorate in genetics at the University of London, but she was not interested in academics—'I wanted to study something that had an industrial application.'

It was then that her father asked her to consider brewing as a career option. 'That was the beginning of a long process of self-discovery,' says Kiran, who also rediscovered her father's role as a pillar of strength and constant guide. 'He said that there was nothing like a male bastion or a gender barrier that one could not get past. As India's first brewmaster, he was keen that one of his children carried forward that legacy. So, I went ahead and did the course and was confident that I was going to be good at my profession.' Kiran earned her master's degree in malting and brewing, from Ballarat College, University of Melbourne, Australia.

Vijay Mallya remembers how determination and focus were the mainstay of her personality, even as a young girl—'She knew what she wanted to do in life. She loved science and was committed to qualifying as a brewmaster. This was almost unheard of as students don't generally like complicated subjects like science. And, becoming a brewmaster was actually taking science to another level. She is probably one of the very few women in the world to be qualified in brewing and certainly the only Indian lady at the time.'

For Kiran, living in Australia was also an important interlude that forced her to build the resolve that still sets her apart. 'I blossomed there and developed the self-esteem I lacked when I was in India,' she says. Australia exposed her to a diverse society and the reality of competition; Kiran gained confidence, being in a man's world and outperforming her male peers.

But there was more inner resilience she would discover when she returned to India in 1977. The greatest challenge that Kiran faced in the brewing industry of the 1970s was that no employer was ready to hire a woman for a job that involved running the brewery, handling labour unions and late nights at the plant. Kiran even approached Vittal Mallya, Vijay's father, who was then chairman of UB. He told her, 'It's difficult to give you a job; this is a man's work.'

Young, qualified, brimming with ideas and fresh from a foreign country where she had found her spirit and voice, Kiran was deeply disillusioned by this attitude. I am curious to know how it felt to be an educated and accomplished woman who was being discouraged only on the basis of gender. Kiran smiles as she responds, 'I think glass ceilings are in people's minds. The glass ceiling is a transparent one, so it's up to you to either hallucinate that it is there or to think that it is not there. [I decided to] break free!'

This decision coincided with a fortuitous encounter with Les Auchincloss, promoter of Irish enzyme-maker Biocon Biochemicals. Auchincloss asked Kiran to help him set up a subsidiary in India, which would supply enzymes to brewers, packaged food companies and fruit juice makers. It was a turning point for the feisty young woman who was learning not to give up.

'I am an accidental entrepreneur—I wanted a career as a brewmaster, and when that did not happen, I had to take on this challenge. I wanted to prove that women should not be looked down upon or be denied opportunities because of any prejudice or archaic mindset. I set up a company, but felt disturbed that in a country where we were really looking for people in science to do more for this country, women scientists were sitting at home,' she says.

It was an attitude that made a marked impression on Auchincloss, who reportedly said, 'She was so focused and had such a forceful personality that I knew she could hold her own.'

Kiran's zeal to work hard for what she wants to achieve has led to widespread respect and acknowledgement of the sheer force of her vision. She earned her name in a field that had largely closed its doors to women, and this has been recognized by leading organizations around the world. In 2016, she was conferred with the highest French distinction, Chevalier de l'Ordre National De La Légion d'Honneur (Knight of the Legion of Honour), marking worldwide recognition for her contribution to biotechnology. In 2017, she was felicitated with an honorary Doctorate of Science (D.Sc., honoris causa) from Presidency University, Kolkata and the AWSM Award for Excellence 2017 by the Feinstein Institute for Medical Research, USA. She also earned recognition and awards from state governments, NGOs, and private organizations through 2018.

## THE BEGINNING OF A DREAM

On 29 November 1978, Biocon Biochemicals and Kiran launched Biocon India as a joint venture, with Auchincloss agreeing to limit foreign ownership to 30 per cent. It was the beginning of a trying time, as it is with any start-up—Kiran was up against many barriers, as she started going about setting up the business in the garage of her rented house in Bengaluru with a seed capital of Rs 10,000; a 3000 sq. ft shed nearby served as a factory.

Kiran was twenty-five years old, had little capital inflow and no experience of running a business. She was also promoting an unknown sector—biotechnology. Financial support was not forthcoming, and qualified people stayed away, not wishing to work for a woman boss. A friend agreed to help out as her secretary. 'Women entrepreneurs have to be able to convince people to back them, to invest in them and when one does, it is a huge responsibility,' says Kiran. 'I was determined to make the venture a success, and kept knocking on doors until people were persuaded to back me.'

That, however, was only one hurdle crossed. When Kiran wanted to procure raw materials, suppliers desisted, saying they preferred to negotiate with a man. Why couldn't she send her manager instead, they wondered. Kiran would tell them firmly that they had to deal with her.

And then there followed infrastructural challenges. A biotech business needed to have some basics in place, such as uninterrupted power supply, water whose quality was assured, sterile labs, the latest research equipment and people with exceptional scientific skills. None of these was available.

As for any start-up, funds were an immediate necessity, but Kiran's chances of raising more capital remained slim. Biotechnology as a sector was yet to show potential and banks balked at lending to an industry that was still in its inception. By sheer luck Kiran met the general manager of Canara Bank at a wedding and brought to his notice the attitude of bankers towards women entrepreneurs. He called her the very next day to inform her that a loan had been sanctioned. This was money that she was in desperate need of to upgrade her premises—the business was outgrowing the garage.

A major breakthrough came in the early-80s when Kiran decided to manufacture enzymes. Within a year, she began exporting enzymes to the US and Europe, the first Indian company to do so, bringing her revenue that she used to scale up her production to become India's largest enzymes company. The next turning point came in 1999 when Biocon started its journey to become a leading biopharmaceutical company, and went on to become India's first and the only publically listed biotech company in 2004.

Kiran was, in effect, using her education innovatively. Or, as Hasit B. Joshipura, former India head of GlaxoSmithKline Pharmaceuticals, one of the oldest pharma companies in the world, says, 'Hers is a business which is deeply rooted in science, which Kiran commercialized. I think the results speak categorically of her ability to blend science and commerce.'

Within a few years of the firm's inception, Kiran had this gut feeling that biotechnology would be transformational and, in 1983, set up a facility on a twenty-acre piece of land on the outskirts of Bengaluru to start operations in this direction. She was lucky to get licences without greasing palms during the Licence Raj days. A senior bureaucrat, who believed in her plans, helped her get the required government approvals. The company soon began to generate impressive cash flows and its turnover reached $2.5 million.

In 1989, Unilever acquired Biocon Biochemicals in Ireland and Auchincloss moved out of the venture by selling his stake. Kiran now thought it was the right time to expand beyond enzymes. In 1994, she founded Biocon's first subsidiary, Syngene International, whose agenda as a research outfit was to offer early-stage development for drug companies. Soon, Kiran also expanded the company's scope to include developing biopharmaceuticals like statins, insulin and monoclonal antibodies. In 1996, Biocon debuted in the biopharmaceuticals segment with the manufacture of statins, a class of drugs used to lower cholesterol.

To generate this sum of money, Kiran's husband, John Shaw, a former textile executive and chairman of Madura Coats, sold his home in London and joined Biocon.

The rapidly growing company needed another major infusion of capital, which was not hard to source now. ICICI Venture, a subsidiary of ICICI Bank, agreed to provide the funds. The father of modern banking in India, Narayanan Vaghul, who was then chairman of ICICI Bank, found Kiran's faith in her idea impressive. 'We had a breakfast meeting when she presented her proposal. She was very young but had a fire in her belly and she believed in her purpose. And when she spoke, I could see that she had the drive to see her ideas through. I asked her to analyse the proposal and submit it to my office in one day as that was all the time I had. We examined the proposal, and sanctioned the loan,' he says to me.

In 2000, Biocon entered the field of specialty pharmaceuticals with the commissioning of its first fully automated submerged fermentation plant. The same year, Clinigene was launched to offer clinical research and development services to other pharma companies. A year later, the US Food and Drug Administration approved Biocon as a manufacturer of lovastatin, a cholesterol-lowering drug, the first Indian company to merit the assignment. The next sphere that Biocon conquered was biosimilars—these use biological processes to develop generic forms of biopharmaceutical molecules. Kiran decided to tackle the huge disease burden posed by diabetes as it was important for an Indian company to offer cost-effective and easily accessible treatment. In 2004, Biocon successfully introduced India's first indigenously developed and produced recombinant human insulin. Biocon thus made a significant difference to diabetes management in the country, and expanded access to insulin by making it affordable.

Deepak Parekh, chairman of HDFC, thinks Kiran's is 'an extraordinary story. She has grown tremendously in stature in the last few years and today she is at the zenith of her career. She started on a modest scale and it is her perseverance and hard work that have carried her to the top.'

He credits Kiran's success to her ability to balance the responsibilities of a scientist and an entrepreneur. 'She has a unique knack for translating an idea into a business opportunity, then mass-scaling it for the benefit of people and making money. She is an ideal mix of a biotechnologist and an acute businesswoman.'

## CREATING HISTORY

In April 2004, Biocon went public with the most remarkable stock market debut. It was only the second Indian company—Bharti Airtel being the first—to exceed $1 billion on the first day of listing. This was a moment of complete triumph because it proved to Kiran that she had finally succeeded in making people understand that building a business was not merely a bricks-and-mortar exercise, but also required knowledge and intellectual property; and the response to the IPO proved that she had given science a business value.

Having an IPO is essential for companies seeking to raise funds but, according to Parekh, Biocon's success was due to the sincerity with which Kiran marketed it. There was the fact that it was a little-known field, or 'the rarity factor' that she needed to conquer—'Her confidence in her research and the quality of her products was evident. So, people believed that it would make for a good investment.' The success of the IPO notwithstanding, Kiran clarifies that her entry into business was impelled by far more than just the desire to make money. She wanted to use her knowledge of science for the welfare of people, to devise innovation that would serve the common good.

As we speak, it is clear that this motive is even more important to Kiran as the years go by. She is keen on consolidating Biocon's contribution to the treatment of diseases, such as diabetes, cancer and autoimmune disorders. She has kept in mind her own milestones for the business—to develop oral insulin and a blockbuster drug, each of which would benefit a billion patients. The quest for exploring newer treatments for addressing debilitating diseases has led to Biocon developing two novel biopharmaceutical drugs. While BIOMAb EGFR® for head and neck cancer is helping meet the cancer treatment challenge; ALZUMAb™, the world's first anti-cd6 monoclonal antibody, has made psoriasis management easier for thousands of patients in India. Biocon is currently developing the world's first orally delivered insulin which is expected to revolutionize diabetes treatment and management. In 2017, Biocon made steady strides in securing approvals from the FDA for biosimilar drugs to treat breast and gastric cancers. Biocon also launched KRABEVA® (Bevacizumab), a key biosimilar antibody drug for the treatment of patients with metastatic colorectal cancer and other types of lung, kidney, cervical, ovarian, and brain cancers in India.

According to Kiran, the biotech/pharma industry and its regulators are not in sync with each other, 'We are hindered by the government's failure to ensure excellent infrastructure and amenities. The delays involved in obtaining clearances add to this as well.'

Vaghul calls Kiran the pioneer of the biotech industry. 'Biotechnology is a nascent industry globally. When Kiran first started, the word biotechnology was not known in India. So, in effect, she gave birth to it, and nurtured it. Most importantly, she thought beyond herself and Biocon. Kiran has become the voice of the biotechnology industry.' It is no wonder that Kiran has been repeatedly featured on multiple lists of the rich and powerful by publications like *Fortune, Forbes,* and Kotak Wealth's Hurun report. In 2018, the Ministry of Women and Child Development felicitated her for being the first Indian businesswoman to reach a net worth of USD 1 billion.

In 2019, Kiran created history when she became the first Indian woman to be elected as a member of the prestigious US National Academy of Engineering (NAE), Washington DC, for her contribution to biotechnology and affordable healthcare in India.

## AN ASTUTE ENTREPRENEUR

Kiran's approach to building Biocon has been fuelled by experimentation and learning, coupled with intense determination. Challenge has always been like grist to her mill, and changing social mindsets major on her agenda. She has said, in the past—'When I was building Biocon, I felt a woman's role in society was not at the level it ought to be. Women were relegated to second-class citizenship where they did not have the courage to find equitable opportunities in the country to help in social development like men have. I felt that we were kind of stereotyped into what we could do and what we shouldn't.'

Particularly to Kiran, entrepreneurship is also about creating value and she takes immense pride in the value she has created especially as a woman entrepreneur. 'I had a supportive family; my father, particularly, believed strongly in women's roles in society. With this kind of backing and the kind of education I received in school, I had a sense of self-belief and self-worth which made me feel that I should play that role. Therefore, when I set about my career path, I was always daring, I always wanted to do something different. I wanted to challenge the idea of a male bastion,' says Kiran, who dislikes the title of 'richest woman in India', which her value of $1.2 billion has won her.

To her what matters is the fact that her growth has been inclusive of other women—'Biocon has about 5000 scientists on its rolls, of whom 40 per cent are women. Many have returned to India from abroad. For my company I wanted women scientists to work, innovate, research and build value. At Biocon, I created this scientific environment for all scientists, not only for women, but I felt that women scientists should be able to come and work here. I realized that there were a lot of women who have BSc and MSc degrees, even PhDs, and then sit at home. It was wrong for India to waste this valuable resource. I feel gratified that I have built Asia's largest biotech company, the seventh-largest biotech employer in the world with a large number of women.'

She also feels strongly that improvement of the condition of Indian women is vital. This is as close to her heart as advancements in healthcare and healthcare access. 'Women are psychologically caught in this trap that they can't do things and they need help with finances. They don't have that sense of purpose or clarity on professional goals. Women often feel responsible for others. But if you are doing it for yourself, you are trying to build something and your responsibility is your own, then you can do it,' Kiran says.

As a company, Biocon has a culture of freedom and encouragement. Everyone at Biocon is on a first-name basis, and everyone, including Kiran, queues up for lunch at the canteen. 'I've remained steadfast on my basic values. The quintessential woman to me is one who is aware of her status in society and contributes to its change. I am not just a woman business leader; I am a business leader in the country. Today I am the voice of biotech, of business in India,' says Kiran.

Others who have walked the hurdle-riddled entrepreneurial path are, understandably, in awe. 'I think that Kiran is an absolutely amazing entrepreneur and has demonstrated against tremendous odds that she can overcome all kinds of obstacles and show creativity in building such a phenomenal company,' says Nandan Nilekani, who is regarded as a key contributor to India's technological development. 'We are both entrepreneurs from non-traditional backgrounds—Kiran's father was a chief brewer at UB, my father was a middle manager in Bengaluru. So as first-generation entrepreneurs we also have a soft corner for our peers, and we like to see India and Bengaluru as hubs for entrepreneurship.'

Listed among the world's 100 most influential people by *Time* magazine, Kiran possesses a rare blend of credibility, grit, determination, global vision, entrepreneurial passion and team spirit—all of which make her an exceptional leader. She, however, believes that leadership comes from within and has to do with vision, purpose, perseverance and a plan for change. Kiran has been inspired by several leaders at different stages of her entrepreneurial journey and believes differentiation, excellence and values enabled them to stand out.

## THE HUMAN TOUCH

Kiran has pledged to give away 75 per cent of her wealth when she dies. She has already donated about $33 million to various causes since 2005—especially in healthcare and education. It is not surprising then, that *Forbes* has named Kiran one of the most generous people in Asia.

Vaghul, himself the chairman of Give India Foundation, says of Kiran's generosity, 'Giving away 75 per cent of one's wealth is noble but, above all, it is the very thought of sharing wealth that ought to be commended. The intent behind the philanthropy is equally important.'

She founded the Biocon Foundation in 2004 to work in areas of health, education and civic infrastructure, with the economically weaker sections of society as the beneficiaries. The gamut of the foundation's work includes offering micro-health-insurance schemes in villages, running primary healthcare clinics across Karnataka and organizing health camps. Each year, the beneficiaries of the foundation's holistic approach number nearly 300,000.

'When I was setting up the foundation, I could have called it the Kiran Mazumdar-Shaw Foundation, but I wanted the company to look at philanthropy in a big way. When I was making a significant contribution to the organization I wanted Biocon to develop an ethos of giving. It doesn't matter how much, it is the concept of giving that matters, and I want every Bioconite to give something as personal philanthropy,' she says.

Another aspect to her unflinching commitment to social causes is reflected in the pricing of Biocon's drugs; many of them cost less than half of other innovators. Kiran is clear that innovation cannot come with prohibitive costs; it has to reach people. 'If one person has lived longer or suffered less because of us, I would consider that as our greatest achievement,' she says.

The emphasis she places on healthcare being a key area for the foundation is rooted in a personal story. Her best friend was diagnosed with breast cancer in 2002, and Kiran was a witness to her fight against the disease, as well as the invasive and expensive treatments she had to undergo. Kiran also experienced the trauma of having her husband and mother diagnosed with cancers, and their battles against it. In 2007, Kiran partnered with eminent surgeon and visionary philanthropist, Devi Shetty, who runs Narayana Hrudayalaya, to establish the Mazumdar-Shaw Cancer Centre at the Narayana Health City campus in Bommasandra, Bengaluru. The 1400-bed centre delivers affordable and high-quality cancer care to patients, especially to those who belong to the lower socio-economic strata.

'Kiran approaches her humanitarian tasks in the same manner that she does her work—quietly and with dedication. The best proof of her philanthropic work is that I am not aware of it; she has done it below the radar,' says Joshipura.

## ALL IN THE FAMILY

From her office, Kiran can look out at the tree under which lie her father's ashes while a photograph of him hangs prominently above her desk. At a time when a patriarchal system relegated daughters to the background, and disregarded their intellect, he had asked Kiran to use her knowledge to do something meaningful. She says she owes a large part of her success to her family. Both her parents were progressive in their thinking and held unconventional views on what they wanted their children to do.

Kiran's husband, John Shaw, is a Scotsman. 'Unless you find the right person you don't want to get married. The criticality of getting married should not come in the way of pursuing what you want to do,' she says. 'We complement each other: I am a scientist and he has a strong financial background. He is a very strong and secure human being and I am fortunate to have such an understanding partner. I was forty-four when we married and had spent my whole life working, so we have no children but that's been a sacrifice I have accepted.'

John Shaw, who grew up in Scotland and moved to Bengaluru in 1991 as the chairman of Madura Coats, has been her steadfast companion in both her personal and professional lives. 'It's professionalism that came into the business in a much bigger way because of him,' Kiran says. 'I was very entrepreneurial, but for a business to scale up, one needs professional systems in place and that's what John helped me do. Because he came from a multinational culture, he shared with us many things that need to be done and which we were not doing.'

An aficionado of art, Kiran's office is filled with paintings and sculptures by Indian and Scottish artists; prominent names in her collection include M.F. Husain and Yusuf Arakkal. I find that the space resembles an office less and a comfortable, elegant living room more, and I am not surprised to learn that Kiran has a yen for interior design. Combining her two loves—brewing beer and art—she has written a coffee-table book called *Ale and Arty*, which explores both disciplines. Travel is another interest—Kiran has nursed a sense of exploration throughout her life and enjoys taking short breaks with her family, especially to the Maldives, Italy and Spain.

For Kiran, a typical day begins by enjoying a workout at home and walking her dogs before heading to work. And it ends with dinner at home with her mother and husband, the news and reading. When she is not brainstorming on expansion plans for Biocon or ways of reducing the costs of life-saving drugs, she dabbles in cooking. I find it singularly surprising that this pioneer loves being in the kitchen, particularly to dish up meals in a jiffy—a *'jhatpat* cook,' despite the occasional class taken on vacation.

Kiran enjoys music and has also acted in a play, *Amadeus*, directed by Arjun Sajnani. Reading and watching movies—especially those that star Meryl Streep, Tom Hanks, Richard Gere, Aamir Khan or Shah Rukh Khan—are other pastimes; *Winners Never Cheat* by Jon Huntsman is her favourite book. (Shah Rukh Khan is a good friend of Kiran's incidentally, and was invited to launch Biocon's first cancer drug. The actor's father died of the same type of cancer that the drug treats.) Kiran also enjoys a special friendship with Sudha Murty and the Murthy family.

Kiran confesses to me that she is given to being sentimental, and still uses the desk she started working at in her 'garage days'. Friendships and close personal associations are very important to her, as is evidenced by the abundance of family photographs in her office. A particularly poignant souvenir is a drawing her nephew made as a child on which he wrote—'If I found a pot of gold I would give it to my aunt for her company to make new medicines for very bad diseases.'

## THE DNA OF SUCCESS

Particularly fond of Bengaluru where she has grown up, built her success and still calls her home, Kiran believes she owes a major part of her inclination towards the scientific temper of Bengaluru, and recalls her joy as a child, frequenting science museums in the city with her brothers.

'I love the city. This is the city I grew up in; took advantage of when I was building the organization; which invested in me; whose government gave me loans in the early days. So, I owe it to my city and community. Any impact that I can make, I should first make in this city,' she says.

To her mind, the growth of Bengaluru from a sleepy, green city into the country's IT hub is an example of the greatest paradox in India—that between the very wealthy and the very poor. While most industrialists refrain from flaying the government for pursuing policies that debilitate industrial growth for fear of a political backlash, Kiran is surprisingly outspoken. 'If you run your business ethically and if you engage with the government for the right reason, why should you be scared to speak up when things go wrong? You cannot speak up when you have something to hide and have taken favours from the government. That has to stop. We have to make this country far more transparent and accountable.'

Kiran heads the Bengaluru Political Action Committee (BPAC), which aims to bring in good governance in the city. BPAC supported good candidates across parties, and Nilekani with his background and philosophy made him one such ideal citizen. He made his political debut in the 2014 general election from the Bengaluru South constituency and worked with Kiran at BPAC. 'Kiran has been at the forefront in the creation of BPAC. She has always said that people who succeed in other walks of life should enter public life and politics. I am very grateful for her backing for my campaign,' he says.

Kiran herself though, does not want to run for public office—'Politics is a huge business all over the world and I don't think people like me fit in.'

Mallya identifies the constraints on Kiran's time, and thus appreciates her contribution to socio-economic causes—'She is very vocal in expressing her views. I am very pleased that she, as one of the prominent citizens of Bengaluru, is part of the action group. The group has made some significant suggestions for the improvement of the quality of life in Bengaluru.'

While she calls herself a proud Indian, Kiran is disturbed with some aspects with which the country has come to be identified. 'India is known to be the most corrupt country in the world, and unfortunately, it starts with us,' she points out. She remembers how, as a young entrepreneur, she used public transport and owned a rickety old car which she often had to push-start. Finding a quicker, easier way to gain wealth had never occurred to her.

Kiran was just thirty-five when she received the Padma Shri in 1989, for her pioneering efforts in industrial biotechnology; this was followed by the Padma Bhushan in 2005.

In January 2013, the US Pharmacopeial Convention put Kiran on its board of trustees and its CEO, Roger L. Williams, said, 'As a businesswoman and philanthropist, Kiran has innovated and campaigned tirelessly for affordable medications on behalf of patients in India and worldwide for decades.' The next year, Kiran succeeded Mukesh Ambani as chairperson of the board of the prestigious Indian Institute of Management Bengaluru. Taking stock of the extraordinary arc of Kiran's career, Parekh says, 'She was unrecognized when she started out, and in a matter of years, has evolved into acquiring a global profile in the pharmaceutical industry. She is on the prime minister's economic advisory council and on the Indo-US CEO forum. Kiran has earned recognition from all quarters.'

The recipe for success, according to Kiran, is simple—one has to be dedicated, determined and not give up. Indian society is quite unforgiving of failure, which is unfortunate, she thinks, because failure is a wonderful teacher—if we wish to learn. 'I think all great entrepreneurs around the world have started with very little. It's just an idea, the conviction that I can do it, and that I can build companies is very important.'

Mallya who calls Kiran his 'elder sister' takes an almost proprietorial pride in Kiran's achievements. 'If anybody talks about gender inequality then Kiran has disproved everyone. She's not just as good but she's probably better than most men that I know.'

Kiran has come very far from where she started but believes that she still has much to accomplish.

'There is a long journey ahead for me. There are many more milestones to cross,' she says. She feels that her legacy is going to be affordable healthcare. 'I certainly would want to be remembered as someone who was a pioneer, who built India's biotech sector, and also as someone who brought in important societal change for women in this country.'

And as Biocon's tagline—'The difference lies in our DNA'—goes, the power probably lies in Kiran Mazumdar-Shaw's DNA.

# DEVI SHETTY

*A compassionate philanthropist, a tireless reformer, a visionary entrepreneur and perhaps the last name in cardiac health, **Devi Shetty** is a pioneer in every sense of the term. He joined hands with **Kiran Mazumdar-Shaw**, making a formidable team with a shared sense of a larger purpose, determined to bring about effective change in the healthcare scenario. Her can-do attitude and sharp entrepreneurial skills, combined with his medical expertise and vision, resulted in the setting up of a 1400-bed cancer hospital at the Narayana Health City in Bengaluru in 2007. The cardiac surgeon talks about his friend and partner and the plans they have to change the world, one compassionate initiative at a time.*

**You have known Kiran for many years and have collaborated with her at a symbiotic level. Tell us something about your association with her.**

I have known her since 1995, when I joined the Manipal Heart Foundation. Kiran was then building up Biocon and I was impressed with the way she worked. We came to know each other over the years and eventually became friends.

For most people who have worked abroad, to return home and see how backward we still were, was undeniably hurtful. There are only so many things one can do. However, there are some who think differently. Kiran is one of them. She started making insulin because she thought that if companies in the US and Europe can make it, we can surely do so in India, as well. It was a major step at the time since Biocon was not a very big company. I really admire her for getting into this without any precedence in India.

**Kiran is looked upon as one of the most important leaders in India today. How would you define her style of leadership?**

Kiran displays a completely unorthodox way of thinking about how this country should be positioned. She believes that India can do everything that anyone in the US or Europe can; in fact, she believes we can do it better.

Her audacious goals are what set Kiran apart. One probably cannot imagine a company as small as Biocon getting into insulin production, which is one of the most difficult drugs to make. Her leadership essentially lies in doing the unthinkable. I think this is the reason she has attracted so many admirers today. Had she not started manufacturing insulin, millions of diabetics in India would not have been able to afford their insulin shots today. Even MNCs had to control their prices, thanks to her—this indirect contribution of hers has had a cascading effect on the whole cycle.

Kiran partnered with me on the cancer hospital project. As she got into investment mode, I noticed that she just took the document and signed it; she never asked what was written in it. I think she has this gift of trusting people, which also sets her apart. But what I admire most about Kiran is the amount of time she has for her close friends, some of whom are ordinary people. I clearly remember, once, when a friend of hers was suffering from breast cancer, she looked after her in a way that was, for a woman of Kiran's stature, unthinkable.

**Kiran transformed a company that was founded on just Rs 10,000 to one that is currently valued at Rs 9350 crore. According to you, what traits have led her to this phenomenal success?**

Kiran reminds me of a wise ice hockey player. The ball is called a puck in that game and she almost seems to know where the puck is supposed to go. She is always a few seconds ahead of the puck!

Biocon was initially an enzyme manufacturing company till they started making high-end insulin products. Kiran has thoughtfully reinvented herself every three to five years to keep herself updated. After a point of time, she got into cancer treatment and cardiology. Her knowledge about the pharma industry is phenomenal. Not only is she updated about latest innovations and technologies, she knows a lot about cancer, sometimes even more than oncologists.

**Kiran has been involved with a number of philanthropic activities, including setting up the Biocon Foundation. As someone who has worked with her in that field, can you describe her philosophy?**

While investing in our company, she did not look for returns. From the start, she was clear that she was putting in money without expecting any returns on her investment. Kiran has stuck to what she said. This has nothing to do with business; it does not give any returns. Besides, she looks after the healthcare of the entire region, paying health insurance premiums for those who cannot.

**How would you describe Kiran's journey in all the years you have known her as she has built Biocon into the company it is today?**

I believe that her company will be among the top few, globally. It is poised to grow that way because she is the only insulin-maker in Asia. The largest growth in the pharmaceutical sector will take place in Asia, Africa and Latin America. I don't see any other company coming up in the next five years since now there are only consolidations; no big players are getting into it. So, Kiran and Biocon will have a virtual monopoly for the foreseeable future.

**Kiran also runs major social service initiatives. What do you think is most inspirational about her?**

Infosys proved to the world that people from modest backgrounds can build companies that go on to be respected the world over. When Kiran created this world-class infrastructure, we knew it was no longer a handicap being in India.

For young Indians, she should be an inspiration because she has proven that being an Indian is not a handicap and starting your venture in India is definitely not a bad idea. You can create world-class enterprises in India and Kiran has proved her point by doing it in the most regulated industry. You have to realize that tomorrow if you start a software company to compete with the world, no one will prevent you from growing. But in healthcare, a lot of people try to harass you on the pretext of regulation. Growth in a regulated industry while making sensitive drugs is a tough task, and she has achieved exactly that. Besides, garnering recognition from the leaders of the industry across the world is definitely praiseworthy.

130

**Several corporate houses are becoming a part of healthcare; they are running hospitals and taking other initiatives. What is distinctive about Kiran's CSR goals?**

Kiran has never believed charity to be saleable. She believes that good business, with a charitable outlook is scalable. She would never ask us to write off bills, she would rather insist upon reduction of the price so that a common man finds it affordable. The idea is that this way, you can help thousands of people because if you make it free, how many people can you realistically cater to? She doesn't just preach but also puts her own money and makes things happen. She has convinced us that she walks the talk.

Kiran is also honest with the highest level of integrity. She is totally trustworthy and a great friend to have. Moreover, she has always believed in thinking big. She believes that ambience makes a major difference to what you produce.

**You are an eminent physician and have vast experience of running public healthcare services. What propelled you to join hands with Kiran?**

The main reason is trust. In any business venture, trust comes first, and then, ideology. Both of us share similar ideologies. We worked towards a common goal of disassociating healthcare from affluence. Once ideologies and trust were in place, she agreed to join hands with us. That's all you need.

**Can you elucidate the ventures you are working towards, regarding healthcare?**

We have built the cancer hospital; now we want to take the Mazumdar-Shaw Cancer Hospital global and we are also working towards the growth of the Narayana Heart Hospital. Whenever we set up a hospital globally, it has, or will have, a Mazumdar-Shaw cancer ward, with the idea that cancer treatment should reach everyone. Cardiac problems and cancer are two devastating health issues. Our greatest gift to the world would be conquering these two diseases.

# ZIA
# MODY

•

As a lawyer myself, I knew one thing — she always has had an enquiring mind, and does not accept things as told to her, but it is her hard work that stands out. At one time she was known as Soli Sorabjee's daughter. Now I'm known as Zia Mody's father. I'm very proud of it and I hope I'll always be known as both—that Zia is my daughter and I am her father.

**—SOLI SORABJEE**

•

*I*t was close to midnight when the BlackBerry rang, shattering the quiet of a corner office on the twenty-third floor of Express Towers, Mumbai (the office has since shifted to Peninsula Towers in Lower Parel). Zia Mody, senior partner with AZB Partners, India's second-largest law firm, was at work. Through her bay windows, she looked down on the flickering arc of Marine Drive, the dark horizon of the Arabian Sea in the distance. Work often kept her back in the office till late into the night.

The caller was her colleague in New Delhi, Ajay Bahl. He had just got off the phone with Sunil Mittal, founder and chairman, Bharti Airtel, who was bidding to buy South African telecom giant MTN in a whopping $24 billion deal, and wanted AZB to be Bharti's adviser in India. Zia, Ajay and their team had an immense amount of work ahead of them.

In 2010, under AZB's counsel, Bharti Airtel eventually acquired Zain Telecom, a big player in North Africa and West Asia, in a $10.7 billion deal—one of the largest cross-border transactions in corporate India. It also cemented AZB's reputation as one of India's most powerful corporate law firms and an outstanding dealmaker.

When I talk to Mittal about Zia, he is effusive—'Zia has a great degree of gravitas. She is looked upon as a very able legal person with much credibility who has scored major successes with almost all leading business houses and banks. More importantly, she has a very strong position in the Indian legal fraternity.'

Another admirer of hers is chairman of the Aditya Birla Group, Kumar Mangalam Birla, who feels confident when Zia represents him, but feels doubly reassured 'when she is on the other side of the table,' as she is very fair, and will never offer advice to a client that could potentially jeopardize a transaction. 'What I like about her is that she is a solution finder rather than a problem maker. She always wants to find a solution that works for her client and for the other side as well. If she believes something is not correct, she will be very outspoken about it. She will never mince her words. I work very well with people like that.'

Conversations such as these, with some of the country's biggest industrialists, prove that it is not just urban myth that Zia is on the speed-dial of India Inc. for every multimillion dollar deal. She does have enviable lineage—her father is Soli Sorabjee, former attorney general of India and a Padma Vibhushan recipient. She may have inherited his passion for law and his ruthless eye for detail and commitment; but Zia has built her career solely by dint of her own sheer hard work.

Anil Agarwal, chairman, Vedanta Resources, agrees. She worked with his team for several months, as AZB were the advisers on Indian law aspects of the Cairn-Vedanta M&A, 'and we credit her legal acumen for this success.' Commending her honesty and exemplary negotiating skills, he adds, 'She also ensured that she was always available as our learned counsel, to give us strategic advice that was aligned with her vast global experience, having deftly handled most of the key mergers and acquisitions for India Inc.'

Yet, when I sit across the table from Zia at the AZB offices in Mumbai, I find it difficult to match the elegant lady in a quiet, but stylish pantsuit and pearls, and her radiance and infectious laugh. That, I realize, is the magic of Zia—she does not need to wear her steeliness on her sleeve; her life and career are example enough of it. She speaks with a quiet confidence in articulate, measured sentences, breaking out from time to time in a warm disarming smile, especially when describing her childhood.

## THE EARLY YEARS

Listening to Zia talk about growing up with her siblings and parents in a sprawling bungalow on South Mumbai's Napean Sea Road, it sounds idyllic. There were long afternoons with three energetic siblings and the best that the world had to offer in literature, poetry, art and music. Her days were spent between classes at J.B. Petit School and learning a multitude of skills such as horse riding, Bharatnatyam and playing the piano. Even as a little girl, Zia displayed all the traits of an overachiever—she would accept any challenge and be very disappointed if she failed at it. 'Anything Zia attempted, she persisted at and excelled in,' says her mother, Zena Sorabjee.

By the age of nine or ten, Zia had decided that she wanted to be a lawyer, just like her father, a choice of career that came naturally to her. 'I was, by nature, argumentative and loved debating and so it was a very natural progression to want to be a lawyer; there was no soul-searching,' she says to me.

Brilliant legal mind Soli had always found his daughter 'self-willed, obstinate and endowed with huge determination.' He tells me, 'There are certain principles which are ingrained in her, some imbibed from me and some cultivated over the years.' Her father's influence meant that Zia did not need to be pushed towards the legal field, Zena tells me. 'Zia was determined from the very beginning. This all began across the dinner table when her father would attend phone calls of his clients. She would be very interested in his cases, she was happy to listen to her father talking about law.'

Her mother's influence on Zia, too, is undeniable. 'I have a very strong view on gender equality, being a Baha'i by religion. I taught her that men and women are equal in the sight of God.' Married at seventeen, and the mother of four children, Zena remains a force of fortitude in the family. Her elder son, Jahangir, is associated with Mumbai Hospital and the youngest, Hormazd, edits *Autocar India*, the country's top automotive magazine.

If her parents were the catalysts for her choice of profession, Zia's personal life was inextricably linked from a very young age to the man who would be her husband, Jaydev Mody; he lived in the same compound as her and has known Zia since he was eight years old. Jaydev's father, Mukund Mody, was a respected lawyer and judge, and his mother, Usha had studied law. The Modys and Sorabjees were friends, which drew Jaydev and Zia closer, and their friendship grew into love quite organically, when they were teenagers. It was to become a relationship that remained unsullied by time or success.

## TAKING FLIGHT

Zia graduated from Mumbai's Elphinstone College and, following her father's advice, gained admission at Selwyn College, Cambridge University. She was thrilled by the emphasis placed at Cambridge on producing thinkers, and the opportunities to discuss, debate and question; her strong foundation in the elements of the law was laid there to be further honed at Harvard Law School where she was next headed.

Her new peers, unlike those at Selwyn, were successful lawyers, government officials, judges, diplomats, professors and doctoral candidates. Their experience and insight were of great value to Zia, who gained a greater understanding of the intricacies of legal systems in countries across the world. Specialising in the United Nations and international law, she often had to read 300 pages of case laws overnight to prepare for a class—'The sheer pressure of being unable to answer correctly in front of the class kept us going.'

By the time Zia passed out of Harvard and cleared the New York State Bar examination to qualify as an attorney, she had developed a keen interest in international law. In 1980 she joined the world's largest law firm, Baker & McKenzie, as a corporate associate in their New York office. In her spare time, Zia enjoyed the best that New York had to offer in art and dance, concerts and plays, theatres and museums.

The time spent working in New York remains a watershed in her life because of the insight it gave her into cultures and practices other than her own. 'You learn that you are not cocooned, you are not isolated. You begin to understand the economic impact of transactions,' Zia tells me. Being a part of complex corporate transactions, such as the acquisition of four luxury hotels in Washington by the Tata group, she developed negotiation skills and understood how to navigate through complicated matters, which still help her in her work as a mergers and acquisition expert.

A key learning at this time was the importance of staying honest and the ramifications that this dictum held. Zia's reputation for plainspeak must come from this early training: 'No one offered an opinion to please the client. It was very important that we kept our reputation intact. If we lost a client in the process, I think it was acceptable. This was how we learnt the importance of a letterhead and being able to justify things and work out solutions when things became complicated and one's integrity was tested.'

This conversation with Zia reminds me of an anecdote business historian and writer Gita Piramal shared with me—'Once as a young counsel [in India], when Zia was getting agitated that her client was not giving her complete instruction, her senior told her, "*Dikra*, don't get upset with your clients. If they don't listen, just charge double." His advice shocked Zia and, at that very moment, she adopted the mantra she still works by—honesty pays.'

Zia has received many awards, all well deserved. The one she most treasures is the ACQ Law Awards which called the firm 'The Most Trusted Law Firm' (2011). 'Clients trust Zia to offer the right opinion and not just please them. Zia doesn't tell them something they want to hear if it is not true. Irrespective of who her clients are, she will give them hard advice,' says Zena.

But what makes Zia peerless is her art of negotiation that she mastered the hard way. With characteristic grace, she credits her mentor Norman Miller—'Earlier I always approached a case with the attitude that the other side was wrong, and I had to win. Miller taught me to be objective and calibrate myself. He always said that one must consider the other party's point of view first because a deal is only a good one if everybody involved is happy. To him, there was no win-loss—there was only win-win or win-and-a-little-win.' Today, her practical negotiation skills and ability to gauge what the people on the other side of the table want have emerged as her trump card in closing the most complicated of deals with success. It comes as no surprise to anyone that *Fortune* named Zia the fourth most powerful woman in India in 2017. Several leading legal circles have repeatedly recognized AZB and Zia Mody as 'Leading Individual' or 'Market Leaders' for Banking & Finance, Corporate and M&A, and Investment Funds in the Asia-Pacific region from 2016 to 2019.

## THE HOMECOMING

In 1984, Zia took a year-long sabbatical from her job in New York to return home. It was not an easy decision to make. She had been doing extremely well at Baker & McKenzie, and loved the exhilarating buzz of life in New York, but she was also keen to marry her childhood sweetheart Jaydev and start a family.

Because her new husband was not keen on relocating to New York, Zia resigned from Baker & McKenzie and moved back home to Mumbai. It helped that the country was suddenly opening up—a promising new India being ushered in by the new young prime minister, Rajiv Gandhi. Coincidentally, her parents moved to Delhi as Soli assumed the post of India's attorney general. It was a time of transition, but there was now the certitude of having Jaydev and his mother, Usha, who were unstintingly supportive of her career. Jaydev's father had passed away young, but the Modys were familiar with a lawyer's life and its unique demands.

When Zia's daughters—Anjali, Aarti and Aditi—were born quite early into the marriage, the family rallied around to support her fully. 'There was a lot of work to be done those days—getting used to a fairly new marriage; being parents; getting settled in a mostly male environment at work; leaving behind my life in New York—and I really struggled.'

The prospect of working in India overwhelmed Zia. From the well-appointed offices of Baker & McKenzie in New York to being a junior barrister in Mumbai, Zia felt she had stepped unexpectedly into a Dickensian world. She had a tiny desk that she had to share; there were no research resources or office assistant. The entrepreneur in her took over and Zia learnt 'to be very, very efficient.' She stopped thinking about what was not available and made the most of what was.

Her practice at the Mumbai High Court under the tutelage of senior counsel Obey Chinoy, taught Zia the importance of precision, thoroughness in research and the art of filling gaps in legal arguments. The greater challenge perhaps was gaining partial admittance into the male-dominated Indian legal fraternity. She recalls how on her first day at work, her choice of work wear—starched white-collared shirt tucked into a pleated skirt, pearls and modest heels—was given the once over before the senior counsel remarked drily, '*Abhi thoda salwar-kameez shuru karna chahiye* (You might need to start wearing salwar-kameez now).' In some desperation to project the desired image, Zia took to wearing glasses even though she had perfect eyesight. Zena recalls that 'she did that to look older or nobody would give her a brief.'

As a young woman junior in the Bombay high court of the 1980s, Zia was largely a misfit. The legal profession was decidedly a male bastion and clients couldn't figure out why their matter should be handled by this young woman '*bachchu*!' The few women peers Zia had were treated with condescension in the courts, and clients kept them at bay.

'One had to work hard to establish oneself. Women lawyers only handled cases to do with matrimony etc. You had to prove that you were better than everyone else, and once I achieved that, my seniors took me seriously. And the only way I could get there was by working very hard and delivering better and better. If a male colleague was using ten books to research a case, I used twenty. That meant that I found a nuance that he had missed. I basically studied hard and was ruthlessly focused on being recognized,' says Zia. And once clients saw how articulate and intelligent Zia was, they took her seriously.

Drawing inspiration from her role model, US Supreme Court judge Ruth Bader Ginsberg, who faced similar gender-based discrimination in the 1970s, Zia continued to toil. Soon, she was moved from handling the 'soft' cases traditionally given to women lawyers to corporate briefs.

Her proud father even went to the extent of wishing that senior lawyers would not appear on a stipulated day so that his daughter would get an opportunity to prove her worth. Zena recalls an incident with warmth:

140

'Once when my husband was visiting the high court in Mumbai, he passed by a court and heard a woman's voice arguing before the judge. He listened for a while as he thought that she was making a very good point. He went inside and saw that it was his daughter.'

## MAKING HER MARK

That was still the predigital era and sometimes, Zia would need to read forty books to draft supporting arguments for a proposition, without knowing whether the Supreme Court had made any recent decisions that would render her argument void.

I ask her what she did if she failed and she chuckles—'It took some time to understand that I had to lose some cases and not take that personally. I used to get very depressed at a loss, as if it was a personal failure. What did not help was the uneven gender equation because it also made me feel that people thought I lost because I was a woman. And I feared I would not be allowed another chance.'

Listening to Zia talk about her anxieties and disappointments with candour is cathartic. Because her energy and enthusiasm—she keeps sixteen-hour workdays in her late fifties—do not allow you to think of her as having any weaknesses or fears. I often wonder if she has defeated the concept of a body clock because every time I meet or speak with Zia, she has the same radiance and spiritedness no matter what she is dealing with that day.

This was the time that enquiries began trickling in from contacts overseas who wanted to set up shop in India. The economy was opening up and Zia's nascent entrepreneurial instincts were catalysed by the possibility of starting her own firm. 'Much to my father's sadness, I stepped out of the courtroom and switched to table practice,' Zia says. She set up Chambers of Zia Mody (CZM) in Mumbai in 1995.

The course her career was now to take would see her emerge as one of the country's top corporate attorneys. She was, in effect, moving out of her renowned father's shadow and carving out her own place in the sun. 'I'd have preferred her to be at the Bar, practising, so she would be known, to argue as a counsel, not merely as a solicitor or a legal adviser. But she prefers the other practice. That's okay, your clients know you, others know you, but when you're in the court, *people* know you, your fellow advocates, judges and others. A lawyer is watched keenly and acutely by the press, by his fellow peers, and others to see how one performs—and that's how one gets recognition,' Soli tells me.

A loan of Rs 30 lakh from HDFC Bank funded her dream. Starting off with a young team of talented lawyers that Zia had worked with over the years, CZM proved its mettle with its first client—international financial powerhouse Alliance Capital. They were able to help Alliance Capital get a foothold selling mutual funds in the Indian market, cementing their reputation from the start.

While soft-spoken and understated, the aura around Zia carries the unmistakable stamp of a strong-willed, independent woman. Naturally I am keen to learn why, after a few years, she decided to partner with a second-generation lawyer, Bahram Vakil, instead of going solo. She says it's because no amount of ambition and energy can replace having a partner who will help you scale up.

Vakil was one of India's foremost attorneys in infrastructure and project finance law; along with his experience, he brought to the firm an enviable client list across important sectors such as power, oil and natural gas, telecommunications and mining. Recounting his first meeting with Zia to discuss the partnership, Vakil tells me, 'There was this history that went back a whole generation. Funnily enough, the meeting that started our partnership lasted for little more than an hour. It was an easy and straightforward decision. Both of us thought that there was a need for a different kind of a management.' He goes on to say, 'I really know very, very few people who have gone from doing court litigation to doing corporate law. I think it goes to show the breadth of Zia's mind and her immense talent, because making that switch is not easy at all. Besides knowing the law and having a passion for it, you have to have practical common sense and be very pragmatic. And she's great in both these areas.'

In 2004, Vakil and Zia brought on board Ajay Bahl, a Delhi-based lawyer and chartered account who specialized in M&As, securities regulations, foreign exchange-related advisory work and tax litigation. Bahl had incidentally interned with Soli. With Bahl on board, the firm was rechristened AZB (Ajay, Zia, Bahram), with offices in Delhi and Mumbai and a young, tech-savvy team that made older Indian law firms sit up and take notice.

Just at the time that AZB was born, international companies were eyeing a slice of India's vast, untapped market, while Indian ones were looking to expand overseas. Zia, with her cross-functional, holistic and multicultural training had been preparing for such an opportunity all her life. Not surprisingly, most of AZB'S early clients were foreign companies keen to do business in an emerging India. When the partners made a three-year plan, they decided on a 50:50 ratio of foreign and Indian clients; Zia made the shift with fantastic skill and ease, drawing on all her knowledge and experience to understand the demands of an Indian client just as well as she did an international one's.

'Zia has carved a formidable niche for herself, particularly in the field of mergers and acquisitions,' says Cyril Shroff, who heads India's top legal firm, Cyril Amarchand and Mangaldas and is an old friend of Zia's, the Shroffs, Sorabjees and Modys being family friends for more than half a century. 'Her career graph has been very interesting. It is rooted in how incredibly hard she works—there are legendary stories about her timelines, hours and tenacity. Zia has also contributed to many aspects of the development of the law, by being on committees, or just by making sure she has her say on key issues.'

The first major overseas deal AZB bagged was advising Tata Steel on its $486.4 million acquisition of Singapore-based NatSteel in 2004. She recalls the firm's excitement at working with lawyers across six or seven countries: 'I was managing a project for the first time in its entirety and not just for the Indian side. We were in collaboration with global law firms, working on a very huge deal on a very tight timeline.'

Impressed with Zia's dedication, Ratan Tata chose AZB again in 2007, when Tata Steel acquired Corus in a landmark $12.1 billion deal, making it the fifth largest steel producer in the world. Unsurprisingly, the Tatas partnered with AZB on the acquisition of Jaguar Land Rover in a $2.3 billion transaction. The association with the Tatas not only enhanced Zia's bid to hit the mark as a leading corporate attorney, but helped her become an active part of a wider transformation that the Indian corporate space was to witness.

'Zia has grown in stature tremendously from when she started. She comes from prominent lineage but where she is today, is all her doing and her hard work. She has emerged in the last fifteen years and has become a force to be reckoned with. She is probably the best of the top two or three legal luminaries any corporate would go to and the first port of call for multinationals,' says Deepak Parekh, one of corporate India's well-recognized faces. It was in a mere three years that AZB grew from a firm with fifteen–twenty lawyers to a formidable bench of over 100 spread across the country.

## WITH HONESTY AND HARD WORK

As I researched Zia's career to examine what made her a universal first pick for such a wide range of people, I spoke to her corporate clients, some of whom are India's brightest legal minds, and also to partners in rival law firms. This is the next best thing I could do to actually witnessing her negotiate a deal. Everyone has a uniform opinion of her, and that opinion is born out of affection, admiration and deep respect for her stellar traits, both personal and professional.

Praise from a competitor of sorts does not usually come readily and Shroff is generous with it. 'Building a professional services firm in India is not easy,' he says, 'especially a new entrant like Zia's. But she's done it, through her focus on quality, ethics, service standards and a modern, efficient approach. She embraced modern economic opportunities—a lot of the other firms died along the way because they never saw the new India and the new opportunities coming in.'

Gita Piramal shows me the bigger picture when she says, 'One of the perks as a journalist is meeting outstanding people. It's my job to find the outliers. In all these years I have met a bare dozen who combine the four magic ingredients of success: clear thought without self-delusion, humanity without paternalistic feudalism, a child's joy for life and humility. One of them is Zia.'

Industry veterans respect Zia for her razor-sharp analytical skills and for always keeping her eye on what is right, which allows her to chart the course to get there.

'The cross-border M&A deals coming into India, or those deals going the other way around, are an AZB speciality, and of course, Zia's speciality. She knows both sides very well from her five years of practice in the US. So, we stand out because of this,' says Vakil. 'Zia is a very straightforward person. Sometimes, when your client is extremely high-profile, one is tempted to sugar-coat it. But, no matter the stature, Zia is very forthright with her view, which is always honest and intelligent. Zia's leadership style is very traditional. She is someone who will lead by example, from the front. She is definitely a workaholic, and this inspires the younger lot who watch her put in the kind of hours she does.'

For Soli, though, it's not Zia's success as a lawyer that he's most proud of, but her courage of conviction, and he narrates an incident that happened when she was mugged in New York. The men were caught and the police needed Zia's evidence to prosecute them. 'People told her, don't go, they'll take revenge on you, but she gave evidence and the muggers were sentenced. She wanted justice to be done—that's what I admire.'

In a lighter vein, he talks about the chinks in the armour of his favourite child whom he immensely admires and adores—her courage evaporates when faced with a needle! 'When the doctor came to give her an injection, she would hide under my bed,' he laughs.

When I speak to Zia about work, it is clear that she loves what she does – being the legal eagle and facilitating a good deal every day. She says, 'Before you start work on a deal, it is important to understand what the client authorizes you to walk away on—what is their buy-in? You must be clear on the essentials of the deal, and what can be traded. If not, negotiations will never end. At this point of my career, negotiating a good settlement and entering a transaction midway to resolve any deal-breakers are what I enjoy the most. I like working in a sensible and proactive manner. And when I have the trust and confidence of not just my own client but of the other party, I am happy. And even happier when the other side becomes a client the next time!'

Zia also firmly believes that the 'cycle of life is round,' and takes seriously the relationships she fosters and maintains as these are not easy to build; but it is clear that she wins the respect of some of India's most successful people not just due to her legal acumen and ability to understand complex business and legal matters, but also because she wins their trust and confidence. There is her close friendship with Mukesh Ambani, who consults her on personal and corporate matters. Other friends include Kumar Mangalam Birla, Raghuram Rajan, Deepak Parekh and Anil Agarwal.

'I respect her being a straight shooter—if I ever need a lawyer, I will approach Zia,' says Shroff. 'It is always a pleasure to have her on the other side, because I know we will be able to have a practical dialogue. We have always closed a transaction because whenever Zia and I deal with each other, we reach an outcome.'

They have worked together on cases such as the Adani-Dhamra Port and Axis Bank. 'It was memorable working with her on the Axis deal because although it was not very huge in terms of value, it was so complicated that the trust and competency between us helped. One deal we worked on had to be closed immediately and we did not have the time to document it before we closed. So we documented the deal two days later. There are not too many people whose word you can trust, but Zia is one of them. This example tells you everything you need to know about her!'

Parekh adds, 'Intellectually speaking, Zia is quite merciless. She will keep peeling off the fuzziness. What makes Zia stand out are her people skills, her ability to explain a problem and the solution in simple language and her enormous capacity for work. She has the ability to advise, not only on strictly legal matters, but on a potential deal's political dimension as well.' For a woman in a man's world, it was both a political and professional nod to Zia's calibre when in 2017 SEBI inducted her to a board led by Uday Kotak. The board specifically advises Indian corporates on various issues related to improving corporate governance standards, improving safeguards and disclosures regarding related-party transactions, and issues in accounting and auditing practices by listed companies and transparency-related issues in Indian corporates.

In my own multiple conversations with Zia, I have admired how approachable she is and how lightly she wears the mantle of superlative success. There is no hubris or arrogance to her. With her team of partners and 250-plus employees, she displays genuine concern and empathy even as her firm wins prestigious awards.

While in the early days, as a leader, Zia would roll up her sleeves and get involved in every routine issue, her role is now evolving to being ever-present as a mentor and guide to AZB lawyers and as a safety net for clients. The openness and transparency built into the firm extend to succession and partnerships, which are typically thorny issues in traditional Indian law firms. Her clients have been awestruck by her accessibility and aversion to 'adventurous' advice. In fact many a time, she has advised clients to drop deals which she found risky because she knows that the clients lean on the firm's judgement, more than anything else.

'Zia's core strengths remain unchanged—how hard she works, her passion for being ethical, and her ability to tell it like it is. I have seen her talk firmly to a client and correct them,' says Shroff. Zia is clear that AZB is not a family firm, and her dream is to institutionalize it further in order to encourage the younger partners to become its future leaders.

For Soli giving it back is as important as success. 'Zia's vision is not only to succeed as a corporate lawyer but also how she trains others— young lawyers need training, need encouragement; we must spend some time for that.'

The other thing AZB has going for it is its amazing gender diversity. And being a young woman entrepreneur myself, it struck a very personal chord. 'Many a time we have Americans coming in who inquire about our "gender mix". They are very particular about whether a firm meets their standard ratio but in our case, they are positively shocked when I tell them that about 50 per cent of our lawyers, at any given point of time, are women. Besides, what adds further to our credibility (and the client's surprise) is that we have so many women partners,' says Vakil. Zia's commitment shines through at every opportunity—in 2019, she partnered with the EdelGive Foundation to launch a program called The Influencers, where Zia Mody, along with other influential women of corporate India, committed to actively assisting in building a gender-just India in collaboration with fifteen major NGOs in India who are doing critical work towards enabling economic and social empowerment of girls and women in India at a grass-roots level.

Piramal, who was also on a list of Twenty-Five Most Powerful Women in Indian Business along with Zia, calls her friend a quiet doer. 'Look at the number of women working at AZB & Partners. I doubt if any of the other legal firms in the top ten would come close to the same level of diversity. Her feminist beliefs are deeply embedded,' she adds.

'Successful implementation, good track record and sound advice are the key qualities that have propelled AZB to its position among the best. Interestingly, Zia's name figures in the firm's middle, Z of AZB, yet she is the mover and shaker. Indeed, the prima donna. What makes Zia stand a foot above the others is that she is accessible,' says Parekh. 'When there is a crisis and you want prompt advice, an appointment with Zia is almost always immediately given. She efficiently juggles her day and readily meets people. This is absolutely necessary and that's why she is so well regarded.' As a successful working woman with a family, Zia encourages younger women to build strong partnerships at home first, in order to balance their personal and professional lives. She also counsels them that creating a stable personal life strategy is crucial for women to handle work and family life with ease. 'I get my energy from God and by my husband's grace.'

## A PATH APPEARS

As I trace Zia's life, one of the greatest lessons I learn is that if you stay true to your deepest desires and are willing to do the work from a place of integrity, a path appears and you will be supported. Zia repeatedly tells everyone that success is a state of happiness; it is a state of self-respect. It is clear that her family has always been her fulcrum, and most poignant to me is the extraordinary support she is offered by them.

Zia truly believes that Jaydev, her husband and best friend, is the reason her career has been as successful because they both, from the start, have worked hard to make sure their marriage has been a win-win partnership. From 1986 to 1990, while they had three children, both he and Zia needed to cement their professional reputations.

The years soon after Anjali, Aarti and Aditi were born were demanding ones. She was only a few years into her marriage, setting up a law practice in India, but she never failed to attend parent–teacher meetings and school performances despite her packed schedule. Speaking for several of her friends who have seen her focus as much on family as on work, Parekh says, 'She is a hands-on mother to her three daughters, all of whom are extremely well educated and excellently brought up.' All three of the Mody daughters are now in their twenties and building careers of their own. Anjali is a married woman and Aarti is now a mother, and Zia and Jaydev are the proud grandparents of a baby boy.

And it's not just the family; Zia finds time for her friends, too. 'When we meet socially, we talk about everything that friends tend to discuss—our next holiday, our families, our professional lives . . . we even bitch about our mutual competitors! We enjoy each other's company very much,' says Shroff.

Just as Zia forged her own path despite sharing the same profession with her father, she is now letting her children create their own paths, too. 'My father is my role model and I am lucky to be able to discuss matters with him because he balances out so much for me. I stopped competing with him many, many years ago. He is better than me—an incredible jurist with an enviable memory,' says Zia, speaking both as an adoring daughter and respectful peer.

Shroff sees a lot of similarity between father and daughter. 'They share a desire to excel. They are both at the top of their game.'

Mittal, who, too, is friends with both Sorabjee and Zia, says he finds them dissimilar in their approach and their personalities. 'Both are legal luminaries and can bring forward good creative solutions to corporate problems. But my own view is that they approach the issues differently and bring to the table their own minds and expertise in dealing with those issues.'

While Zia's demanding work life does take a toll on quality time with family, they vacation together often. She admits that as someone who is so busy that her hairdresser and tailor come to the office, leisure hours are rather limited, but her other interests are cooking, watching romantic movies and reading. Like her father, she is a jazz aficionado.

The Modys share a passion, too, for one of Zia's earliest loves: horses. She remembers being at Mumbai's Mahalaxmi Racecourse as a fifteen-year-old, being courted by Jaydev. Her friend, Shanoor Forbes had once said that Zia always picked out ill-tempered horses that no one else wanted and went on to win races with them. Jaydev now owns over forty racehorses. and Zia says the thrill of the races can still make her sit on the edge of her seat.

She has also authored an acclaimed book, *10 Judgments that Changed India* published by Penguin Random House. Piramal says reading Zia's book made her respect her old friend even more. 'In her research, Zia would have looked at so many cases before finalising her selection.'

## OF FAITH AND PHILANTHROPY

Meeting Zena in the house where Zia grew up, I am allowed a rare and privileged glimpse into her world. Elegant and graceful, Zia's mother shows me newspaper and magazine clippings about her daughter that she has filed away. They are both followers of the Baha'i faith, a monotheistic religion that does not lay emphasis on rituals, but on giving back to society, especially to those less privileged. This is the cornerstone of Zia's deep commitment to philanthropy.

Family and her devotion to the Baha'i faith, known for its beautiful Lotus Temple in Delhi, take up a lot of Zia's spare time. Not many people know of her contribution to the building of this temple. Piramal says, 'The temple took twenty years to build, partly because it would accept donations only from Baha'is. When Zia returned to India from New York in 1984, she devoted time, funds and energy to the project. It was completed in 1986.'

She and Zia bumped into each other a few times on Mumbai-Delhi flights during this period and Piramal was struck by Zia's passion for the project and her faith. She says, 'Zia's mother, grandmother and great-grandmother were all Baha'is but her father is a Zoroastrian, and her husband is a Hindu. She became a Baha'i at the age of twenty-one. I believe almost all her giving goes to the Baha'i Fund.'

Zia was a trustee of Barli Institute, an Indore-based NGO, which works for the development of rural women and is funded by the Baha'is. She is also a board member at Teach for India, which trains volunteer teachers and places them temporarily at government schools across the country. Zena is clear that Zia's greatest strength is her commitment, whether to a cause, or her own work. 'She has to be on top of everything, which means that she should know the latest rules and regulations. She needs to know about everything so that she isn't lost or unaware of anything before she's gone to sleep. For her to stay up to date requires a lot of reading. She doesn't get much sleep because she is working overtime all the time.'

Indeed, seeing Zia get through a day is awe-inspiring. Routinely in the office until 3–4 a.m., she used to rush home in her self-driven Volkswagen Beetle and be back in the office by 10.30 a.m. Vakil jokes, 'I think Zia is the only person I know who brings two *dabbas* to work—one for lunch and one for dinner.' Colleagues and clients can always reach her, and whether she is jetting across the world to client meetings and closing new deals, at a lunch, a social event, or on holiday, her BlackBerry is always buzzing. After decades, she does wish to step back a little but tells me the problem is that the next exciting deal is always around the corner—'What do you say no to?'

'She is always smiling, always jovial. I've never ever seen her upset and I've never ever seen her down and out. It is commendable that she has this kind of a temperament despite the pressure of running a large firm and functioning as per the timelines within which lawyers must produce opinions, reports and advice,' says Parekh.

I believe the answer to that lies in something Zena said to me about her daughter, when I asked her what she thought Zia might want to ask God if she met Him. Without skipping a beat, she answered, 'Are you pleased with me?'

# JAYDEV MODY

*It's been a marriage based on love and commitment that was as precocious as it was enduring. **Zia** and **Jaydev Mody** met as children, and they have, in many ways, grown up together, and he has been able to watch her evolve and achieve phenomenal success over the last four decades. Theirs has been a partnership of the truest kind, honesty, mutual support and crackling chemistry animating it. They invested in building demanding careers—Zia is one of India's top lawyers, Jaydev runs a company that is one of the biggest players in construction and gaming—while also raising three accomplished daughters. Jaydev speaks with admiration about her, 'the greatest effect' that marriage to Zia has had on his life and the rare symbiotic relationship that they share.*

**You have been a part of each other's lives for over five decades. What was the young Zia like?**

She was absolutely stunning, and bright and fun. We got along so well and had great chemistry. All of this is still the same—nothing has changed. What she is today, she was then. Maybe she was more fit because she worked out more, which is something she has little time for now. Otherwise, Zia remains the same—hard-working, trying to make things happen, honest, truthful and straight—litigations, settlement, that has been her forte right from the beginning and it is still so.

**How has she evolved over the years?**

Even as a child, Zia was very strong-willed and very serious about whatever she did. If she learnt to play the piano, she followed through until she passed the examinations at the final level. She used to ride a lot then, and in her early teens she was a top-class rider. From the time we were young, whatever she did she would do fabulously and perfectly. This has never changed.

Even at Cambridge and Harvard, she did extremely well, and got the best job she could in Baker & McKenzie in New York. At her age, she was probably the best lawyer. She used to go to court and argue. She was doing chamber practice. She is more of a solicitor today. Then she moved and completely changed her legal career from being a counsel to going into a firm, and hers is one of the top firms in the country today.

151

She is very, very committed and nothing comes easily in the process of getting to the top, so she has worked extremely hard. Also, being a woman in a male profession like law has always been kind of a challenge, and then to make it to the top in the full 100, not just among ten women, is extremely difficult.

**Are there any fun stories to do with the days when you were courting her? How did you propose to her?**

In those days, there was no television and we were outdoors a lot. I think she proposed to me or, at least, I think that's what happened. I don't remember now whether she proposed or I. We decided to get married when we were sixteen or seventeen. We always knew that we would marry.

**What is Zia like as a mother?**

When Anjali, our first daughter, was born in 1986, I was very busy; and so it was with our second and third daughters too, who were born in 1987 and 1990. I would say that that was the toughest time in my life, and even for Zia. She would go to court, then meet clients, come home and spend whatever time she could with the babies. Since I worked for myself, I would take some time off in the evenings to be with them, and then go back to work. Zia tried very hard and did whatever she could to spend time with the kids in those days, and we took a lot of holidays with them.

**She faced many struggles to get noticed when she first moved back to India from the US. Was this only to be expected of the working culture here at that time?**

Nobody was saying then that one couldn't be a lawyer as a woman, but people agreeing to have a twenty-nine-year-old representing them in cases worth crores of rupees was an issue. People didn't feel comfortable for some reason and I think that all she needed to do then was to be able to open her mouth and speak to the client. The moment she did that along with the senior sitting there, they took her seriously. So all she needed was the opportunity. And she worked hard to get the opportunity.

**What have been the reasons for Zia's success and the phenomenally inspiring career she has built?**

She works very, very hard. She knows more about the matter at hand than the other people in the room, because she reads, studies and researches a lot. Most lawyers get someone else to do that for them, and get briefed. For Zia, it's all about research and understanding the issue herself. That's been her strength really.

When Zia started out in India, she was alone. Then there was Chambers of Zia Mody, and now there is AZB, that's the way it went. The big change she has made for herself is to go from being a lawyer to a promoter and entrepreneur, because to run a firm of this size you need to be a businessperson as well—merging, bringing other firms in and other people together. Building this huge law firm needs administrative and entrepreneurial talent. There are so many other things that have gone into it and she learnt all of it on the job.

**Zia has fostered several friendships and trusted professional relationships with some of the country's biggest names, from the Ambanis to the Birlas and Tatas. What draws people to her?**

She is extremely honest. There are no two sides to her. She is very committed, loyal, bright and warm. These are the endearing qualities that I think draw a lot of people to her.

She is very genuine. Her advice is very instinctive and she says it in a fun way. Zia has a fabulous relationship with Mukesh [Ambani], who would blindly trust her. She is a dealmaker. There are lawyers who will complicate matters to justify their existence, but her thing is to get to the deal and cut through the crap, to make it practical, commercial, acceptable to both. She is fair, so people on the other side also trust her, which is very important. Zia creates the right environment to make sure that the deal actually happens and it does not go into a loop.

**She talks about having no work-life balance: so how much of a family person is she?**

Zia has zero work-life balance. She just can't do it. She doesn't have the time to do it, and she does what she can. Zia may have the chance to slow down in the next few years but for now, I think we have all accepted it. Our daughters and I are happy with the holidays we take and we understand that given the work she does, balance is impossible. She does not sleep for more than four to six hours a day and does not exercise. Our daughters are all a good mix of Zia and me—they work very hard but, I think, having seen their mother's life, they balance theirs out more. They have friends, they party and they focus on work when they have to.

**What is your vision for her? What makes her happy?**

I think she should do what she wants to do and when she is ready to slow down, she should do other things, because this is not all that there is to life. Zia is interested in so many things, like philanthropy, but has no time for it. She needs to get fit, and work out to stay healthy. I hope we will travel a lot at some stage, because we love to. We have a house in East Africa, where I spend a lot of time. We just bought two tiger lodges in Satpura and Pench.

Pursuing her goal and getting there is what gives Zia the most joy. Then on the personal side, holidaying with the children and me also makes her very happy. She enjoys it a lot. Other than that, she is just very happy working, frankly. It never tires her out.

**Zia and you have built companies from the ground up. She is very clear that she could not have done any of this without you. How has she influenced and supported you in your own journey?**

We have been very supportive of each other. Even though I am extremely competitive, I am a little more balanced than she is. We accept each other's needs. I know what she needs to do for herself and I let her do it. And similarly, she knows what I need to do for myself and she never interferes. We will always interact and tell each other what we think is the best way to get to whatever we want to do, but we let the other find their own way. I think that's been very important.

The greatest effect she has had on me is to make me aware of governance and being completely 100 per cent legal at all times—even if irregularities are rampant in our country. But to stay completely legal and not do anything that is even 1 per cent off, is something she has drilled into me, and it has been very difficult to do, but it has become very important for me now.

## What can young women learn from Zia?

Work very hard, be absolutely committed and don't think that because you are a woman, you can't do it. You can. If people think you cannot, that is their perception and not your reality, so it should not affect you.

# SWATI
# PIRAMAL

•

*When you think of Swati, you think of an incredible joie de vivre. She enjoys being alive and has immense curiosity in everything around her. She has a tremendous capacity to learn and the desire to get involved in a whole spectrum of things. Whatever she puts her mind to, she does very, very well. Swati represents two things for the Indian woman in the global community: one, she accepts no limits and sets her aspirations very high; and two, she is not local, she is not parochial, and is at home whether she is doing philanthropy in a village here or serving on the board of overseers at Harvard University. It's this global sensibility that Indian women in particular seem to embody—when they do it well, they do it very, very well.*

**—ANAND MAHINDRA**

•

*E*very legendary story begins with a dreamer and their dream. That of the Piramal Group is no different. Its patriarch, Seth Piramal Chaturbhuj Makharia, came to Mumbai from Bagar, Rajasthan at twenty-eight, with Rs 50 in his pocket. His destination was Lower Parel, where there were the textile mills on which Mumbai's industry ran. Seth Piramal became a successful commodity trader and then, in 1920, bought Morarjee Gokuldas Mill from a wealthy freedom fighter, laying the foundation of what is now one of India's most illustrious business empires.

Just short of a century later, the land that resonated with the bustle and clank of mills is now Mumbai's new midtown district, punctuated with high-rises, and throbbing with new industry. It is still here, though in a plush block of offices, that Seth Piramal's legacy continues. And one of the people who carry on that sacred legacy for generations to come is his granddaughter-in-law, Dr Swati Piramal.

It is hard to find adequate adjectives to describe Swati so I am going to start by stating fact. Along with her husband, Ajay, she turned a textile-centred business into Piramal Healthcare Limited—renamed Piramal Enterprises in 2012—a Rs 21,000-crore conglomerate that works in pharmaceuticals, real estate, financial services and packaging. What's more, her commitment to scientific research and technology had made the healthcare division the biggest name in patents and drug discovery in India. Her two-decade-long work in disease prevention has helped her business scale meteoric heights, while her commitment to providing affordable healthcare to the underprivileged has made her one of the most respected names in the world. The company's new drug application for molecular imaging for Alzheimer's disease won US FDA and European approval in 2015 showing the success of the R&D portfolio. She was the only woman on the Prime Minister's Scientific Advisory CSIR Council from 2003–13 and also served on the Council of Trade and the board of CSIR and IIT Bombay. Formidable, blindingly sharp, dynamic, gregarious, multi-passionate and multi-talented, Swati is who she is, and the rest of us can only hope to measure up.

'In India you have people who are focused on business, but I think both Swati and her husband Ajay have a very keen sense of social responsibility,' says billionaire Dilip Shanghvi of Sun Pharmaceuticals. 'They want to make a difference, they want to do things—not only in business, where they are extremely successful, but also in things which will make India a better country, and society a better society.'

Swati is the first woman I interviewed for this book, which makes her story even more distinctive for me. I remember waiting for her at the glass-and-chrome headquarters of Piramal Enterprises in Lower Parel; the room displays a collection of rare Shiva-lingams; framed verses from the Bhagvad Gita; artwork by acclaimed Japanese designer Eriko Horiki; contemporary Indian art; and an assortment of bonsai. I think of what ace lawyer Cyril Shroff said to me about Swati—'You can see, in her office and her house, the kind of painstaking attention she pays to tiny details. She brings great sophistication and a sense of care to every situation.'

When she walks in, dressed in a fine chiffon sari and a pearl necklace, Swati exudes a rare combination of elegance, serenity and power. This is, after all, the celebrated woman with a Renaissance temperament—a healer and an entrepreneur who synergizes all of her interests, passions and expertise to create significant change.

## THE HEALER AND THE ENTREPRENEUR

On the face of it, there is little that links a stethoscope and a spreadsheet. One focuses on a single heartbeat, and the other charts profits and numbers. In Swati's world, though, the numbers game is influenced by a higher purpose. The seeds of this philosophy were sown young by two incidents—a deeply personal one that birthed the idea, and a public one that catalysed it.

When Swati was twelve, a young cousin had an allergic reaction to a vaccination; his little body turned blue, and the hysterical family summoned their doctor, who saved the boy's life with a single injection. Swati still remembers how her family's outpouring of love, respect and gratitude for the doctor awed her—'It was then that I decided to become a doctor. I had always believed in helping people, especially by taking responsibility for their health. I had always been drawn to medicine and I considered healing the sick to be an irreplaceable reward for one's efforts. This incident confirmed it for me.'

Swati went on to earn her MBBS degree from the University of Mumbai. Soon after she graduated, she saw a little girl who was crippled by polio in Parel—'I shuddered to think that she would never run or even walk properly. For me it was an extremely sad sight. I knew I had to do something.' Her nascent passion for public health and inherent compassion were kindled, and combined with her singular brand of creativity and confidence.

Swati got together friends from medical college and drew up a strategy. It was not enough to set up a polio vaccination centre—they also had to fight superstition to raise awareness. Through door-to-door visits, street plays and song-and-dance routines in Marathi, the group managed to convince people that all they needed to do to battle the polio virus was give their children three doses of vaccine. To succeed, Swati suggested a gift for every family that got children all three shots. She was married by then, and convinced her father-in-law to donate bales of cloth from the family's mills. Within months, mothers across the neighbourhood were dressing their children in the colourful cloth they had won. Ten years later, the polio centre was closed; Parel was declared free of the life-threatening disease.

Looking back now, Swati says to me, 'It was the first time I realized the value of public health and I was determined to know more. Early intervention will always lower your cost of prevention. I live by this realization and apply it in my work in healthcare.'

## THE KNOWLEDGE BUSINESS

To learn and to apply knowledge in every possible way are intrinsic to Swati, and the roots of it were sown by her father, a textile mill owner with an unusual love of reading. In her middle-class Gujarati home, books were precious and she inherited her father's voracious appetite for books. From her mother, Swati learnt to seize the day, and always stay optimistic and cheerful. Her family was progressive, encouraging Swati to come into her own.

She married Ajay Piramal—who had courted her for several years with a determination to match her own—when she was a final-year medical student. The youngest scion of the family that owned Morarjee Mill, he came from a home as open-minded as her own. Although the Piramals are a Marwari business-owning family, there was nothing conventional about them. Ajay's parents were unstinting in their support of Swati's ambitions. When she was accepted by Harvard School of Public Health for her postgraduate degree, Swati was already a young mother but the Piramals encouraged and helped her with her decision to continue studying.

'In the old days, only men from Marwari families worked in the business, and the fact that Swati was not only permitted but encouraged to take on responsibility outside the house speaks very highly of the family. Ajay's mother also supported Swati, even though she was not a working woman herself,' says Ranjit Shahani, managing director, Novartis India Limited, and an old associate of the Piramal family.

Gopikrishna Piramal, Ajay's father, was a far-sighted industrialist and patriarch. Through the 1970s, he made important acquisitions—from VIP to Kemp Pharma. He also entrusted entire businesses to each of his young sons—Ashok, Dilip and Ajay. So, at twenty-three, Ajay found himself appointed managing director at Miranda Tools, a small company that made cutting tools for engineering firms. The elder Piramal also recognized his youngest daughter-in-law's enormous potential, and promised Swati he would open a hospital for her.

Unfortunately, he passed away at fifty-nine, leaving his family bereft; it was the first of many tragedies that would test their mettle. Ashok stepped in to fill his father's role and honoured the promise made to Swati by building the Piramal Memorial Hospital. Swati plunged headlong into the vocation and tells me she was 'doctor, accountant, marketing manager—24x7.'

Simultaneously, the Piramal brothers split the family business, with Dilip branching off on his own with VIP Industries and a few others, and Ashok and Ajay handling the rest, including Morarjee Gokuldas Mill and Miranda Tools. On 18 January 1982, sixteen days after the settlement, the textile industry was brought to its knees by the most crippling labour strike post-independent India had seen. The textile strike was never really called off. It fizzled into oblivion, bringing to a tragic end what once was the pride of a new India.

By the end of 1982, both Ashok and Ajay had lost much of their inherited industry. 'It had been our family business for over a hundred years. We were nearing bankruptcy and had no office. Those were difficult times,' Swati says to me. Adding to the chaos and sadness was the fact that Ashok—who had assumed the roles of family patriarch and business head—was diagnosed with malignant, progressive cancer; he passed away in 1984, leaving Ajay and Swati the responsibility of looking after Ashok's family—his youngest son just three years old—and taking over the family business. This was the time that forged strength and conviction into their marriage.

At twenty-nine, Ajay found himself appointed chairman of the Piramal Group. 'Everybody said he was too young, but I told him, "You can do it, we can do it." It was really a low point in my life. Everyone warned us that the journey would not be easy, but Ajay took over the group,' Swati says. Over the next few years, the couple worked to bring the crumbling business back on track. Ajay followed his father's route of diversification, with Swati as his knowledge partner. One industry that drew their attention and passion was pharmaceuticals.

In 1988, the Piramals heard that an Australian pharmaceutical company, Nicholas Laboratories, ranked forty-eighth in the Indian pharma sector, was scoping out potential buyers. Ajay staked his claim to Mike Barker, who was in charge of making the sale. While admitting that he knew nothing about the industry, Ajay promised him that Nicholas would be one of India's top five pharmaceutical companies under the Piramals' ownership. Barker was impressed by his gumption and they struck a deal. 'We were simply full of enthusiasm, determination and brimming with new ideas,' Swati says to me.

She was thirty-two, and Ajay, thirty-three. They had crafted a clear vision, fighting down any doubts or fears about taking a 100-year-old business into uncharted territory. 'We entered the pharmaceuticals industry, which was a knowledge industry, from the commodity-driven textile industry. We realized that concentrating on immediate goals and not faltering on delivery was what we needed to focus on. This basic approach helped us strengthen our company and move to our expansion plans through acquisitions.'

A decade later, in 1998, when Barker had retired, Swati and Ajay paid him a visit. They carried with them the annual report of Nicholas Piramal, which had become India's fifth-largest pharmaceutical company; Ajay had made good on his promise. By 2010, the Piramals sold a portion of the company they had bought for Rs 11 crore at Rs 18,000 crore (approx $4 billion) to Abbott Laboratories, in a deal considered landmark by the international pharmaceutical industry.

## THE PERFECT PARTNER

As I spend more time with the Piramals and their friends and family, I glean that this is not an ordinary marriage by any measure. They are partners in every sense, whether as husband and wife who share a resilient bond, or as peers who have fought many battles to build a phenomenal business empire. To not only be spouses and parents, but also step into a boardroom and play to one another's strengths while balancing out weaknesses, requires an inordinate amount of maturity and trust. What strikes me as extraordinary are the deep reserves of respect and happiness that they maintain for each other's successes, without a whisper of jealousy or competition.

'One needs both the hard-as-nails business side as well as the heart. Swati is a very genuine person and shows the same degree of respect and care for everyone, regardless of their position. She was the power that pushed Ajay and gave him his reputation as the 'takeover tycoon'. Ajay also gave her the support to pursue her interests and her own career,' says Shahani.

Swati prefers calling their partnership seamless: 'There are no boundaries between the work that Ajay and I do. My prowess lies in science, research and technology. His proficiency seals dynamic deals; it helps us configure a long-term vision and maintain that drive. We have grown together through hard work. There is no formula, except the passion to succeed. We dream and follow our dream.'

Those close to them, who have seen them evolve into a power couple and the Piramal Group into a global brand, emphasize the keen sense of balance they both bring to the table. Legendary banker Narayanan Vaghul who serves on their board, says, 'Ajay has been doing a lot of deals these days and you won't find Swati commenting on those deals. But she holds her ground on research which is her area of expertise. Who influenced whom is difficult to say in a couple. Maybe both have had a mutual influence.' Anand Mahindra, chairman and managing director, Mahindra Group, corroborates—'Swati has this tremendous research capability. Her ability to drill down, investigate something, weigh its pros and cons, apply analytical skills are very clear. That's why I think, in their business, Ajay has asked her to look at those areas of their investment, particularly in the areas of technology.'

A good example of their synergy lies in how they have grown in pharmaceuticals. One of their major decisions was to shift from manufacturing branded generics to exclusive products with patents at a time when many multinationals were coming back to strike manufacturing and research deals with Indian pharma companies. The Piramals focused on products backed by intellectual property rights, moving steadily towards their vision of indigenous drug discovery and licensing. 'Our dream is to discover a drug in India and take it to the world. It takes ten or twelve years to do this, and out of the 100 times you try, ninety-nine times you fail. I want to be the one to succeed,' says Swati. 'So this business is not for the faint-hearted. But you have to dream today about tomorrow, only then will you succeed. I believe that failure or rejection should not demotivate you, it should, instead, force you to persevere.'

Vaghul identifies this quality as her defining leadership trait – 'Swati has a deep commitment towards research and development.' This attention to research is what Shroff, managing partner, Amarchand and Mangaldas, emphasizes, too—'What I find most inspiring about her is the sheer amount of care she invests in everything. She researches everything extensively, brings her knowledge to effect and implements it. She is a perfectionist.'

## RAISING THE BAR

In 1998, when the Piramals acquired a research centre in Mumbai from Hoechst Marion Roussel, many eyebrows were raised but they stood firm in their intention. Swati tells me that the firm conducts its entire R&D in that facility and it is the origin of Piramal Healthcare's patents. It is interesting for me to learn that of the 400 scientists working there, fifty focus on Ayurvedic cures.

Between 2000 and 2010, the Piramals spent around Rs 1200 crore on R&D. Through a series of dynamic global acquisitions, Piramal Healthcare, under Swati, has helped place India on the global map of discovery and innovation. With a remarkable portfolio of over 350 patents and twenty drugs in various stages of clinical trials the world over, her vision of making India self-reliant is steadily garnering strength. 'When I started R&D, people said that no Indian knew how to innovate, they did not know how to file a patent, and if they filed a patent, anything that they did during a clinical trial would not be accepted by the West. At Piramal Enterprises, we have busted these myths today. We have R&D in many countries and people are respecting us for our innovation,' she points out.

Swati stays aware that the work they do as a company is an uphill battle because healthcare is a complex industry, which requires them to pay attention to every minute detail. 'Trying to get the best in the world is not easy,' she tells me. 'It starts with a few million dollars' worth of investment and we are at the end of a decade of a learning curve. Instead of giving up, based on the dismal public health figures, one must rise above it. Like a lotus. And focus on the higher purpose.'

Hasit Joshipura, managing director of GlaxoSmithKline, says, 'Swati has become the company's scientific face, its spokesperson. Yet, she comes across as someone who effectively combines a scientific understanding with the values of compassion and humanity. Both of these are critical to being a very successful healthcare professional.' This is true because, at the heart of it, Swati remains a healer, with a clear interest in serving the community. Her interest in public health, as Shahani points out, 'is one dimension of this commitment to serving the larger good, evident in the manner in which she has personally looked into lifestyle diseases, diseases of the central nervous system, diabetes and cardiovascular diseases—and set up several networks through which to address them.'

While her vision is trained on the larger goal, Swati also has the incredible capacity to track the smaller stories simultaneously. A survey in around thirty–forty schools soon after her polio eradication campaign in the late-70s revealed that a vitamin D deficiency had led to every teacher having osteoporosis. 'So we did public health programmes in osteoporosis, epilepsy and chronic diseases, such as diabetes and hypertension.' And then there are the individual gestures of gratitude—'When my team and I invented a new medicine for arthritis called Rejoint, it was a huge success. People would come and thank us. One person came and touched my feet—these are prized feelings.' In 2017, Piramal Swasthya, an initiative of Piramal Foundation, launched a community-based cancer screening programme, DESH, to detect cancer early and reduce mortality in Assam under the guidance of Swati Piramal. It touched the lives of an estimated 1.5 million men and women.

Piramal Capital is the company's financial services unit, focused on lending to the real estate and education sectors. The group is also foraying into security technology and information management. What Swati and Ajay are very clear about, though, is that work goes beyond business. For them, their growth has been tempered all along by a commitment to both spirituality and philanthropy, which places Swati's favourite metaphor of the lotus in a much brighter light.

## LIVING BY THE GITA

On my first visit to Piramal Towers, when I step out of the elevator on the tenth floor, a verse from the Upanishads greets me — *You are what your deep driving desire is, / As your desire is, so is your will, / As your will is, so is your deed.* The scriptures, especially the Bhagvad Gita, form the company's doctrine of faith. Over my time spent researching and writing this profile, I understand just how all-pervasive its influence is, starting with the fact that all boardrooms are named after Arjuna. 'Arjuna was a man who had to learn, had to persevere, cultivate humility, fight for *dharma* and things that are right, and never give up. These are attributes that we need in business. The Bhagvad Gita is so relevant even today,' Swati says.

How the Gita and other scriptures came to become the Piramal Group's cornerstone forms a telling story. Swati and Ajay's son, Anand, was in Venice as a young student to study history and architecture. He fell in love with the city and his subjects, but was reminded by his teacher that his own country and culture had far more richness and texture to it. When Anand returned home, he began classes on the ancient Hindu scriptures with Swami Satvika Chaitanya, a young priest from the Chinmaya Mission, explaining the ancient text. Soon, his parents joined him in his weekend classes. Swati is deeply grateful for Anand's epiphany, which led all of them to a bedrock of faith.

Even their company logo echoes the ancient and sacred *gyanmudra*—three fingers that symbolize values of *gyan* (knowledge), *karma* (action) and *bhakti* (devotion). These are the core principles on which Swati bases every decision; it is completely organic for her to base her business practices on them, too.

Vaghul believes that 'the way in which Piramal Enterprises could evolve in the next few decades will represent Ajay's and Swati's value systems. The secret to the success of their leadership is their spirituality.' He is involved with the Piramal Group—and other organizations—on their activities in the corporate social responsibility space; the Piramals' social contract wins his praise and appreciation—'The Piramals will lend their name to any worthwhile cause as against the narrow-thrust philosophy followed by some other businesses. They will take up a water initiative in one village, education in another and ambulance services somewhere else. Swati is an exceedingly compassionate and dynamic woman, and there is much in her from which others can learn.'

With me, Swati talks with enthusiasm about the philanthropic aspect of their work. A particularly important piece is their involvement with the award-winning NGO, Pratham India, of which Ajay is the chairman—'The idea of Pratham India was introduced to Ajay by Narayanan Vaghul. He was totally fascinated by this initiative of accelerated learning whereby an illiterate child could be imparted the joy of being able to read and write within a few weeks itself.' Their work has contributed to helping more than 3.3 million children nationally.

Boosted by their success with Pratham, Ajay and Swati established the Piramal School of Leadership, which helps headmasters develop leadership skills—'We train the headmaster as he is the natural leader of so many teachers. The Piramal School of Leadership is a private initiative but it is in partnership with the government. Today, thousands of schools across the country have benefited from this and the ideas have been adopted in many states and internationally, too.'

In 2006, the Piramal Foundation was established, with a Grassroots Development Laboratory in Bagar, Rajasthan; the mandate was to find answers to some of the toughest problems in rural development. Focusing on issues of national relevance, the Piramal Foundation has impacted more than 50 million people.

## THE WORLD OF WOMEN

While Swati is a qualified medical professional, she has never formally studied business. She does not have a business degree but studied business courses at Harvard Business School and the Harvard School of Public Health. Everything that she has accomplished in that sphere has been the result of her keen intelligence and ability to absorb complex topics. While the Bhagvad Gita has been her sheet anchor, she's learnt on her feet, according to Joshipura, with her strong scientific bent and 'a very good understanding of the business side which makes her a very effective business leader in the healthcare industry.'

An excellent example of this skill is Swati's time as the head of ASSOCHAM, one of India's most respected industry chambers; she was the first woman president of the ninety-three-year-old association. Unfazed and self-assured, she drew from her vast experiences and values. She tells me, 'Knowledge is the most powerful tool. I made it a point to be equipped with information beforehand.'

As president of ASSOCHAM, says Swati, she was completely clueless about the Indian economy, 'but I could welcome the president of Indonesia by doing my homework on the Indonesian economy in detail. Similarly, before my meetings at the RBI, I would meticulously prepare on banking and other regulations so that I had an answer to everything that was being discussed and hence, no one could argue with me over the facts and understanding of the situation. I know how to search for deeper knowledge and understanding of a subject I am curious about. I have always had the innate curiosity to learn about things.' Clearly, what she learnt from her father about teaching oneself instead of waiting to be taught is something she is diligently practising even today.

Vaghul, who remembers seeing her in action at ASSOCHAM where he had been invited to speak, says, 'Two things about her struck me. One, the people in the room accepted her leadership; and, two, the finesse and crispness with which she summed up the deliberations gave insight into her persona as a leader.'

Elected as a member of the 350-year-old Harvard Board of Overseers, one of Harvard's two governing bodies, Swati won the election, which was earlier lost by the likes of Barack Obama and Anand Mahindra.

A working mother from the start, she discusses parenting with the same keenness and clarity that she does medicine—'When one is a parent, one does not know immediately what's right and what's wrong until quite late—but for the children, one has to walk the talk, one has to live the values passed down to them. Aside from getting good grades, I wanted them to learn values such as leadership, a social conscience and respect for elders. Of course, business was dinner-table conversation.' Swati has taught Nandini and Anand to look beyond an Ivy League education and a corner office, to consider the greater questions they can find answers to.

Speaking of her family life, Swati tells me, 'Of course, when I began working flexitime after having kids, the guilt of leaving my children was terrible. Every working mother experiences it. When my daughter was a few years older, she told me, "I'm so glad you are a working mom." That wiped away any shred of guilt. There are certain moments when work and family conflict, but I try to be there for people whose special occasions I miss, and make up for it.'

A graduate from Oxford University, with an MBA from Stanford, Nandini worked with consultants McKinsey & Co. before joining the family business. She has worked tirelessly to implement solutions to India's drinking water crisis within the Sarvajal project. A graduate from Wharton Business School and the University of Pennsylvania, with an MBA from Harvard Business School, Anand is today an executive director at Piramal Realty. He played a decisive role in founding Piramal e-Swasthya, a rural start-up with an aim to democratize healthcare through technology and sustainable business models.

'Nandini and Anand will chart their own course, taking off from what Ajay and Swati have done. They are very focused business people, very intelligent and they both have a strong sense of values,' says Shroff, who has known the younger Piramals all their lives. Vaghul finds that Anand is well groomed for the group's social initiatives, having shown a great deal of resourcefulness in that area. 'Both her children, Nandini and Anand, have imbibed the best from both parents—business acumen coupled with deep respect for others and their viewpoints,' adds Shahani.

In December 2018, Anand got married to Isha Ambani, daughter of Nita and Mukesh Ambani, sealing their years of friendship into a family bond. They got married amidst great fanfare at Mukesh Ambani's residence Antilia, while the pre-wedding celebrations happened in Udaipur.

## THE CONNOISSEUR

When I speak about Swati to a wide range of people, including powerhouses like Nita Ambani and Rajashree Birla, not only do they talk about her with the greatest respect and affection, but they also allude to how talented and fun she is.

The Piramals' home in Mumbai is not only well appointed but also has a touch of the unusual, such as an old dhow that Swati had restored, and often hosts parties in. She is also very passionate about Greenwoods, their residence in the hill station of Mahabaleshwar. They acquired the century-old heritage structure in 2006 from Vijay Singh Patwardhan, Maharaja of Sangli; built in the Maratha–Victorian style, it has been restored with the greatest attention to detail.

'She certainly is a host. When you enter her house you can see her touch everywhere, whether it is the welcome at the doorstep or the treats served at the table. And she runs a super-efficient house, which is not easy because she is working 200 per cent of the time! I don't know how she does it,' Shahani says. Artist Krishen Khanna, one of whose paintings has pride of place in Piramal Enterprises' boardroom, is most impressed with Swati's 'great collection of Persian miniatures.' Invited to the launch of the Piramal Art Foundation, the artist tells me, 'The food was just exceptional. I have never eaten anything better.'

To Swati, though, keeping beautiful homes, hosting people and cooking are part of what makes life rich and interesting. Being a connoisseur extends, for her, to every area of her life. Her mother, Arunika Shah, was a cordon bleu chef, which instilled an early love for fine cuisine in Swati. Mastering family recipes and gathering new ones as she travels is her passion. She tells me that she has learnt some of her best recipes from the unlikeliest of sources, such as a carpet seller in Kashmir who taught her how to make kahwa, an aromatic Kashmiri tea.

'People are most enthusiastic when you ask them to share their traditional recipes,' she says. At home, she is known to cook multi-course meals for family and friends—'Food is about three things—taste, taste and taste. I love to cook and experiment all the time.' The sunny kitchen in her house is most often full of guests, helping make the meal. 'Everyone lets down their guard and there is bonhomie,' she says.

Ever generous with her skills, Swati is also the author of cookbooks, including one on Zen cooking and another on healthy food, which she collaborated on with the late and legendary Tarla Dalal. That book, *Eat Your Way to Good Health*, was ahead of its time with its focus on nutrition and well-being, rather than weight loss.

Books form an important part of Swati's life. She reads voraciously on business, science, medicine, history and poetry, but her true love is for rare books. From Mumbai's Chor Bazaar, Delhi's Jama Masjid, and ancient markets in Egypt and Marrakesh, Swati has curated an incredible collection of vintage editions. These include volumes by sixteenth-century Hindu poets and also recipe books, handwritten and put together by Sir John Malcolm, a governor of Mumbai in the nineteenth century. 'These books are more important to me than all my worldly possessions. I am generally a person who is very curious about everything—right from my area of expertise to nineteenth-century literature. If something catches my attention and interest, you will find me researching and reading up about it until I get to the bottom of things and have explored the topic enough to my own satisfaction,' she says.

As is her wont, Swati brings to the world of literature the same sense of synergy and enquiry that she does to medicine or business. For the launch of *The Light Has Come to Me*, she put together a son et lumière show of the same name. When she stumbled upon Tagore's tribute to his friend and scientist Acharya Jagadish Chandra Bose—on a vinyl record in a flea market in Kolkata—she commissioned lyricist Javed Akhtar to rewrite the verse in Hindi and Pandit Jasraj to sing it. It is now the corporate anthem for Piramal Enterprises, and to commemorate the decision, Swati composed *Dance of Life*, an opera on ancient science in India performed by Mrinalini and Mallika Sarabhai. An occasional poet, she dedicated a book of haiku verses to her late brother-in-law on his twenty-fifth death anniversary, and tells me she always has a small notebook with her, in which she writes down her own lines of verse.

Spiritually inclined verses by Sufi and Bhakti poets like Rumi, Bulleh Shah, Malik Muhammad Jayasi, Kabir and Tulsidas, add richness to Swati's speeches and public presentations. One such recitation moved BJP veteran L.K. Advani to tears as she brought alive a sixteenth-century Sufi poet from Sindh, taking him back to memories of his birthplace.

She has a keen love for horticulture, which is fuelled by her knowledge as a scientist. For Swati, a love for botany began early in life, when she learned about photosynthesis at school. A perfect blossom requires a lot of factors working in harmony, and it never fails to amaze her. To promote this love for horticulture among others, she hosted the Vaikunth Flower Show in Thane, Mumbai for three consecutive years between 2016–18. The flower show featured a lot of local, regional, and seasonal flowers that caught the attention of many who visited the show. Emboldened by the response to the show, Swati showcased a cricket-themed pavilion titled 'India: A Billion Dreams' at the Chelsea Flower Show in collaboration with the British Council, to celebrate India and UK's horticultural history and love for the game in 2018. It won a Silver Gilt medal.

## THE ETERNAL SEEKER

At the time that I am interacting with Swati, she channels her love for education and finesse with technology into an online education project. Initiated by Harvard School of Public Health, the course is being offered to students the world over, free of charge. Swati and Ajay have helped form two new research centres for their alma mater—the Harvard Business School and the Harvard School of Public Health—in India to enable the transfer of knowledge across borders. 'Our country has lakhs of doctors but very few who are trained for clinical research and trials. This course will help in bridging the gap. Through this, a doctor sitting in rural India can take a course from one of the best institutes in the world and interact with peers and colleagues from across the world. All they need is an Internet connection,' says Swati.

Her concern for public health and welfare prompt me to ask Swati if she considers joining politics at all. She replies, 'I did aspire once to become the Union health minister—but now it is a family joke,' she says with a smile.

'I wanted to be in the government because their policy can affect the lives of thousands of people. And I want to do things that have an impact.' When she says that, it seems like it was not so long ago that she was at Parel, the young medical student, out to eradicate polio. 'I want to recommend a whole bunch of policies, not just one, regarding investing in innovation and affordable drugs, and making sure one's regulations go out on time.'

For my part, apart from all the discussions on medicine, politics, art, literature, philanthropy and women's rights, the most pressing question is how Swati gets so much done in 168 hours a week. 'I don't waste time. I don't know when I last went to the movies. I don't go to kitty parties. Replying promptly to someone—on email, texts or calls—increases a person's productivity. Besides, nothing gets me down, I am always looking for something new to do: that is what leads to progress,' she says. 'I love what I do, which is why I do it and it never feels like work.'

Tracing her inspirations through her writings, speeches and conversations, all of them echo in some way to two key forces—the mathematician Srinivasa Ramanujan, the very symbol of perseverance, and the Mahatma's exhortation to 'be the force' that one wants the country to be. When I ask her for her own goals, she says, 'To reduce the burden of disease. What I have done is only one drop in the ocean. What remains to be done is still huge. My dream is to find a new drug for cancer and diabetes.'

And what is her idea of happiness? She returns to her favourite poet, Rabindranath Tagore, who translated these lines written by a medieval Indian woman poet. They echo in everything Swati does:

I salute the life that is revealed and that is hidden and the life of surging sea of fire;
the life that is tender like a lotus and hard like a thunderbolt;
the life full of joy and life weary with its pains;
the life eternally moving, rocking the world into stillness;
the life deep and silent breaking out into roaring waves of happiness.

# AJAY PIRAMAL

*Sitting at the helm of the formidable Piramal Group, **Ajay Piramal** is one of the wealthiest men in the country today. Wonder boy-turned-tycoon who transformed his inheritance of an ailing textile mill into a billion-dollar conglomerate—his story is a standing example of industry and public life. For close to four decades, much of his strength and inspiration has been drawn from **Swati Piramal**. He talks about his wife's extraordinary strength of character and values—those that have held him, their family and the business aloft.*

## How does a power couple like Ajay and Swati Piramal make a partnership work?

The most important factor required in making a partnership work is to have unstinting confidence in oneself. In our case, I think we complement one another. I have strengths that Swati does not, and what she brings to the table, I cannot. So, for myself, I don't even try and compete in the areas where she excels. She serves on the prime minister's council of advisers, and she is a Padma Shri awardee. I am neither, but I am happy and proud of her achievements. It's the yin and the yang—people need to remember that.

## Can you list some of Swati's attributes and practices that have an impact not just on her own growth and path, but also yours?

Swati, inherently, is a very creative person. Her thinking on an issue and her approach towards an opportunity have always been unique. And this creativity goes beyond business, into food, literature, art, even gardening. Swati's life and career are replete with examples of this.

The second aspect of her success is sheer hard work. She is forever willing to not just put in that work, but also tie together the smaller details to make sure it pays off. Swati also has a great sense of self, impelled by supreme confidence in her own knowledge and understanding of a subject. She is, thus, able to hold her own, whether it is in a board meeting or among global leaders. This takes a lot of strength and conviction.

Moreover, she is an optimist, who is unafraid of facing challenges and it is this courage that has influenced me considerably. Through her, I have learnt to appreciate life more, and take bigger, bolder decisions – all with a positive attitude. She has been an inspiring and inclusive leader who has never relied on hierarchy, but has always believed in getting everyone on board on an equal footing, for the best possible results.

### Let's do a bit of time travel—when did you first meet her, and what drew you to her?

I met Swati in 1972, when both of us were very young—she was seventeen and I was eighteen. She was—and still is—much more outgoing than me; I am a bit shy and reserved. I remember her being this bubbly person—full of ideas and always up for a challenge. Though she belonged to a business family, she had decided to study medicine. Actually, I think the first comment she had made about me was that we were entirely different from one another and that I was not her 'type!' That said, we did finally get married!

### What is Swati like, as a wife and mother?

Swati is a very strong person with extremely clear views on what is right and what is wrong and that makes her a very supportive partner and family member. Not only has she been a thoroughly involved mother, always there for our children, she has also instilled fundamental values in them—leading by example. Now, in fact, I see those values in our grandchildren as well. Even for my parents, her parents and our extended family, she has been a source of strength.

### The two of you co-authored *The Light Has Come to Me*. What role does spirituality play in your life, and your marriage?

It is the basis of our existence and forms the foundation of my life. Spirituality not only influences the way we live as a family, but has also inspired the values of our group—knowledge, action, care. I am a firm believer of the importance of one's daily actions.

### You are known for large acquisitions and Swati has her own commendable body of work. Tell us how you collaborate in business.

We have different ways of working, so we let one another be. We may not always agree on everything, but we do come together on the most important aspects. I like to think that Swati listens to me if I have a stronger point of view on an issue, and the truth is, many times, I let her do what she thinks is right.

Swati has been very supportive towards me and her encouragement makes me see the glass as half-full always. If I am in the middle of a big acquisition, for instance, and there is, invariably, a lot at stake, things may or may not go my way. What keeps me level-headed in that situation is Swati's expression of unflinching confidence in my judgement. That, to me, is very important.

**The 1980s were a trying decade for you, in business and for the family. What is Swati like in a crisis?**

From 1983 onwards, it was a very difficult time for us. My brother [Ashok] was diagnosed with cancer all of a sudden—he was young, as were his wife and children. Being a doctor, Swati was deeply involved in the management of his treatment, which was done between India and the US. Swati was a rock for all of us at that time.

When my brother passed away in 1984, I was twenty-nine. I suddenly found myself thrust into the roles of head of family and business. My sister-in-law, who was in her early-thirties, and her young children needed a lot of support. It was here that Swati stepped in, giving me the confidence and encouragement I needed, while also caring for my brother's family. There were several rough spots but she helped everyone navigate them.

**You have been at the helm of many major acquisitions but the first two were of Nicholas Laboratories in 1988 and Roche Products in 1993. I am interested in knowing what that process was like for you, and how Swati helped you.**

Swati was very supportive through it all. She vetted the ideas with me and convinced me that I could do it. She was there through the several rounds of complicated discussions, which took eight to nine months to close. When we acquired Roche, she was very involved in managing the business—both branding and research and development. Swati has also been indispensable in the process of bridging our foreign partners with the government. Pharmaceuticals is a sensitive industry and issues such as pricing, new product approvals and intellectual property need to be handled well, which is what she does immaculately.

**You believe in *seva* and working towards eradication of diseases. Swati has said if she ever got a chance to be health minister, she would take it up . . . Your thoughts.**

The healthcare business that we are in is geared towards working to alleviate human suffering to the largest possible extent. Swati has always believed in this mission and, in fact, she started a polio eradication camp right out of medical school. Over the years she has been deeply involved in each of our initiatives such as the Piramal Swasthya programme. Swati has been driving that, apart from being involved at the policy levels of several government initiatives aimed at ensuring that healthcare and medicine are available to every Indian.

As for her ambitions, I think they are commendable and I have always encouraged her. My belief is that one should try and do something more or better each new day. That is how one progresses.

**You believe that 'values create values.' How have Swati's values of warmth and compassion boosted the group economically?**

Rock-solid values, over the long run, create economic values. In the beginning, however, there may be a cost. Let me use the example of respecting intellectual property rights as a pharmaceutical company. At a time when almost all Indian companies did not adhere to this value, we decided to adhere to it as a group. So, even as we acquired businesses, we never duplicated their products. In the short term, there were losses because we did not export. But in the long run there has been phenomenal value addition, because every multinational that wanted to exit India would come to us as the first port of call. And when we wanted to sell to Abbott, we got the highest-ever valuation in the world for any generic, till date. All of this, because of our values.

**What can young women of India emulate from Swati Piramal?**

Swati's work and work ethics are the biggest source of inspiration—she has done so much in so many varied fields, be it medicine, business, art or culture. And yet, her feet have always been firmly planted on the ground and she has stayed humble, even as she strives for so much more.

# PRIYANKA
# CHOPRA

·

*Priyanka is unique in her own space. There is a lot of resilience, fortitude and passion in everything that she does. She is an incredibly warm person, very giving of herself in many ways . . . in terms of just being there for you. There is a can-do atmosphere that she tries to inculcate and she wants everyone to have fun. She has the ability to actually believe that anything is possible—she has shown that with her never-say-die attitude.*

**—SIDDHARTH ROY KAPUR**

·

*Hazaron khwaishen aisi ki har khwaish pe dum nikle/Bahut nikle mere armaan lekin phirbhi kam nikle.*

Ghalib and contemporary Bollywood seem an unlikely combination; but in the glitzy, global world of twenty-first-century Hindi cinema, there is one star who can appreciate the depth of these lines effortlessly. The fact that Priyanka Chopra is an aficionado of Urdu poetry—she can write and translate verses—is just one surprising aspect of the versatile star's personality. Beauty queen, model, actor, singer, style icon, blurring the lines between India and the world, she is the perfect mascot for today's fearless, multi-hyphenate generation.

As I consider the Padma Shri award winner's many winning performances—playing boxer Mary Kom as powerfully as the punches she pulled in the film *Aitraaz*, reinterpreting the vamp as seductress and not a tramp; and the heartbreakingly vulnerable, autistic Jhilmil of *Barfi!*—I am amazed by the breadth of her repertoire. By the standards of Bollywood's mainstream crop of light-eyed, alabaster-skinned, leggy beauties, the petite and dusky Priyanka is truly more like a pretty girl next door. Put her in front of the camera, though, and she turns into a stunner; those smouldering eyes, bee-stung lips and full-blown confidence give plain-vanilla beauty a run for its money.

It's a clear day when I meet her at her airy, sunlit duplex apartment in Andheri, a Mumbai suburb that houses much of the film and television crowd. Priyanka is just out of a meeting; dressed in the classic combination of blue jeans and a white shirt, her hair in a ponytail. The only movie-star concessions to her look are subdued make-up and red heels. She greets me warmly, and as we begin talking, I am impressed to find that PeeCee, as she's known, remains unaffected by the magnitude of her achievements. She is honest, articulate and devoid of arrogance. Instead, Priyanka has that disarming ability to look me straight in the eye and make me believe that she has halted every important task for this interview— a trait that has won her a legion of fans in India and abroad.

I start our interview by asking her which of her qualities are her own favourites that set her apart from her peers. 'My courage and conviction,' she says, without any hesitation or pretentiousness. 'These can be seen as belligerence and rebellion sometimes. But if I choose to do something I stick by it, whether it works out or not.'

Is her superstardom a result of a childhood dream, pursued with this conviction, I ask. Priyanka laughs, telling me I'm wide off the mark—'No, never in my wildest dreams did I think I would be an actor.' Her dream was to be an engineer and she studied seriously. 'But then at seventeen, I won the Miss World pageant and my life changed completely. I suddenly grew up. Movies started happening and I began my learning process—how to act and what was required to be a star. Slowly, it became my profession. And now I am doing music and starting again right from the beginning. It was never planned. I am destiny's favourite child.'

## A NOMADIC CHILDHOOD

With parents who were both doctors in the Indian Army, Priyanka has been used to moving home, city and country from a very young age. She was in boarding school by the third grade, in the US by the seventh, and travelled the world in between. 'The best part of my childhood was being able to become somebody else every two years.' Today, the ease with which she adapts to every situation and her shape-shifting personality have been largely influenced by those formative years.

'When she was young, she loved being in front of the mirror all the time,' says cousin Parineeti Chopra, who is also a Bollywood star. 'She would put on my dadi's [grandmother] dupatta, or my mom's bangles, and perform for everyone to watch. My dadi would ask why Priyanka was always dressing up. Little did we know that she would become a beauty queen and an actor.'

Her sojourn in the US came about quite by chance. While holidaying with an aunt in Boston, she took an iq test that gained her admission to a school where she studied for the next three years. Those were good times except for the occasional racist remarks from some students and her own sense of diffidence, in the context of American life. She took all of this on the chin though, and started building her inner resilience and focus.

After three years in the US, Priyanka came back to Bareilly to finish school. Her newly minted confidence meant she scandalized her conservative family with her short dresses, and when she won a local May Queen beauty pageant, Priyanka attracted dozens of unwanted, sometimes seedy, admirers.

Listening to Priyanka tell the story, as colourful as any screenplay, it seems to me like the May Queen pageant and subsequent fan following were actually just a trailer. Priyanka agrees and tells me that a few months later, when she got a call from the Femina Miss India organizers, the spotlight's glare was unavoidable. 'I was dumbfounded. My mom and my brother had entered me into the contest without my knowledge.'

Younger brother Siddharth remembers how shocked they all were by the sudden turn of events—'We had merely sent her pictures for the magazine, but we didn't expect her to win. Of course, my mom had a very big role in making her participate in the pageant. Since my sister was preparing for her Class XII board exams, mom had to discuss it and convince dad first.'

The pageant turned out to be a cakewalk for Priyanka and by extraordinary coincidence, the judge who put a question to her in the last round was her favourite star Shah Rukh Khan. Perhaps it was her inner determination that was manifesting her deepest wishes or perhaps it was a glimpse that the universe was giving her into her future profession. 'SRK asked me whether I'd rather marry a businessperson who'd buy me diamonds, a sportsman who'd make me proud or—with his trademark wry humour—an actor like him who'd ask me multiple choice hypothetical questions. I picked a sportsperson,' she tells me. And would it be the same today, I ask. 'Absolutely. I can take care of myself financially; I'd like to be with somebody who'd make me a proud wife—a man I can look up to and respect.'

When asked if winning the title changed things dramatically for his sister, Siddharth replies firmly, 'She definitely evolved after Miss India, but right from her younger days, she always had a certain poise and a positive attitude. Miss India just refined all those qualities.'

The victory was followed in a few months by the Miss World crown in 2000—a double whammy made even sweeter by the fact that the eighteen-year-old Priyanka was the youngest Miss World ever.

## LIFE AT THE MOVIES

In the first decade of the new millennium, winning a beauty pageant also won you a ticket to Bollywood and it was no different for Priyanka who decided to move to Mumbai to explore the flood of movie offers she was receiving. Her conservative father agreed on one condition—that she would be accompanied by her mother. 'My parents have put so much of their time and resources into me,' she says. 'When I became Miss World, my mom had a successful career as a physician and she had to quit it all to be with me because I was so young. I always remember that because she was in her forties. For her—and my dad—it was a big change. My entire family moved because they didn't want me to be alone. I was my dad's pet; his belief and pride in me has been a huge contributing factor to my drive and focus.'

The young pageant winner was conflicted about working in films but her family's support propped her up—'At that point, Bollywood was a leap of faith, but one that I was willing to allow myself. I had a long conversation with my mom, and we decided that I should take the risk rather than regret years later that I had not given it a shot.'

Priyanka's first offer was a heavyweight—a lead role opposite Bobby Deol in Abbas-Mustan romantic thriller, *Humraaz*. It fell through, however, and she eventually debuted in *Thamizhan,* a 2002 Tamil film, which had not been her ideal launch vehicle. The following year was better and Priyanka made her Bollywood debut with the Sunny Deol-starrer *The Hero: Love Story of a Spy* and starred in *Andaaz,* which won her the Filmfare Award for Best Debut. The critics, however, remained unimpressed and a spate of underwhelming films like *Plan*, *Kismat* and *Asambhav* at the beginning of 2004 did not help.

What did, though, was *Aitraaz*, directed by the acclaimed duo Abbas-Mustan. Priyanka played Sonia, a go-getting character who stops at nothing to achieve her ambitions, be it a loveless marriage to a much older tycoon or a false sexual harassment suit against her married ex-boyfriend, played by Akshay Kumar. Given Hindi cinema's legendary classification of women into fragile heroines or immoral vamps, *Aitraaz* was a risky choice for a newcomer. It paid off when Priyanka won the Filmfare Award for Best Performance in a Negative Role in 2005.

Film critic and author Anupama Chopra says it is just this 'tandem spirit', this fearlessness that sets Priyanka apart from the rest. 'She was so brave to take on that role of Sonia in *Aitraaz* at the time when it could have obviously popped a perception and one does not do negative roles like that early on. And at that time, it was extremely bold of her even though the film was rejected by the audience.'

## THE SWEET TASTE OF SUCCESS

By 2006, Priyanka had established herself as a critically acclaimed actress and one of Bollywood's top heroines with starring roles in blockbusters like *Krrish* and *Don*. But success and failure continued playing hide-and-seek, and she was written off again after a spate of unsuccessful movies like *God Tussi Great Ho, Chamku* and the colossal flop, *Drona*. And then, to turn the tide, came Madhur Bhandarkar's *Fashion*. 'Whenever we meet, even today, she says, "Madhur you have really been a turning point for me in my career,"' the director tells me. 'She carried the film completely on her shoulders.'

*Fashion* was a brave choice for Priyanka. Few actresses then would have sullied their 'heroine' image to play the dark role of an ambitious small-town girl who claws her way up the ladder in the modelling world, and sinks into decadence before finding her way out again. It took Priyanka six months to say yes to the part—her fearlessness at making the difficult choices helped her turn a deaf ear to the naysayers; as Bhandarkar points out, she was unafraid to 'take the bullet on the chin'.

Eventually, Priyanka's hard work and top-notch performance paid off—she won a National Award for *Fashion*, making her the youngest actress ever to win one—'It was crazy, I was in a state of shock for a really long time. When President Pratibha Patil was about to hand over the medal to me, I kept thinking that I would trip and fall. My whole family was there. It was really a very big deal.'

According to Bhandarkar, 'She is a very, very intelligent girl. I won't call her a method [actor] but she wants to know the graph [of her character]. She wants to know the story thoroughly—what exactly is she doing as the character, what was happening in the previous scene, what is about to happen next. She gets into the skin of the character and is absolutely focused.'

There was no looking back for the feisty actor thereafter—her role in *Fashion* made her the first choice for film-makers with women-oriented scripts. With Vishal Bhardwaj's *Kaminey* in 2009 and *7 Khoon Maaf* in 2011, Anurag Basu's much-talked-about *Barfi!* in 2012 and the Sanjay Leela Bhansali-produced biopic *Mary Kom* in 2014, Priyanka became the new poster girl of offbeat cinema.

Alongside these, she also did mainstream films that set the box office on fire in India and overseas: Dharma Productions' *Dostana* and *Agneepath*, Farhan Akhtar's *Don 2*, Rakesh Roshan's *Krrish 3* and Yash Raj's *Gunday*.

'For me, her growth or her biggest achievement has been in the balance that she manages to strike as an actor. There is nothing that she can't do,' says Parineeti.

A lot of this evidently stems from Priyanka's clarity on what she wants in her career. She has experimented with challenging roles in offbeat films, yet at the same time she is not dismissive of commercial cinema and tells me she enjoys being part of box office hits. At the same time, she takes every role seriously, doing a serious amount of homework, whether it's for *Mary Kom* or the *Don* franchise where she trained in boxing and martial arts respectively—or *Barfi!*, for which her research included spending time with differently abled people.

Her brother, Siddharth attributes much of this propensity for hard work and, more significantly, dedication, to their parents. 'They have both been very hard-working and dedicated in their lives. [The same qualities] have led to Priyanka's success today. She has played a variety of roles which have required a lot of preparation. One of the toughest, according to me, was Mary Kom in which there were intense training schedules that she had to undertake. Most people would just give up that sort of a training regime, but she was determined to see it through and she did.'

I ask Priyanka if there's a particular method to the roles she chooses. 'I am basically a spontaneous actor, though a bit of method is required everywhere. Of course, prep is required for every role, but on set, all of it goes out of the window; so I would say spontaneity, above all else, is important,' she explains.

Priyanka, for her part, is excited about the contemporary period of Hindi cinema with its author-backed roles for women—'It's a great time for a female actor in Indian films. We are doing parts that are written for us, and written so well. While *Barfi!* as a film was about Ranbir's [Kapoor] character, I had an incredible role to play in the film even though I was there for only 40 per cent of its duration.'

'I loved her in *Barfi!*,' says Anupama Chopra. 'I really, really enjoyed her performance in *Mary Kom*. It is amazing when you realize that she is actually not a trained actor. She came via the beauty contest route. That is quite incredible. And I like that she has not been afraid.'

*Barfi!*, released in 2012, is a role that's really close to Priyanka's heart. It won many of the big awards, despite the fact that she shared some with Vidya Balan in *Kahaani* that year. In fact, when I quiz her on the three achievements that she's really proud of, she responds without hesitation, 'My National Award, making a music album and starring in *Barfi!* I was really scared I would not be able to pull it off.'

Incidentally, so was director Anurag Basu, at least initially. Unsure as he was, he did not announce the casting till he'd put Priyanka through a three-day workshop—after which he was not only convinced of her ability but really glad that he had chosen her for the role. When the film was released, Priyanka earned an overwhelming response from critics and peers.

'There is a lot of resilience, a lot of fortitude, and a lot of passion in everything that she does,' says Roy Kapur, who has produced many of Priyanka's box office hits, including *Kaminey* and *Barfi!* 'When she commits to something, she is there for you more than 100 per cent. She backs it up completely, she never lands up unprepared, and she just gives her all to what she is doing.'

As this book goes to print, Priyanka is winning accolades for her thoughtful performance as a conflicted wife and daughter in Zoya Akhtar's family drama *Dil Dhadakne Do*, besides the many awards for *Mary Kom* that are coming her way.

Anupama Chopra says, 'She made it in the industry despite having no godfathers in the business and just came out of nowhere. She had talent and that is what I like. I think she is willing to put herself out there, to be afraid, to be criticized, just to try something new, and that is pretty amazing.'

Sanjay Leela Bhansali's period romance *Bajirao Mastani* opened in December 2015 to critical acclaim, while her next, *Jai Gangajal* with Prakash Jha, received lukewarm responses. She made her American television debut with ABC's FBI show, *Quantico*. Playing the lead—the only South Asian actor to have done so in an American series—Priyanka's portrayal of Alex Parrish won her much praise and accolades, including multiple People's Choice Awards and spots on the top late-night shows on American television, over its duration of three seasons.

Riding high on the success of *Quantico*, Priyanka made firm inroads into Hollywood live-action films, debuting as antagonist Victoria Leeds in Seth Gordon's action comedy *Baywatch* opposite Dwayne Johnson and Zac Efron in 2017 and another release at the 2018 Sundance Film Festival, *A Kid Like Jake*, a family drama about gender variance starring Jim Parsons and Claire Danes. In 2019, Priyanka starred as a yoga ambassador in Todd Strauss-Schulson's comedy *Isn't It Romantic*, which starred Rebel Wilson in the lead role and was released on Netflix.

Priyanka is set to star opposite Chris Pratt in the action film *Cowboy Ninja Viking* and will portray lawyer Vanita Gupta in courtroom drama *Tulia*, an adaptation of the non-fiction book *Tulia: Race, Cocaine, and Corruption* (2005) based on a 1999 case of racial injustice that took place in the city of Tulia, Texas. Back home, she will be seen on-screen after a break of three years in Shonali Bose's *The Sky is Pink*, co-starring with Farhan Akhtar and Zaira Wasim. The film is based on the life of Indian motivational speaker Aisha Chaudhary, who died aged nineteen in 2015 after contracting the respiratory illness pulmonary fibrosis during a bone marrow transplant.

In a bid to promote regional talent and cinema, Priyanka set up her own production house called Purple Pebble Films in 2016. Her first production, a Marathi comedy-drama, *Ventilator*, gave her a chance to debut a Marathi song sung by herself, and went on to win three National Film Awards in the same year. She is now in the process of producing over a dozen regional films in various languages under her production company and developing a sitcom for ABC based on the life of Madhuri Dixit, in the capacity of an executive producer. I wonder if Priyanka is exhausted with the scale of work she takes up every day, but clearly, she is indefatigable.

## PEECEE: THE VOICE AND THE GLOBAL SUPERSTAR

Priyanka has music in her genes: her father, Ashok Chopra, was a good singer, who left audiences spellbound when he appeared on a television music show along with his star daughter. He loved Hindi and Urdu poetry and vintage film music—tastes he passed on to Priyanka. Her schooling years in the US, meanwhile, exposed her to western pop and hip-hop—she loved Tupac and The Fugees.

This passion didn't go unnoticed when she began acting in films. Her first co-actor, Vijay, and her director heard her humming on the sets of *Thamizhan* and urged her to record a song for the film. Priyanka, though disinclined, finally did it; the same unwillingness made her turn down the song *Tinka Tinka* in her 2005 film, *Karam*, though she did record an unreleased song for *Bluffmaster* the same year for her friends, composer duo Vishal-Shekhar. She sang *Chaoro* for *Mary Kom,* which made it her first playback song in Hindi films. She believes that her reluctance could have been at a subconscious level and that destiny was actually preparing her for a larger stage—her international music launch that happened in September 2011.

Following her career, I have always felt that this launch highlighted Priyanka's amazing confidence. Iconic as actors in the Indian film industry are, none of them have ventured into uncharted territories the way Priyanka has at an international level. That kind of drive requires self-belief and a risk-taking ability, which she has in plenty. 'I don't like doing what is expected of me—that's very boring. Music wasn't a plan. I hadn't thought of a singing career—it was Universal that approached me. So, I gave it a shot very exasperatedly and it seemed like an interesting project so I thought why not go ahead?'

Incidentally, Priyanka's name was suggested to Anjula Acharia-Bath of Desi Hits (the music company that collaborated with Universal) by Salim-Sulaiman, who had done some Lady Gaga remixes for the company. The first Bollywood star to do a music crossover, Priyanka went on to surround herself with the best and most powerful players in the music business: Jimmy Iovine (Interscope Records) who launched the careers of the Black Eyed Peas and the Pussycat Dolls, and Troy Carter, CEO of the talent management agency Atom Factory who manages Lady Gaga. She was also signed on by Creative Artists Management, a Hollywood talent agency that has virtually every top Hollywood star on its roster.

'It is great. It is brave,' says Roy Kapur about Priyanka's foray into international waters. '[But] it is something that not many people would do when they are so well established in their home country, but that again is testament to the fact that she likes to try new things.'

Priyanka goes back in time to the recording of her first debut single with famous rapper and seven-time Grammy award winner, will.i.am. Iovine was keen that she and will.i.am do something together, and what emerged was *In My City*, a song that Priyanka co-wrote. Inspired by her own nomadic childhood and her journey from small-town girl to celebrity, the single was chosen by the National Football League network as its theme song for Thursday Night Football and debuted on 13 September 2012 in a TV spot for the show. A day earlier it was launched in India where it proved to be a triple platinum success, selling over 1.3 lakh copies in its first week.

The blazing start was followed by many more accolades—a Best International Debut award at the People's Choice Awards India; a featured artist on *Erase*, an EDM song produced by The Chainsmokers; a second single with celebrity American rapper Pitbull called *Exotic* that went on to become No. 1 on iTunes India; and a third single that was a cover of Bonnie Raitt's *I Can't Make You Love Me*.

In 2017, Priyanka collaborated with Australian DJ Will Sparks for an EDM song *Young and Free*, which she also wrote.

Priyanka maintains that music is simply an extension of her creativity and she is willing to take the risks that come with making a career of it.

## THE STYLE AND BRAND ICON

Given her sex appeal, glamour and extraordinary success, it was inevitable that Priyanka would become one of the leading brand ambassadors in India.

I ask Priyanka how she chooses her brands—is it merely a commercial decision or is there any kind of an underlying ideology? 'There has to be a brand fit, like I wouldn't be brand ambassador for a health portal, for example, because it doesn't make sense: I am not a healthy person, I am not a fitness freak; I eat only when I remember to and also eat junk food. I like to be involved with brands that I believe in.'

It is hard to believe that Priyanka is that insouciant about fitness and wellness because she certainly does not look like the average slacker. Always toned and fit, and sexy in the way that only the most confident women are, she is a style icon, too. On screen, off screen, 24x7.

Whether she's wearing a curve-hugging gown, a sari or just jeans, Priyanka knows how to style her super figure to perfection. She brought in a certain casual, edgy vibe to the way Bollywood actors dress, with her ripped jeans, casual T-shirts and short skirts. While it took Priyanka some time to find and embrace her personal style, it is now clearly a marriage of high street and couture, and Indian and global.

The same conviction that colours her association with brands extends to Priyanka's interaction with social media and her philanthropic causes. She understands the value of networking and dialogue, and has taken to the new media like a fish to water. She has also written columns and the occasional piece for the media. So can we hope to see her in yet another avatar in the future— that of a writer? Priyanka muses over the question and says, 'I wouldn't put it past me.' True to her word, in June 2018, Priyanka announced that she will publish her memoir titled *Unfinished*, which is scheduled to be released in 2019 by Penguin Books in India, Ballantine Books in the United States, and Michael Joseph in the United Kingdom. Apart from that, Priyanka's maiden venture as an investor in social and dating application Bumble, which has been launched in India in December 2018, aims at driving social change and women's empowerment by letting only the woman make the first move in heterosexual matches. India is the first country in Asia to get Bumble.

Priyanka's columns—which include contributions to the *New York Times* and the *Guardian*—have addressed subjects such as female genital mutilation, and trailblazers like Malala Yousafzai, whom she admires deeply. The opinions she expresses are not mere lip service. Apart from the many charitable causes she's taken up—health issues such as thalassemia, polio, cancer, leprosy and tropical diseases and social ones like female foeticide and infanticide—Priyanka has launched her own foundation for social and philanthropic work.

'One of my biggest achievements is that I have created my own foundation called the Priyanka Chopra Foundation for Health and Education,' she tells me. 'All these years I have worked a lot with UNICEF. For the last five years I have been UNICEF's Goodwill Ambassador officially, but unofficially, I have been associated with the organisation for more than eight years. We have done a lot of good work together. Before that, I worked a lot with the girl child because I really believe in the education of the girl child.'

Priyanka was appointed as the global UNICEF Goodwill Ambassador again in December 2016 and received recognition on multiple power lists from multiple agencies for her contribution towards social causes between 2016 and 2018.

## BEING PEECEE

The second time I meet Priyanka, it's in my home city, Kolkata. She's shooting for *Gunday* and is getting her make-up done for the role of Nandita, the 1970s' cabaret dancer with whom both Ranveer Singh and Arjun Kapoor fall in love. In real life, too, Priyanka has had no shortage of suitors and relationships though she is famously discreet about them. Given that she's led what seems like a charmed existence where almost everything she touched turned to gold, I wonder if she ever went through the normal period of struggle that most actors do.

Priyanka gives me an interesting answer—'The struggle still continues; it's just that it changes form. There is no way that any human being can live a life without struggle. Success is a validation but it doesn't mean you are validated for life. No, Bollywood isn't as easy as people think it is. But then life itself isn't easy.'

It certainly has not been for Priyanka over the last few years. Her beloved father was diagnosed with cancer in 2009, and never really stayed in remission. Always daddy's little girl, she held his hand through the illness; when I met her on the *Gunday* sets, he was still alive but suffering, and I could feel her pain as she spoke to me about it. When he died, Priyanka was a pillar of unstinting strength and support for her mother and brother. Talking of those difficult days, Siddharth says, 'She stood by our mother and me, no doubt, but it was very trying for her as well. My dad and she were very, very close. They would share everything so it hit her pretty hard when he passed away, but she maintained her level-headedness and focused completely on her work. I don't think she has got over the loss, but she is still putting her best foot forward.'

Priyanka returned to the sets of *Mary Kom* a mere four days after her father's death. While her colleagues marvelled at her strength and resilience, the fact is that work was a very necessary refuge for her to get away from painful memories. 'I didn't want time to think,' she told Karan Johar on his show. 'I'd work like crazy, reach home really fatigued and crash.'

Talking to Priyanka, it was crystal clear to me that for her, all the fame, success and money in the world were nothing compared to family. To date, the last forty-five minutes before bedtime are exclusively for her family. When her father was alive, she'd sit between her parents, watching a soap opera, reading a book or just lounging around. When her father fell ill, she reversed roles and became a parent to both him and her distraught mother. Two years after his death, she has learnt to cope without him and has immersed herself in her career once again.

Zoya Akhtar tells me that she is one of the rare actors who is actually sensitive to what a film-maker might be going through. 'I never felt weird talking to her about anything. She was like a buddy and she is very smart, she is very glued in to your process as well. So she is very sensitive to what the film-maker is going through. Usually it is always you worrying about the actor, but she really cared about what was going on with me.'

I ask PeeCee what her most important lesson in the industry has been. She pauses and answers, 'My advice to anybody coming into show business would be the advice my mom gave me when I came here myself. I really lived by it and survived because of it. Nothing in life is do-or-die—we are very lucky to be in the twenty-first century where we can switch professions, be whoever we want, put a finger on a place on a map and go there. The world is your oyster—so don't be restricted in a bubble. Every single day with the kind of pressures that we deal with, one can get really bogged down. But I have learnt not to wallow in self-pity and say that my life is screwed and terrible. I have learnt to be positive despite the drawbacks. Yes, there will be days when you don't want to get out of bed, but you make yourself do it. And then you look at the sun and say, "Shine on me, I'll still look up at you."'

She is candid about the drawbacks that come with fame, telling me that the biggest downside of an acting career is loneliness. 'A lot of people think that just because you are an actor and in the glamour business, it's a very easy life. No, it's not—there's stress, and I don't mean physical stuff like being on a plane 300 days a year or having to always look pretty and presentable. But that's the kind of pressure that comes with being a public person. That's really hard—the constant public glare, speculation, judgement, living under the microscope—all of it is frustrating. But again it's the price you pay to be where you are. You are in the limelight and you cannot say you don't want to be recognized. You would be lying, but you can control how much you want people to know about you.'

Perhaps it is strange, but then again, the movies have always taught us that we often find the things we are meant to on the road we take to avoid them.

Priyanka Chopra and Nick Jonas met each other at the Met Gala in 2017, soon after which they started dating. Nick Jonas is said to have shut down a Tiffany store to select the perfect ring, and he bought a home three months before he proposed to Priyanka Chopra. Like every girl who has dreams of a princess wedding, Priyanka and Nick got engaged in a roka ceremony in Mumbai in August 2018 and were married in an elaborate ceremony that lasted days at the Umaid Bhavan Palace, Jodhpur. They had a Christian wedding on 1 December and a Hindu wedding on 2 December 2018, after which they had wedding receptions at Delhi and Mumbai. Priyanka and Nick's wedding truly took the world by storm and ensured that the world saw Priyanka and India in a new light.

A couple of years ago, her favourite co-star Shah Rukh Khan called Priyanka the shero (she+hero) of the industry for her ability to be a woman and the hero of the film simultaneously. While that is true, she is so much more than an actor. She's a storehouse of talent; she's also a brand who has reinvented herself beautifully every few years, almost like an accomplished entrepreneur.

# RANVEER SINGH

*Both were complete newcomers to the industry, relying on talent and tenacity to build a career. Both have been up and down the roller coaster of success, winning the masses and critics over eventually with their ability to rule over the screen. It is fitting, therefore, that **Ranveer Singh** considers **Priyanka Chopra** a co-star, peer and friend who he has an immense amount of affection and respect for. He talks about Priyanka's talent, collaborative spirit, courage and ability to always push the boundaries and shine brighter.*

## What are your thoughts on Priyanka as a friend and as a co-star?

Priyanka is really vivacious, spirited and full of energy. And I don't just mean physical energy—I mean that she has a lot to give. She is a people's person, who will be at the centre of attention and yet not hog the limelight.

What impresses me is that she uses all these strengths to her advantage— she works a lot, works very hard and multitasks. I admire that, and have learnt a lot by observing her. She inspires me because she does so many things at the same time, and manages to do all of them perfectly. So I would say she is a model for modern women.

## Shah Rukh Khan calls Priyanka 'shero', and believes she is the only one in Bollywood who can be described as one.

I like that she has the self-esteem and confidence to unabashedly receive praise. And yes I totally believe she deserves that title. She started out young, and has worked very hard for many years, so she deserves all the accolades she enjoys today. Priyanka is one of the most powerful women in the industry— there is no doubt about that, and she has earned it. She is very determined to make a mark with what she does.

## How would you chart her growth from being considered a trophy girl in films to doing mainstream and offbeat roles such as in *Barfi!*, *Mary Kom*, among others?

194

Priyanka had to get her foot in the door somehow, and she did this by taking any role that came her way. But with her talent, it was inevitable that at some point, she would be recognized and the roles would get better. You have to make yourself get somewhere, before you can become successful. She is blessed with talent. When that talent was explored by various film-makers, it was showcased in the most memorable performances in Hindi cinema of all times, which really puts her in a very elite league of performers.

**Despite her success and the accolades, Priyanka still doesn't consider herself to be a Bollywood insider. What do you think of her standing in the industry?**

If she feels like an outsider, then maybe that is [how she plays] the game, but she is very much a part of the industry. When I started working with her, she was one of the leading stars, and what was wonderful to see was how warm and gracious she was with both Arjun [Kapoor] and myself. That was the time when we were relatively new in the industry, so it was really nice of her to be so cool with us, not impose her seniority on us and just have fun with us. She made our working experience really fun.

**How uplifting is she as a co-star?**

One aspect about Priyanka as a collaborator is that she understands what teamwork really means. It is about *jugalbandi*. It is about playing off each other and collaborating with each other's energies. And she has that collaborative quality—she is not a selfish and an individualistic performer. That's what is really lovable about working with her because we know that she puts her best foot forward to make the film look good, and she doesn't compromise. She is a team player first and foremost.

**What would you say are the qualities that distinguish Priyanka from the other leading actors that you worked with?**

All of them do it their own way and each has a different process. What I find about Priyanka is that she is extremely versatile—she can be Jhilmil [*Barfi!*], she can be Mary Kom, etc. She can fit into the mould of any character and is very comfortable in any kind of genre, in any space. She can be a real mass entertainer, too. I think her range is very exceptional.

**Priyanka is India's only crossover international superstar, who is also a successful musician and is debuting on television. Can you talk about that a little bit, as a colleague and a friend?**

We are really proud of her. She has got the talent and it is not defined or limited by the culture that she is working within. Her talent clearly connects with everyone from Bihar to Boston. She has taken a very brave step and done something that no one has done before—becoming an international pop star. Plus, Priyanka can act in any language, sing and dance, so she is really an all-rounder. She is a real powerhouse performer, and although she has just started, I feel she is going to do extremely well in the times to come as she explores these frontiers. It is only going to be upward from here.

**What qualities of Priyanka's do you think young India can emulate, professionally and personally?**

Priyanka is a model modern Indian woman and everyone can emulate her sincerity and passion for her work. She constantly pushes herself out of her comfort zone. And this is true of modern Indian women, as well, not just actors.

# KAREENA
# KAPOOR KHAN

•

*Kareena is a thinker and has very strong values. She has never allowed her looks, position or lineage to get to her head. She makes room for people she loves in her life, and that includes me. While being financially independent and successful, Kareena chose to be in a relationship. In an industry that believes marriage is the end of an actress's career, we got married—across religions—and she has continued to work and do very well. All of these are important lessons for women—that you can achieve all your goals, and still enjoy your life, if you open yourself up to that thought.*

**—SAIF ALI KHAN**

•

'*I*'ve always lived from the heart and don't think of myself as karmically blessed. Even as a child, I wanted to be the biggest movie star I could be. And I wanted a fairy tale romance. Being Kareena Kapoor Khan is who I am, and it is very important to me.'

Sitting across from me is an alabaster-complexioned, green-eyed beauty, dressed in track bottoms and a T-shirt. It is 9.30 p.m., and we are in the Noor-Us-Sabah Palace, a hotel in Bhopal where Kareena is shooting. If she is exhausted after a long day at work, I have no way of knowing because she is completely present, with no traces of stress or arrogance. The apprehensions and fears that had niggled at me before I met Kareena dissolve within minutes. Curious, chatty, candid and utterly charming, everything about her is proof of her supernova stardom, and both the lineage she was born into, and the one she has married into.

'I have watched her as an actor and a person over the years, and I think she is incredible, way ahead of everyone else. She has always been beautiful and a good human being, which reflects in her work as well,' says her doting husband—and Bollywood star—Saif Ali Khan.

One of the few women members of Bollywood's 100-crore club; the star of forty-six films over fifteen years, including the super-successful *3 Idiots*; a fashion and fitness icon who endorses twenty-two brands and has designed a capsule clothing collection; a begum; and a scion of Bollywood's first family, Kareena is a woman who owns her place in the world, but lightly.

## TO THE ARC LIGHTS BORN

'My whole family is in the movies. So being an actor was something that just came naturally to me, which I am proud of,' Kareena tells me. 'And I've worked very hard to prove that I am not just glamorous.'

Despite her illustrious last name, Kareena's path to success has not been smooth or easy. To start with, women in the Kapoor family have traditionally not been encouraged to work. Kareena's mother, Babita, had been a popular star in her own right when she met, and decided to marry Randhir Kapoor, eldest son of the late and legendary actor Raj Kapoor. After their wedding in 1971, she stopped working in films.

The couple has two daughters—Karisma, and Kareena. Called Bebo by family and friends, Kareena's name was inspired by the protagonist of Leo Tolstoy's classic, *Anna Karenina*, which Babita was reading while she was pregnant with her second child. Though she and Karisma have dramatically different personalities, the sisters are very close and supportive of each other. Growing up, Kareena was the brat who was always plotting mischief and speaking her mind, while Karisma (called Lolo in the family) was composed and reserved. And the younger sister idolized the older, following her around everywhere she went.

'Bebo's always been a daredevil, the more outspoken one,' Karisma, ever the indulgent older sister, says. 'I'm the kind of person who wants to be correct in life; Bebo has been just the opposite. Even as a child, she was more of a rebel. If my mother asked us to go out, do something adventurous, I wouldn't but Bebo would. She was the talkative one, the one on the dance floor at parties, the one always ready to pose for pictures.'

Indeed, her sister and mother have been the two steady anchors in Kareena's life. A strong, determined and sensible person, Babita inculcated several practical and very valuable lessons in her daughters from a young age. The rebel in the conservative Kapoor household, she had been one of the most glamorous actors of the 1960s; her father was a Sindhi character actor, Hari Shivdasani, and her mother, Barbara, was English. (Kareena's striking beauty is often attributed to this genetic mix.) As a child, Kareena was fascinated by her mother's of-the-moment churidar-*kurta*s, and the way she wore her hair in a bouffant.

The girls were also very close to Babita's English mother, Barbara, who formed Kareena's first association with glamour. She would watch her grandmother get dressed every evening to go to the club: 'I watched every step of her routine and was especially fascinated by the delicate way in which she applied her lipstick. As soon as she left, I would dress up and dance to a song, begging my mother to watch me.'

While her family teases Kareena for having had starry airs since she was a child, she remembers herself as a tomboy who was never allowed to be difficult or fussy. She does not deny being a bit of a drama queen—she has Kapoor genes—but her parents did not indulge any starry airs. With her mother's firm gaze always on her, Kareena's childhood was filled with friends and ordinary fun. She studied at Mumbai's Jamnabai Narsee School and at

Welham Girls' School in Dehra Dun; the boarding school experience is not something she remembers fondly, however, and says she agreed to go only for her mother. A bright student, she never managed to stay out of trouble, always fighting for people she was close to—a trait she still has.

This idyllic childhood was set against a storied, uneasy family history.

The Kapoor family's deep roots in Bollywood are traced back to Kareena's great-grandfather, Prithviraj Kapoor, one of the pioneering stalwarts of Indian cinema and theatre, a very successful actor-director-producer, who established the legendary Prithvi Theatre, he featured in landmark films such as *Alam Ara*, *Sikandar* and *Mughal-E-Azam*.

Prithviraj's son, Raj Kapoor, took up his father's mantle and crafted a dazzling career as an actor, director and producer. His brothers, Shashi and Shammi, were also successful actors. The Kapoors, with the exception of Shashi, had a strong patriarchal streak; the daughters of the family were 'married off' and the daughters-in-law—successful actors like Neetu Singh and Kareena's mother Babita—were made to give up their acting careers for domesticity. It was against this background that Kareena and Karisma, with the active support of their mother, revived the glory of the Kapoor name on the screen after it had been stagnating for a decade. But the journey wasn't easy—it involved a bitter separation between their parents, heartbreak and struggle.

When Babita walked out on Randhir with their daughters in tow after he refused to let Karisma act in movies, life changed dramatically, says Kareena—'My mother has seen troubled times; my sister had to struggle when my parents weren't together. Money is incidental in my career, but I value it a lot. My mother still looks after my finances and occasionally tells me not to waste money on shopping and expensive restaurants. She single-handedly brought us up, we're very attached to her and I don't think I can function without her.'

Kareena was quite young when Karisma began her acting career and the times she accompanied her sister to film sets were momentous for her. She did not go too often, because her mother wouldn't allow it. Whenever she did, Kareena was fascinated by the world behind the scenes and the hard work that went into making a film. In that sense, she was just like any other star-struck child, she says—'Lolo was sixteen when her movie career started. I was fascinated by her new life—the costumes, the choreography!'

201

The added advantage, she confesses, was being around some of the hottest actors of the time, who were Karisma's co-stars. Kareena admits that around her favourites, she'd be 'blushing from head to toe'. The starry-eyed young girl would tell anyone willing to listen that she, too, would become a famous actor one day. Salman Khan, she says, was one of those who not only indulged her but believed in her dreams.

Another industry insider who was supportive of the young Kareena's ambitions was fashion designer Manish Malhotra, who is close to both sisters. He says, 'In 1990, I was a costume designer in the movies, and was [working] with Karisma. Bebo was nine then—a pretty, chubby girl filled with admiration for her sister, wide-eyed about the glamorous world of movies and absolutely clear that she was going to be a star.'

It was a while before Kareena answered the call of the arc lights. After she graduated from Welham, she studied for a Commerce degree at Mumbai's Mithibai College and then headed to Harvard University for a short course in information technology. On her return, Kareena enrolled at Government Law College, Mumbai. Amid all of this chopping and changing, she decided to stay faithful to both her original dream and her family's legacy—acting. After being mentored and trained by Kishore Namit Kapoor, a respected acting coach and a graduate of the Film and Television Institute of India, Pune, Kareena began her Bollywood journey.

## STARDUST IN HER EYES

In 1999, Kareena signed her first movie, *Kaho Naa Pyaar Hai*, which was director Rakesh Roshan's venture to launch his son Hrithik; no one could have predicted its smashing success and Hrithik's rise to Bollywood superstardom, which continues even today. The film could arguably have altered the course of Kareena's career, but she backed out of it soon after it was begun. It was a controversial move at the time, but Kareena had an unlikely debut film in her kitty—J.P. Dutta's *Refugee*, which would also launch the Bachchan heir, Abhishek.

Even as the industry and audience expected to see Kareena in a run-of-the-mill romance, *Refugee* (which was released in 2000) was a serious film set against the backdrop of the 1971 India-Pakistan war. The debutante's role was challenging but showcased her acting genes, and tremendous screen presence. 'She took that leap into offbeat territory right from *Refugee*,' says Karisma admiringly. 'And then she did *Chameli* so early on. She's always dared to be different.'

In 2001 came the movie and the role that solidified Kareena's position in the industry as not just a stellar actress but also as a feisty, stylish young girl who could have fun. As the air-headed, style-obsessed, pouty megalomaniac Poo in Karan Johar's monster hit *Kabhi Khushi Kabhie Gham*, Kareena won the hearts of audiences worldwide with her comic timing and sartorial chops.

Karisma says, 'Kareena is one actor who can just give of herself completely. And I think that is why she is every director's dream. That vulnerability in her eyes and her ability to cry at the drop of a hat—these are her strengths.'

But fate is a fickle mistress; after three celebrated performances there followed a series of forgettable films like *Jeena Sirf Merre Liye*, *Khushi*, *Fida* and *Hulchul* to name a few. A little hesitantly, I ask Kareena about the grey years from 2001 to 2004. Her eyes soften—'I never want to think of those years. Of course, I was unhappy. I would cry and wonder why my films were not doing well. But I realized there is something like the 'right time', especially in Bollywood. It happens to everyone. It's also true that you would not have been interviewing me if I'd got everything on a platter – it's the inevitability of life. If I hadn't gone through that phase of despair and struggle, the euphoria of the post-*Jab We Met* phase wouldn't have existed either. Geet was born out of all that.'

Geet, the effervescent and utterly lovable girl that she played in *Jab We Met*, Imtiaz Ali's delightful 2007 caper, turned her fortunes around instantly; the role won Kareena her first Filmfare Award for Best Actress. In the four years before Geet came her way, and commercial success was elusive, Kareena made her mark in parallel cinema. She played a hardened, yet lively young prostitute who forges a strange bond with a yuppie banker in Sudhir Mishra's *Chameli*. It was a calculated move meant to negate the bad press she was getting as her commercial films flopped. The gamble worked, as for a brief while Kareena was the darling of alternative movies with roles in Mani Ratnam's *Yuva*, Govind Nihalani's *Dev* and Vishal Bhardwaj's *Omkara*. By the time *Jab We Met* hit gold—much of it because of Geet—Kareena had to her credit critical acclaim and box office credibility.

Despite many bouquets and brickbats over the years, Kareena has remained bold about her choice of roles with movies like *Ki And Ka*, *Udta Punjab*, and *Veere Di Wedding*. Every role was vastly different from the other, but Kareena brings her spunk and versatility to each of them with ease.

Saif analyses Kareena's success for me succinctly—'Kareena has a great sense of discipline and that makes all the difference; I believe that discipline plays an important role in proving one's professionalism. What you do when you are not working, though—what you eat, how you sleep, how you take care of yourself, how you see yourself—all these things play a big role in defining you as a person. She wins on those fronts, too.'

Kareena is clear that there is much more work ahead—'I will eternally want to prove myself as an actor, even though I've been doing it for the last fifteen years. It's not the success that I'm chasing—it's because I enjoy the making of a film and acting. And I don't know anything else apart from acting. That is the only thing I've done besides watching movies, and I'm proud of it.'

## A GAME CHANGER

Kareena and I meet the next day, which happens to be February 14. She is in her trailer on the film set in Bhopal, and over her favourite snack—chilli cheese toast—we chat like old girlfriends, even though we met barely twenty-four hours ago. I realize that Kareena is a mix of all the women she has played on screen—she has Geet's effervescence, Poo's magnetism, Chameli's street-smartness and the alluring mystique of Dolly from *Omkara*, all blended with her own femininity and charisma. We talk about everything from the best detox salads to facialists and the latest fashion trends. Kareena has a quicksilver persona and while she is happy to chat uninhibitedly, she also protects her boundaries with her rapier-sharp tongue.

It's this bluntness and occasional lack of tact that won Kareena some enemies among her peers in an industry where sugar-coating and brown-nosing are widespread. She often said exactly what was on her mind in the media, and was considered a difficult colleague. But that was then. 'Now I'm much more mellow,' she tells me. 'I think being settled and a bit older has helped. When you're content with work and at home, it also makes you calmer.'

While one of her transformations has been an intangible one from a candid young woman to a wiser, unruffled star, a parallel journey has been far more visual. Both began with one movie—*Tashan*, a fast-paced, action-packed script that needed Kareena to be less of an actor and more a sexy star. There was one scene that gave her the heebie-jeebies, though—she would be expected to rise up from the sea in an echo of Bond girl Ursula Andress's iconic scene in *Dr No*. Kareena balked at the thought of being caught flabby on camera.

She began working out in earnest, but failed to find her sweet spot. And then, via recommendations from friends, she met Rujuta Diwekar, a little-known nutritionist who is now one of India's biggest names in her field. Known for her firm but practical approach to wellness, Diwekar cleaned up Kareena's diet—with its Punjabi staples of cream and meat—and introduced her to simple, wholesome preparations. 'Kareena kept, and still keeps, her diet simple—dal, rice, sabzi and the local food of whichever place she is in,' Diwekar tells me. 'She wants it to be fun, and will not do anything where she feels deprived. She's the only woman I know who does not feel guilty about enjoying her food. She is passionate even about drinking her cup of tea.'

With Diwekar's support and gruelling sessions of yoga, Kareena soon whittled herself down to a figure that was to become a catchword in the country's pop lexicon: size zero. Though Kareena is happy about the association between her and the American dress size (which actually borders on stick-thin), she points out that she was never size zero in the strictest sense. The image of a lithe Kareena rising from the sea in a lime-green bikini will perhaps remain one of the most iconic images of Hindi cinema and she credits *Tashan* with two of the biggest moments of her life—she became a part of popular culture, and found her soulmate in her co-star, Saif Ali Khan.

Today, Kareena is a working mother in the glamour business, with a hit radio show that focuses on all kinds of women's issues and activism related to infant mortality and post-partum healthcare. She's still breaking barriers across the board. Nobody tells her what a married woman or mother can and cannot do.

## A PRINCE AND A GENTLEMAN

As Kareena and I talk, she breaks off every so often to check her messages. 'Sorry, I'm addicted to my phone,' she laughs sheepishly. As if on cue, her phone rings. Kareena's eyes light up—it's Saif. They have not met for some time, and she has a brief, affectionate conversation with him. This is the perfect cue for me to broach the subject of her personal life and Kareena is more than game to talk about it.

Ever since she was a child, she tells me, Kareena had two desires: to be the biggest movie star ever and to have the perfect fairy-tale romance. 'I unabashedly wore my heart on my sleeve and it was a nice ride till I finally met Saif and we fell in love,' she laughs. 'Yes, and as it turned out, he is a prince, which fits my fairy-tale metaphor perfectly, but he didn't have to be one—I mean, he would have been just as charming without his title.'

Saif first met Kareena when she was a young girl on her big sister's film set. In his own words, he was bowled over by her beauty and asked someone who she was. They were co-stars in *LOC* and *Omkara* but had never spent time together until they began shooting *Tashan* in Ladakh. Kareena confesses that she thought Saif a very attractive man, and the fact that he made her laugh was a big plus.

'I think timing is everything. I met Kareena at a point in my life when I was ready to consolidate and build in every area of my life. She brought a great sense of stability; I felt like we were able to create a solid foundation on which I could build emotionally, financially and professionally,' says Saif.

As they began shooting in the stunning and isolated landscapes of Ladakh, Saif and Kareena were healing from failed relationships, which brought them closer. Unalike as they are, their chemistry and relationship grew in the magical, inexplicable manner that the greatest love stories have. Kareena was bowled over by Saif's forthrightness, sense of humour and love of adventure; he was charmed by her liveliness and childlike personality. They decided to live together. Kareena says to me, 'Saif and I moved in together because I was ready to leave my mother's house, and if he and I did not live together, we would barely meet. There were some raised eyebrows, especially since I am from the Kapoor *khandaan*. But I was always honest about it. In Bollywood, the tried-and-tested formula always works, so why not try and test a relationship? I didn't see anything wrong in it.'

Yet, the decision came as a big shock for her mother, Karisma remembers. 'It was for me too, to some extent. Our family is slightly conservative but then we accepted that this was Bebo: all heart and all sentiment. Besides, she has this incredible ability to always know what is right for her. She is led by emotion and instinct but, touch wood, her decisions have always proved to be positive and wise.'

Five years after they began living together, Saif and Kareena were married on 16 October 2012. It was a quiet affair—a *sangeet* and civil ceremony at Kareena's Bandra home, followed by a lavish dinner in Mumbai and a *Dawat-e-Walima* in Delhi hosted by Sharmila Tagore, Saif's mother. For two Bollywood stars from famous families, the celebrations were discreet and understated. Kareena says it was important for the couple to protect their privacy and tells me they had threatened their families that they would elope if their wedding was turned into a media circus.

When I speak with Saif about their marriage, he says, 'When two actors are in a relationship, no matter what the intention is, there is a great deal of uncertainty. Our wedding resolved that. For me it is very important to feel calm about the person I am with, and not distracted or worried. If one is happy at home, it shows on one's face, and in one's work. Kareena has made me feel secure about our relationship, so I am happy being with her.'

## SCENES FROM A MARRIAGE

Saif and Kareena are, in so many ways, a modern, fuss-free couple. She did not even entertain the thought of quitting movies after her wedding, and neither has she begun to play safe with her choice of roles.

'I'm an actor first, my films are a part of me, and people love me because of them. I know I am now Kareena Kapoor Khan, and with that comes a lot of responsibility towards my in-laws, but this has nothing to do with my career. A lot of people had actually advised me not to get married because there's this idea that married women are not accepted in the industry. But I think there's nothing sexier than being a married woman.'

Saif is effusive about how Kareena has changed his life. 'She has been a good influence on me, and inspires me to get things right – whether it's being disciplined about fitness and food, or how much to party. We share a healthy equation of likes and dislikes.'

When I meet Kareena in Mumbai, months after our time spent together in Bhopal, she has just finished a gruelling session of Ashtanga yoga in her well-appointed home in the upmarket neighbourhood of Bandra. Of course, she has that post-workout glow and is tanned from a recent vacation, but I discount these facts as I admire her chiselled beauty. Again, her face is free of make-up; she is dressed in her yoga gear and is barefoot. She greets me with a bear hug and as she fills me in on the latest gossip, I feel as if I'm at a slumber party with a girlfriend—only there are no scratchy pink pyjamas in sight. We start off by talking about her marriage, and she tells me that the delightful truth is that she and Saif have introduced each other to a different way of living. While she brought balance, wellness and fulfilment into his life, he has shown her a whole new world. Reading books on world history; spending time in Gstaad (the Swiss haven favoured by royalty); frequenting members' clubs in London; and hobnobbing with European and Persian royalty, Kareena now views life from a privileged lens.

While their love story does seem like something out of a fairy tale, it has not been easy—and both are honest about this. For one, Saif was a divorced father of two when they met; from his former marriage to actor Amrita Singh, he has a daughter, Sara, and son, Ibrahim. Kareena is clear that while she truly is very fond of the children, who treat her home like theirs, she is not a mother to them. 'It's not something they or Saif would want from me,' she reasons. 'They have a wonderful mother who is bringing them up. And Saif is a great father to them. I want his focus to be on his children, and when we have kids, they will all be siblings.' But she's quick to add that having children is not something she and Saif have discussed. 'I need to be mentally prepared. For me, having a baby is not a means to solidify a marriage.'

As luck would have it, Kareena gave birth to her and Saif's first child, Taimur Ali Khan Pataudi, in December 2016. Taimur is one of India's favourite celebrity babies today. The Indian paparazzi monitors every move he makes, sometimes resulting in hilarious situations.

Saif is very appreciative of Kareena's sensitivity towards his kids. 'Her proximity to Sara and Ibrahim happened organically and the fact that she took her time to get to know them has left a lasting impression on me. And as for me, I have no qualms about confessing that I am very difficult to live with. She makes it look easy and manages so well that I myself am really amazed. She knows how to get me to do the right thing without nagging, or complaining. So when she does complain, I think very carefully about it because I know something must be really off for her to talk about it.'

## THE GOLDEN GIRL

Of course, Kareena is a successful, popular actor but she is also celebrated for her sartorial choices and the wide range of endorsements that come her way. She is also known to set fashion trends with how she dresses both on and off screen. For example, as Poo, she introduced young women to the toniest global brands and her pairing of *patiala-salwars* and T-shirts as Geet changed the definition of casual Indian wear for an entire generation.

Kareena's style icons include her mother, grandmother, sister and, now, her mother-in-law. While she admires their elegance and understatement, she is not afraid to go big. She is not a fashion victim or snob, though—'I can be extremely stylish in my Zara T-shirt. I don't need to wear Alexander McQueen to really be stylish. I will, sometimes, but I don't need to. Comfort is style and attitude is everything.'

Always canny and ahead of the game, Kareena was one of the first Bollywood stars to create a capsule collection for a fashion brand (Globus) and to endorse and write books. She played a huge role in the writing and promotions of Diwekar's first book, *Don't Lose Your Mind, Lose Your Weight*, which rode the post-*Tashan* publicity wave as well. And then Kareena wrote her fashion-centric memoir, *The Style Diary of a Bollywood Diva*, (co-authored with Rochelle Pinto); it was published in 2013 by Penguin Books India.

More than her successes and high-octane oomph and beauty, I am moved by the love and loyalty Kareena gets from her family and friends, for her honesty, authenticity and reciprocal reserves of commitment and affection. Karisma cannot praise her beloved sister enough. 'Once, anxious about a problem I was facing, I called her. After talking to me for about ten minutes, she said, "You know, I'm on a harness, like twenty feet in the air, can I call you back?" That's the kind of person she is.'

Her friends tell me she is great fun to spend time with, and has her share of quirks. Gossip is her weakness, which is a Kapoor family trait, and once she becomes a friend, she always stays one. Her affections are not fickle, but if you don't hold her interest, she will not pretend to care about you. An intensely private person, she stays off all forms of social networking, considering them nothing more than an 'added responsibility'. Every once in a while she takes a quick trip to her favourite city, Paris, to get away from her busy life.

That's where the mystique of Kareena lies—she is an old soul living a modern life. While it might be easy to think of her only as a star, she is truly a woman of today who lives by her rules, is brave in her choices and embraces life, work, love, family and friendships with enthusiasm. 'We need girls and women to be independent in India today,' she tells me in one of our conversations. '[Women] need to have strength, confidence and the passion to achieve what they want to. There are so many restrictions on us in our society and country that we have to fight back, to become who we want to become. At the same time, it is important to respect tradition. In my own life, I have never done anything against the wishes of my family but I have also been brave enough to stand by my own decisions.'

So the finest role she plays every day is that of Kareena Kapoor Khan.

# KARAN JOHAR

*Karan Johar and Kareena Kapoor Khan are almost like siblings. Their friendship runs deep and warm, strengthened over decades through a shared history. Both are Bollywood's offspring. Johar's father was a successful producer; Kareena belongs to the first family of Bollywood and has married into royalty. As if these connections were not subliminal enough, they have both been an inalienable part of each other's careers. Like two friends who just know what the other is thinking, Johar and Kareena share an unmatched bond, based on understanding and a mutual acknowledgement of talent and ambition. Johar describes his friend and would-be-sister, and why he thinks Kareena is the most talented, and most real, of all Bollywood's actors.*

**Did you see the reflection of a star when you first interacted with Kareena?**

I think Kareena was born to be a star. I have known her a very long time, and used to see her on set as a young child who would follow sister Karisma around. She used to try on Karisma's wigs, or look at the costumes Manish Malhotra had made for her sister. She always looked happy and excited to be there. This love for cinema has always been in her.

I clearly remember seeing Kareena at a party, when she was seventeen, standing next to her sister. She had the body language, aura and charisma of a star herself. I knew then that she was ready for the movies. Kareena has stardom in her—you see it when you meet her, when you watch her on screen and even when she has experienced failure. She has a lot of patience and nothing touches her.

**Kareena made her debut in 2000 and is now known as 'the 100-crore star'. As a friend and peer who has worked with her, how would you assess her personal and professional journey?**

I think her instinct is her greatest strength. Whenever Kareena has chosen her roles instinctively, she has done very well; it is when she makes calculated moves then she does not. And she has evolved phenomenally. Though we all knew there was a fantastic actor in her even in her first film, *Refugee*. The role of Poo in my movie, *Kabhi Khushi Kabhie Gham* that she played so well—with that adamant pose—that made her very famous. And then there was *Chameli*, which too highlighted the actor in her.

Her breakthrough, though, was definitely *Jab We Met*. I think Kareena and Imtiaz Ali have great chemistry as a director and actor. As Geet, Kareena carried that movie—as a viewer, you invest in her story, and laugh and cry with her. Unlike most mainstream movies, in which the male lead shines out, Geet was the star of *Jab We Met*. Kareena managed to win over the Punjabi heartland with her portrayal of a bubbly, funny, smart and sensitive Punjabi girl and really set off a trend.

From then on, there have been the blockbusters, like *Golmaal* and *Singham*, and there have been the quieter films, like Govind Nihalani's *Dev*. I find that Kareena's brilliance stands out, like tiny gems, in these [*Dev*]. That is what is exciting about her as an actor—she can surprise you.

**Kareena refused films like *Kal Ho Naa Ho* and *Goliyon Ki Rasleela Ram-Leela* that went on to be super-hits. As a film-maker, what do you think her considerations are when she says yes to a role?**

If you ask her, Kareena will agree that she has made some surprising choices—both good and bad. I don't think Kareena is bothered by those decisions, if she does look back on them. I always tell her not to see them as mistakes because this is life and we never really know how our decisions will turn out. Maybe the films would not have worked for her? The most important thing here is that Kareena does not dwell on the past, she has no regrets—for her, it's always about looking ahead, and thinking about tomorrow. That's her attitude.

**Kareena has been in movies that have broken box office records, but has also had her share of failure. What is your observation?**

Yes, that is true, and that's because she has always had work come her way. You only feel failure when it hits you hard professionally. That has never happened to Kareena. Even when things were at their worst, she was shooting other movies and being offered new ones—there was a lot of hope. She has been working non-stop throughout her career, and has the support of her mother and sister, who give her a lot of strength.

I would say, actually, that Kareena's personal lows—as when maybe a relationship did not work out as hoped—hit her much harder than her professional ones. She has always been a star—against all odds—and no box office verdict has affected that.

**Kareena often says that you are one of her closest friends both in and outside of the industry. Describe for us the dynamics of this friendship.**

Kareena and I really have a soul connection. I don't have a sibling, but if I could choose one, I would pick her. I really feel short-changed by the universe that she is not my sister because I think we have the chemistry that only the best siblings share. I am very protective of her, and I feel like we have a connection from another life.

We've had one ugly fight, when she turned down *Kal Ho Naa Ho*. It was very out of character for me to react the way I did—we tore into each other and were deeply hurt. I remember that for a year, we would pass each other sometimes without even an acknowledgement. We moved past it, however, and are more deeply in sync than before even.

Of course, we're both very busy people who are working all the time, but no matter how long we don't speak, Kareena and I don't lose that bond. We can pick up where we left off. She knows she can depend on me like family and I know I can, too. She lives in my heart, and will always remain there.

**Does she have any quirks that we don't usually read about or know of?**

Like me, Kareena also loves to gossip. We message one another bits of news but we keep it to ourselves, which is great. The third person who loves all this is Ranbir Kapoor. I call Kareena and Ranbir the Information and Broadcasting Committee—she is the gatherer of the news and he is the broadcaster. Both of them are so curious.

The thing that most people don't know about Kareena is that she asks the weirdest questions. If you put her in a room with a lady who is over fifty years old, she will ask them how much they pay the people who work in their house, or how many people actually work in their house. She asks my mother questions like this and I can promise you that no other leading actor ever does so. Kareena also always wants to know what you ate at your last meal and what you intend to eat at the next one. In fact, the retinue that is always with her—hairdresser, make-up artist, stylist, etc. I call them 'Kareena and her Catering' because she wants to know what they are eating, just ate or will eat!

**How does Kareena stand apart from her contemporaries, many of whom are your friends, too?**

There is only one Kareena Kapoor. That combination of beauty and old-world charm is incomparable. Kareena does not have to work too hard. She is a star, she has that aura, and fantastic opportunities come her way naturally. Her presence, lineage and talent contribute so much to anything she is associated with. She is the only actor we have now who can go from playing a young girl who is full of energy and also play a stoic, more emotional character, too. I feel like she has an internal scale—you can place the marker at two, or five, or ten and she will do what you need her to do. That is what makes her distinctive—that ability to bring intensity or quietness, opulence or simplicity to each role. She can be moulded as an actor, which is incredible.

**Kareena has shone in a gamut of roles, but if you were to cast her in one that she has never done before, which would it be and why?**

I would love to see Kareena in the story of a modern marriage. To be more specific, I'd like to see her play an average middle-class working woman who is living through the ups and downs of a marriage in India today. An evolved, mature story that looks at the reality of couples in our country. I think she would be fantastic at something like this.

**Kareena has been both a trendsetter and an inspiration to many young women, from her fashion choices to fitness and the roles she plays. How do you think she views that responsibility?**

214

I don't think Kareena is out to inspire anyone, I think she is out to live her own life. But by doing that, and because of the way she balances all aspects of her life—career, marriage, family, legacy, etc.—she has become an inspiration.

The fact that she has chosen to continue working after she got married has been great because she broke the myth that married actors don't get work. She is married, and roles are still offered to her. Kareena works hard, she works all the time, but manages to be a great daughter, sister, wife, daughter-in-law, friend, etc. at the same time. I think she has a beautiful relationship with Saif's kids, which is great. Kareena is a modern woman who walks tall and does her best every day. What's more inspiring than that?

**What do you think of Kareena's companionship with Saif Ali Khan and what are your hopes for her future?**

Saif has transformed Kareena's life because I think he has got her to live her life in the best way possible. From teaching her about fine wines to introducing her to literature, or how they travel, he stopped her from plateauing in the way she lives. I almost feel like Saif has been a teacher to her. My greatest hope for her is that she remains exactly who she is. I hope she always works in the movies and also plays the role of a mother.

# ANAMIKA
# KHANNA

*One of the reasons that women designers have such great resonance is because they design for a woman's body and Anamika is true to that spirit more than anybody in this country. She will take an embroidered piece and make a little jacket, have a little drape that is half-sari, half-dhoti, half-something. Her style has its quirkiness and twists but always had tremendous understatement.*

**—TARUN TAHILIANI**

*T*he lights are dimmed. The tasteful ballroom is full of fashion's finest, but the audience is restive; no one is expecting too much from the debutante designer of the next show. As the music crescendos, the lights go back up and a tall, slender model in a bridal *ghagra* walks down the ramp, a *dupatta* cloaking the head, face and top half of the body, echoing a *ghunghat*. As the veil rises, higher and higher, the audience lets out a collective gasp. The wearer of the gorgeous *ghagra* sans *choli* is male—Acquin Pais— and the designer has caught their attention in a vice grip.

This was 1999, at the first-ever Lakmé India Fashion Week; and the designer Anamika Khanna, the youngest and newest in a line-up that included everyone from Rohit Bal to Tarun Tahiliani. And yet, the petite, quiet, but resolute designer from Kolkata had the audience on the edge of their seats. Choreographer and fashion legend Prasad Bidapa, a friend of Anamika's, chuckles as he recalls her unusual debut. 'It was spectacular and I've never forgotten the moment.' With that drum-roll start Anamika was on her way, and she never looked back.

It was not easy for a rank outsider to even get a foot in the door in an industry as incestuous as the Indian fashion fraternity was in the 90s. The fact that she is now one of its brightest and most beloved members is proof of Anamika's gumption, talent and tenacity. I have had the pleasure of knowing her for many years—our families are friends—and thus, this profile is especially easy and difficult to write, having seen her journey up-close as a friend and objectively, as an admirer of Indian fashion. Anamika has always lived life – personal or professional—on her own terms. And she has grown from a shy young girl with a quirky sense of style into one of Indian fashion's ambassadors globally.

## THE EARLY YEARS

When Anamika was three months old, her mother, Shakuntala Jain, moved with her to Assam, where her father managed the tea gardens owned by the family. Anamika's childhood was idyllic—'Assam was a different world. I had rooms full of toys; there were rabbits scampering about in lush green lawns. I still remember the domestic help and *chowkidars* who were so fond of me. They would dress me up in outfits and jewellery. I loved it.'

When it was time to start school, Anamika moved back to Calcutta with her mother and new baby sister, Suruchi, to the family home in Burrabazar, a Marwari neighbourhood in central Calcutta. Anamika attended Mahadevi Birla Girls' High School and she was a good student.

'Micky [as Anamika is called in the family] was a happy-go-lucky child. She rarely cried and was always very independent,' says Shakuntala, admitting that the demands of life in a joint family prevented her from nurturing Anamika's inherent artistic skills. 'Even as a child, she was very good at drawing and sketching. If you gave her a pencil and sheet of paper, she would spend hours by herself quite happily. I remember giving her reels of thread and she would be occupied for hours.'

This remains true even today. Anamika's day starts early, she sketches for two hours in the morning and reaches her workshop by 9.30 a.m. That said, she did not study art or design as a student at Loreto College, Calcutta, moving instead from the sciences to liberal arts. All along, though, she indulged in a lot of craftwork, making gifts for others, or needlework for school projects; her friends in college would come to her with fabric that she then sketched designs for. A dream she always nurtured, however, was to take up Indian classical dance professionally.

'I think it's in my genes,' she tells me. 'My *nanisa* [grandmother] and mother were perfectionists and would constantly be stitching or embroidering. I was inspired by them. Their clothes and shoes were always the finest, and I still remember the fabulous trench coats and safari jackets my mother owned.'

It was her friends who recognized that her talent and ability were extraordinary, and they encouraged her to submit her sketches for the Damania Fashion Awards. Her 'amateurish sketches' of an Africa-inspired line won Anamika the Young Designers Award in 1995; she shared the honour with her friend—and now designer/stylist—Aki Narula.

Suhani Pittie, Anamika's youngest sister, who is a successful accessories designer, remembers that occasion vividly—'I remember her first show of the Shoowa collection. I was not allowed inside because I was underage. The next day her picture was in the newspaper! I cut out the clipping and pasted it on my cupboard next to a picture of [cricketer] Jonty Rhodes.'

Receiving the award gave Anamika the much-needed sign that she had the talent to make it in fashion, and she decided to pursue a career with focus. While she had the skills and the determination, she lacked a mentor, and a formal degree. At this point, Vibha Kejriwal, a close friend, stepped in to partner her. Both of them worked hard and long to put together a collection of pieces to sell at a local exhibition. They opened for business at 9 a.m. and by 11 a.m. all the pieces were sold out.

Even as Anamika's nascent career was being met with such success, her personal life had taken on its own trajectory. At nineteen, she went against her family's wishes and married Vijay Khanna, who she had met through mutual friends when Anamika was in the twelfth grade, and she knew that despite her family's disapproval, he was the one she would spend her life with. Vijay pursued her until she relented.

Even though her family were angry with Anamika's choice of husband—Vijay is Punjabi—the Khannas were and still are unstintingly supportive of the couple. A fact that Anamika remains grateful for—'Without their unconditional love and support, it would be impossible [for me] to do what I do. I didn't even know what a metre of fabric was; but once the challenge came up to put up a collection, I took it up.'

While Anamika holds that her strength and courage are rooted in Vijay's support, he says to me—'Anamika taught me discipline. Anyone can see what hard work is if one spends one week with her. Her talent is the result of her hard work. I have never stopped her from doing anything and she never did anything that I would not like.'

A businessman himself, Vijay is that rare man who is comfortable with the spotlight on his wife. Anamika says, 'He is my rock. Vijay is very mature and the balancing factor in my life. He understands that fashion is like any other industry, and it's not just about glamour, partying and socializing, but it is hard work that counts.'

Looking back she says, 'It was probably the toughest phase of my life when my parents did not accept my marriage. It was devastating to think that I had lost them.' Eventually, her family came around to accept their daughter's marriage and embrace Vijay into their world. 'Anamika's father really doted on her and so when she left to get married the whole family was in a state of shock. Her father missed her the most and eventually we gave in to her decision. She has always been a strong-willed person,' says Shakuntala.

The wonderful fact is that Anamika's business is supported by her father, which allows her the time and space to be creative; and both families help her in every way. 'I feel guilty that I don't have enough time for friends and family,' Anamika tells me.

## ONWARDS AND UPWARDS

Anamika and I are in her workshop, on the upmarket Lansdowne Road, south Kolkata. Talking with her and watching her work, I am reminded of the long journey that has brought her here. After she won at the Damania Fashion Awards, Bidapa encouraged Anamika to send her designs to boutiques and they were picked up by two pioneering women—Yashodhara Shroff, who owns Ffolio in Bengaluru, and Kavita Bhartia of Ogaan in New Delhi. Once she was on that radar, Anamika's work got picked up by other designer stores—'My work kept expanding and I worked harder and harder, teaching myself the nuances of cuts and colours, and devouring every fashion book or magazine I could lay my hands on.'

Fashion commentator Bandana Tewari adds, 'I have seen women wear her jackets with trim pants and boots in the winter and her kaftans are so modern they come across as Indo-Greek dresses. The way she cuts them is reminiscent of the draping culture of our country. She remains true to that.'

Closer to home, Suhani has been influenced by her older sister and inspired by Anamika's work ethic to set up her own label—'Ana has achieved it all through hard work and talent. I've seen her go through the grind and I respect her for all her courage. From her I understood the value of a work ethic and I try to be as focused as her. It is the biggest compliment when she likes my work because she has very high standards and expectations from herself and from me.'

Those expectations really got scaled up when Anamika had her twins on Diwali at the age of twenty-five, even as she was still building her business. The boys are the light of her life, and she has always been a hands-on mother to Viraj and Vishesh. 'Even more than my career, my twins have moulded me into the person I am today. My babies' arrival and their total dependence on me made me look beyond my own needs and wants. Today, I have not only become more accommodating, but also more sensitive,' she says. Vijay tells me that her motherhood mantra has been—'Busy or not, kids always come first.'

Media-shy, Anamika has always maintained the practice of keeping her head down and working hard, which her friend Kalyani Chawla, vice president, Marketing and Communications, Christian Dior Couture India, says can be 'kind of frustrating as a friend. She has been a dedicated mother to her boys and nothing else really mattered to her. I want her to grow because she is capable of doing much more. Having said that, I personally love her for who she is.'

'She is like a little girl who is warm, yet embarrassed because of the attention she is getting. She is very humble and cannot take compliments. It almost seems that she does not want to accept that she is a famous designer,' says Tewari, with great affection.

Anamika is up at 6.30 a.m. and finds her 'me time' then to think design; her mother tells me—'Her kids have all the attention of their mother; she has refused important shows and events, prioritising their exam times.'

While Anamika may love her boys and she is a fantastic mother, she has in no way tied them to her apron strings. A strong independent person herself, she has taught the boys the same values—'I think it is important to be there for your children, to listen, understand and to solve their problems. But they must learn to be independent, too. Whatever they want to achieve in life, they have to on their own. I want to be friends with them and for them to feel comfortable telling me anything.'

Adults now, they completed their studies at the University of Southern California. 'I wanted to give them wings. Always serious sportsmen, golfers now, I support every decision they make and want to stand by whatever career path they choose. If design it is, then I want them to fortify themselves with the knowledge first.'

## BUILDING THE BRAND

When Anamika started working, the fashion industry in India was really a large community, rather than an organized body. Her most well-known peers were Rohit Bal, Tarun Tahiliani and Ritu Beri. She remembers the time for me—'It was somewhat chaotic. There was no concept of creating a collection, there were no fashion weeks, and there was certainly no one to direct us. Everyone had to fend for themselves and, in that sense, everyone was unprofessional.'

As Anamika's brand has grown over fifteen years, so has the business of fashion in India. There is now a proper universe that balances out the creativity and the commerce, and she has made an indelible mark on it in many ways.

'Everybody in Kolkata has a very distinct look, with their borders in hundreds of multi colours, and what Anamika has done is redefined that. She uses some of those techniques, in her unique style, which is very complex and individualistic, and her contribution to the Indian fashion industry has been precisely this,' says veteran designer Tarun Tahiliani.

Tewari backs him on the fact that Anamika has a very distinct aesthetic, which is what sets her apart. For example, in a certain collection—'In the last walk down the runway, about twelve women took to the ramp in *malmal* saris in basic colours with a stripe on the border—very traditional concept but in a modern vocabulary and in the most beautiful fabric.'

Technically, too, Anamika's work is flawless, Tiwari points out—'The way she cuts her fabric, that combination of structure and fluidity is typical of Anamika's style. Her patterns and designs blend the traditional and modern and one's first visual recognition of Anamika Khanna's work is the silhouette [of every piece].'

In 2004, after her brand was firmly established on the Indian landscape, Anamika launched her global ready-to-wear line, Ana-Mika. It was showcased at London Fashion Week to much acclaim and stocked at Harrods' Knightsbridge store—a first for an Indian designer.

'I was not surprised at all when Anamika went international. She wears western clothes with great elegance and panache. She understands the need to create a global product using Indian textiles, techniques and embellishments which can be worn anywhere in the world. Savvy investors are already eyeing her label and I expect Ana-Mika to be a globally recognized label in the next five years,' says Bidapa.

Anamika had a very significant career milestone in 2007, when she was selected along with Manish Arora and Rajesh Pratap Singh by Chambre Syndicale de la Haute Couture and Fashion Design Council of India to be the first Indian designers to show at the prestigious Paris Fashion Week. Nervous when she heard, and then motivated by the enormity of the opportunity, Anamika painstakingly put together her Spring/Summer 2008 collection, which she still considers her best.

When she got to Paris, though, she was in for a rude shock—'My stylist threw out things I had worked on for months and I was in tears. She would say, "This lehenga is too ornate, this bag is unnecessary, this drape is too much," and she edited everything out so I thought I had nothing left to show. But the result was fabulous. The show was crisp, precise with not a single extra thing.'

With a big smile, Anamika acknowledges that it was that stylist who taught her a crucial lesson, which has influenced everything she does now—minimalism. 'As Indians we don't know where to put a full stop. We want everything on our outfits, we consider more to be better, but in actual fact it is beautiful when it is simple and clean.'

What is delightful and instructive about Anamika's aesthetic, however, is that she marries this minimalism with a sense of irreverence, which adds an element of fun. It is not surprising that one of her style icons is Madonna—'Anything that Madonna does always starts with having fun. I have always admired her transitions, that madness about her.'

This unorthodox turn to her work means that unlike other Indian designers who routinely add Indian embroidery or embellishment to western silhouettes, Anamika reinterprets Indian silhouettes in a western context. For instance, she reinvented the Indian salwar as cargo pants, and wrapped a skirt around the churidar; from the toga-sari to the sari-pants, she is always able to surprise the industry and the market with her designs.

Take, for example, the collection she presented at the HDIL India Couture Week in 2008, which had everyone mesmerized. It was inspired by the drape of the Indian dhoti, and Anamika used fluid fabrics like chiffon and georgette to focus on drape and movement rather than her signature of embellishment and embroidery. She also rebirthed the sari by clinching it with a belt, draping it over trousers and creating a stunner. 'The sari can be a little cumbersome to wear on a daily basis, yet it really is the best garment in the world. What I have tried to do is improvize a little and make it modern,' says Anamika. 'I realized if you are from India and your designs don't have an Indian soul then you are no one. But you also cannot just offer a *ghagra-choli* to the client. You have to improvize and add something of your own to it.'

'I think Anamika is one of those few designers who represent India in such a glorious traditional yet modern avatar. You can wear her clothes in Mumbai, Paris or Nairobi, and feel like the most stylish person in the room,' says Suhani, who believes that her sister's work is the perfect representation of today's woman. 'Women today all over the world take great pride in tradition but are ready to soar into modern skies. Ana's clothes give you the confidence to be this woman.' This observation turned out to be completely on point, as 2018 witnessed Kim Kardashian and Oprah Winfrey don Anamika's creations for magazine shoots and truly cemented her position as a local designer with global appeal.

Tewari tells me that if she was shown something from Anamika's first collection to the last one, the common factor to identify all of them by would be the use of colour and the consistency of design—'She is very intelligent about the way she mixes structure and fluidity, and she does that in most of her clothes.'

While Anamika designs both prêt and couture, she is still the most well known for her trousseaux. With pieces that combine the traditional with the modern, her bridal creations are the most coveted and win extra points for being practical enough to be worn even after the wedding, to perhaps a decadent cocktail party.

'Every girl has dreamt of *the* wedding dress. Sometimes a girl will come to me and say she wants to get married in her grandmother's old sari, and I think that is so beautiful. I really get involved in making the old sari the best it can possibly be. There are emotions there, which is what I like. I wish more girls like that came to me,' she says.

One of Anamika's biggest fans and someone who wears her designs often is the young designer Masaba Gupta, who says, 'I am hugely inspired by Anamika Khanna. You don't see her around much, and she is not somebody who is trying to do aggressive PR and trying to make sure she is in every paper and magazine and her clothes are everywhere. But she still has so much value because she stands for what she believes in.'

## EVERYBODY'S DARLING

As I speak to her peers, family and friends, it becomes very clear to me that Anamika has, in her own quiet and unobtrusive way, won an army of fans, supporters and followers within and outside the industry. Shakuntala believes that this is because of Anamika's gentle nature, above all else— 'Anamika is extremely soft-spoken, she is very polite with her customers and talks to them personally, which most of the other designers hardly do. These attributes have helped her earn a lot of love and a good name. The amount of effort she puts into her work has also made her a favourite with people.'

Anamika acknowledges that she does have a way with people—'I am polite and look after the bride and the family that comes with her. I am interested in what they want. Somebody who comes to my store is treated like a guest, not just a customer who is going to spend money; that is the difference.'

Chawla says, 'I find it amazing that someone like her calls me every now and then and asks me what I think she should do. But, that's her! She values opinions and is not shy to ask for yours. She stays real and humble, which is so refreshing today. And to me that is beautiful.'

Sanjiv Goenka, vice-chairman of RPG Enterprises and one of Kolkata's most respected industrialists, says, 'She is one of the most creative people I know. A warm and wonderful human being and a hard taskmaster, who reinvents her designs and creations every season.' He, along with other industry giants such as Ravi Todi, have helped Anamika grow her brand, and their families remain her loyal clients.

Tahiliani adds, 'Where would you find a designer who is a friend who will invite you to lunch at the studio, introduce you to embroiderers in Kolkata and call a hundred people for an event you are doing? In this industry this is very rare.' Their association goes back a long way, to when Anamika was starting out and Tahiliani and his sister, Tina Tahiliani Parekh, supported her via their store, Ensemble. 'My personal equation with Anamika is fantastic. Besides the fact that we are born on the same day, a decade apart, we have always got along in the most supportive way. If Anamika has a problem in Delhi, she'll call me to send somebody from my studio to go fix it and if I'm doing something in Kolkata and need help, I will call her.'

Similarly, Anamika speaks of her peers—older, younger, or her contemporaries—with much warmth but worries about the manner in which young designers approach the business. 'Most of the new fashion designers are lost and confused. I think a lot of them are just jumping into the profession because it looks easy and glamorous. I don't know how many fashion designers there are today in the true sense of the word. For the majority the attraction is the exposure to the West and money.'

## HER MUSE

So who wears Anamika Khanna and how would one describe her quintessential muse? The answer is given to me best by Tewari—'A thinking woman who is neither hungry for nor a victim of fashion. When you buy an Anamika piece, you are buying the idea of an emancipated woman. Thinking women find it very easy to dip into fashion without feeling they are being victimized by it. Her brand connects because she is sincerely related to her brand philosophy.'

This concept of fashion comes with a story, and design that is not ruled by trends or external compulsions. Freedom is the key.

Anamika considers Sonam Kapoor her muse. 'Even if Sonam is wearing rugged denim and a cotton top, she will pull it off with great elegance. She has style and intelligence. She relates to my aesthetics and is very fashion conscious,' says Anamika. When the actor walked the ramp for the first time, it was as a showstopper for Anamika, wearing a pair of sinuous dhoti-pants and a zardozi top. With an increasingly global market and a rise in the number of women who are looking for reinterpreted traditional garments to suit a modern woman, Anamika Khanna is now a force to reckon with. A number of Bollywood starlets and society women have worn her designs for various kinds of appearances but Sonam Kapoor and Deepika Padukone continue being her most steadfast muses. From walking the Cannes red carpet to accepting her National Award, Sonam Kapoor has worn Anamika Khanna on some of the most memorable occasions of her life. It is perhaps fitting that both stars chose to wear Anamika's designs even at their wedding festivities. Sonam and sister Rhea Kapoor created a wave of sorts when they wore Anamika's designs with the mark AK-OK at Isha Ambani and Anand Piramal's wedding.

She finds women who make an effort to look after themselves, and who find the confidence to express their true selves through fashion, very sexy – 'You may be wearing something very ordinary, but if you walk into a room, and are able to hold a genuine conversation during which your eyes sparkle and you smile, that is sexy.'

'Anamika is probably the only person I know who eats, sleeps and dreams design, and works extremely hard at making it all happen. We all know what a terrific artist she is but it's inspiring to see her always strive to do better and never say "this is it",' says Suhani. 'I have seen Ana tie knots to the garments as the model is just about to get on the ramp. This yearning to do better and never be complacent is the key to her success. She never gives up, she never gives in and she loves what she does.'

## THE EVOLUTION

In the two decades that Anamika has worked in the industry, she has, of course, evolved personally and professionally; and though she is at the top of her game, the challenges have not stopped coming at her. Fashion has grown more competitive and the stakes are high for every designer, but particularly for someone like her of whom much is expected.

'Previously, if I had a fashion show or a commitment I would have panic attacks, but as I am getting older I am calmer. I don't obsess about trends any more,' she says, but admits that creativity also comes out of stress and it can only flow when one is inspired. 'I am a perfectionist, but also very disorganized. Even now, my show may be tomorrow and a design will only come into my head today. I create from scratch, from just a feeling, an emotion sometimes. Inspiration can come from anywhere for me, but I'm fascinated by the heritage my country has. Success is relative; there is a long way to go still.'

While her work takes up most of her time, Anamika has managed to find time for philanthropic work, be it an association with the Tata Medical Centre, raising funds for children suffering from cancer, or the Akshaya Patra Foundation. It matters, she says. 'I am blessed to be in a position to be able to use my resources and make even the slightest difference.'

An emotional person who is happy to be away from the hurly-burly of the fashion world, Anamika lives and works in Kolkata, the city she owes everything to, and her only flagship store is based there, too. 'You are away from the madness [in Kolkata] and don't feel the pressure like you do in Delhi or Mumbai. It's very calming here. But of course on the negative side, your choices are also limited,' she says.

'Kolkata not only gives her geographical distance, I think it gives her the philosophical and ideological difference from the rest of India, where she does not have to cater to a particular fashion ideology,' says Tewari.

A loyal patron of her brand myself, I know that Anamika has, in her silent and sure way, changed the way traditional Indian garments are worn. I tell her that she gave me the permission, with her exquisite designs, to accessorize less and allow the outfit itself to accessorize me. She nods in appreciation and says, 'My designs are always subtle, they never scream for attention, they are not revealing and are very individualist. I want to dress women to look super-feminine, super-hot and super-sexy. But when your outfit is overpowering it doesn't work. For me the outfit doesn't define me, I define the outfit.'

That encapsulates the timelessness and elegance of Anamika Khanna's work. She aims to leave behind a legacy that transcends all barriers of time and location, and it's not hard to imagine that she will only grow her brand into a bigger, more meaningful and globally transformative one. A true change agent, my friend Anamika is not one to be taken lightly.

# SONAM KAPOOR

*The relationship between an artist and her muse is special.* **Sonam Kapoor** *and* **Anamika Khanna** *have, over a decade, crafted a deep and meaningful association, between actor and designer. Together, they represent the best of modern Indian femininity and speak a bold, bright, new language of fashion whose vocabulary has been created by Anamika's talent and articulated by Kapoor's beauty.*

## Sonam, you are Anamika's muse and wear her label very often in your public and personal life. What draws you to her work?

Anamika is a true artist but besides that, she is a mother, wife, woman who works—I think playing all of these roles makes her craft even more beautiful. When such a complete artist creates garments, they are feminine, but also cutting-edge and detailed. They are extremely beautiful pieces of art, which are made with great thought and effort.

Anamika is a sensitive artist who creates designs and sets trends for the sake of art, not money. Anamika's aesthetic is a combination of modern and traditional elements, which is similar to my personality. I feel like I am a modern girl, but also a traditional Indian one at heart. So her designs really speak my truth.

## How has Anamika influenced and inspired you in your own journey and stardom?

As two people who collaborate often, Anamika makes me want to constantly reinvent myself, because that is what she does. Every film that we do together, every show she does, every outfit of hers that I wear—we try to project something different, which pushes me to be different. That is quite amazing.

## She calls you her soul sister and favourite woman. What do you and Anamika have in common, which forms the basis of this very important relationship you share?

We are both about art and craft. We both don't run after the money. Like me, Anamika does not think about her work as running a race. Both of us are focused more on building a legacy and I think you only achieve that when you don't follow the beaten path but you make your own.

Anamika has the mind and method of a true couturier. She adds that personal touch with clients, which makes everything exclusive and beautiful—her clothes, and the experience of buying them. And, of course, Anamika and I have formed an emotional connection over the years.

## How much do you think Anamika's design and styling have contributed to brand Sonam today?

I would say, quite a bit. Anamika styled me for *Delhi-6*, *Mausam* and *Prem Ratan Dhan Payo*. I only associate myself with brands and people that I believe in. And I associate with Anamika because her designs match my personality and she stands for everything I believe in. Her clothes are beautiful, and of impeccable quality, and when I wear them, I send out the message that this is the kind of work that I endorse.

## What, about her and her aesthetic, would you say, distinguishes Anamika from other designers?

Anamika's knowledge of and command over colour, cut and embroidery are very rare in India; she has the temperament, knowledge and aptitude that most other Indian designers lack. She pushes the boundaries of fashion, but never to a point that you don't feel feminine or beautiful in her clothes. This is a very rare balance to strike. She is always doing more but retains the essence of her art, which celebrates beauty and femininity.

## Your first time walking the ramp was for Anamika—what made you agree to do it? And which of her designs that you own, is your favourite?

I have always chosen to walk for designers whose clothes I love Anamika, Rohit Bal and Tarun Tahiliani. I could not say no to Anamika when she asked me; I love wearing her clothes, and I hope I can wear them always. And I don't know if I can manage to pick a favourite, but the pink dhoti-sari that I wore at Cannes in 2014 comes close.

**How would you describe Anamika's contribution to Indian fashion today?**

The Grecian drape, the dhoti-sari, the belted sari, the lehenga-sari, crushed silk, fine cotton, capes—all of it was Anamika. She has been a front-runner in reimagining Indian silhouettes, and changing the way people look at those clothes. Anamika is a trendsetter, which I think is quite brilliant. She is not inspired by anyone; she is inspired by India and the strong, modern Indian woman.

# SHOBHANA
# BHARTIA

*Shobhana Bhartia and* **Hindustan Times** *have an interesting correlation between themselves and it would be difficult to gauge which excels the other. To the reader,* **Hindustan Times,** *the brand, might stand out in a distinct light. But in industry, political, bureaucratic or even business circles, Shobhana often far outshines the very brand she has helped revive. I remember Shobhana attending meetings, always being such a lucid and vocal editor. She carries an air of fearlessness about her, and to my mind this is what has helped her maintain steadfastly her position as one of the finest media moguls of India.*

**—SUBHASH CHANDRA**

On 18–20 Kasturba Gandhi Marg, New Delhi, stands a historical building: Hindustan Times House. Silhouetted imposingly against the sky, it reflects a legacy of ideals and values that buoyed the nation's struggle for independence. And today, it represents the vision and aspirations of a new India.

Started as a voice against British colonialism, the *Hindustan Times* was launched on 26 September 1924 by Mahatma Gandhi. In 1933, the newspaper was acquired by legendary industrialist and humanist Ghanshyam Das Birla, who had played a role in its founding. Under G.D. Birla's leadership, the *Hindustan Times* became a respected and iconic national newspaper, with Devdas Gandhi (the Mahatma's son) serving as managing editor for over two decades until his death in 1957.

My thoughts are sepia-toned with this lineage and history as I make my way up to the second-floor office of the chairperson and editorial director of Hindustan Times Media. The space is formal, well-lit, spacious and modern, with a minimalist touch and no frills. A large work desk, accompanied by a smaller one on the side, clearly emphasizes that this is a place of work, above all else. Art by Satish Gujral and Krishen Khanna are the only embellishments. It is an office that is tranquil, not extravagant; and classy, without being pompous. And its occupant, of course, is the suave businesswoman, media baroness and ex-parliamentarian, Shobhana Bhartia.

I thought my research on Shobhana was pretty comprehensive when I sought her interview. I came in armed with an entire repertoire of knowledge on her life and work. She was a girl about my age and belonging to a traditional Marwari business family (just as I do) when she decided to take the hitherto unprecedented plunge into the world of media. This is where the similarities end. Shobhana was then a twenty-nine-year-old mother of two boys in their sub-teens. Aware as I am of the tremendous amount of disapproval that such unconventional moves would generate even now in conventional Marwari clans, I cannot honestly boast to claim that I fully fathomed what it must have meant to achieve this remarkable breakthrough back in the 80s.

Shobhana is said to have nagged her father, Krishna Kumar Birla, for years with her daily ritual of critiquing HT's news content. Until one day, K.K. Birla called his youngest daughter to his office, challenging her to prove her place. Convincing her father, it seems, had been the easy stage of this journey for Shobhana because, once she was a part of the institution, there seemed to be no dearth of critics all along the way. 'Initially, people felt that maybe I was going to the office only to pass my time and that I would eventually get bored and pack my bags or start doing something else. But when you stick it out, they know you're here to stay, and then after a couple of years, they start taking you a little more seriously,' she says.

I don't think I'll ever forget my first meeting with Shobhana. Dressed in an elegant cream-coloured sari, she greets me warmly. There is no bluster about her—she is perfectly poised and graceful, and I think of author and politician Shashi Tharoor's words—'Shobhana can hold her own intellectually, within any group—national or international. Her vision is clear and she is extremely pleasant to work with because of her openness to ideas and accessibility. In Shobhana Bhartia, you have the rare combination of an Indian woman professional, an international-standard manager and a news media executive with a clear sense of mission, all rolled into one.'

## FAMILY VALUES

Born into the royal family of corporate India, the illustrious Birlas, on 1 January 1957, Shobhana grew up in a newly independent India. Her grandfather, G.D. Birla had been a close associate and supporter of Mahatma Gandhi; the leader had, in fact, been living at the Birla residence in New Delhi when he was assassinated on the fateful day of 30 January 1948. (Birla Bhavan is now Gandhi Smriti, a museum dedicated to the Mahatma.)

'Ghanshyam Das Birla, my grandfather, was a strong-willed patriarch,' Shobhana recounts. 'In fact, both my father and my grandfather were powerful personalities, and, therefore, I was always slightly intimidated by them.'

A doting, yet meticulous father, K.K. Birla would chalk out his three daughters' daily routines with a healthy mix of fun, games and academics. 'Of course, my father was also very indulgent. Though he was a towering personality, it was my father we turned to every time we needed a little bit of pampering,' she says. The last-born of three sisters, by the time Shobhana was twelve, her older sisters were married, and she was the only child at home.

Her grandfather's long-standing relationship with Mahatma Gandhi and Jawaharlal Nehru, and her father's lifelong association with second-generation Congress stalwarts such as Indira Gandhi, made young Shobhana privy to the inside stories that shaped modern India. Shobhana reminisces how as a young girl she would listen wide-eyed to 'dinner-table conversation that recalled the many facets of life during India's struggle for independence or the state of the world.'

Despite growing up in a house brimming with luminaries and prominent guests, for Shobhana, her father was the true hero. 'My father was very close to Indira Gandhi, so I would hear a lot about her determination and what she stood for. I think I was really influenced only by my father, not by any political entity.' K.K. Birla, who was very involved in his business, worked right up to his passing, two months before he turned ninety. By then he had time to thoroughly evaluate his daughter's performance. When I ask Shobhana if she thinks her father was proud of her, she says, 'He did sometimes mention how proud he was of me, and he also said so in his autobiography. Nothing gave me greater satisfaction than trying to meet his expectations.'

K.K. Birla's influence is best evidenced in Shobhana's leadership of one of the largest media conglomerates in India. No matter where she is in the world, she scans the headlines on the front page and signs off as the editorial director before the paper goes to press every night. She might not be involved in the paper on a daily basis, but her total involvement in the editorial strategy and coverage makes Shobhana institutional in lending direction to the editorial division. Shobhana's looking at HT with 'microscopic lenses' has been her USP over three decades, bespeaking her strong work ethic. Just as her sharp eye does not miss proofing errors, she stays aware of developments across the world even as her professionally run editorial department translates them into leaders, news stories and features.

'She takes a keen interest in the editorial strategy and coverage on a regular basis so it's not a question of one story in which she is interested. She likes to know what we are doing and gives suggestions that we, in our capacity, take or don't take. That's how it works,' says Sanjoy Narayan, former editor-in-chief of the *Hindustan Times*.

Her grit and determination, Shobhana believes, are inherited from her mother, Manorama Devi. Never judgemental in her interactions with diverse people, Manorama taught young Shobhana through her deeds, more than with her words. 'Even if she did not approve of something you'd done, her commitment and love for you would stand undeterred. That is something which kept us all together and I am still learning that,' she says.

239
•

Despite her lineage and the Birla family's social stature, Shobhana's upbringing was simple and fairly typical of predominantly patriarchal Marwari families. A student of Kolkata's prestigious school, Loreto House, Shobhana believes that her academic days were 'a great leveller, and my surname was inconsequential.' The Bhartias have two sons—Priyavrat and Shamit—and Shobhana was a hands-on mother, staying home with her children until they were teenagers.

One of the earliest lessons she taught herself, Shobhana tells me, was to never assume the significance of one role over the next: 'I think it is important to remember that being a professional shouldn't have to mean discarding any other aspect completely. I think it's nice to be able to be sensitive and relate to family and friends, and yet have a clear vision of what you want to achieve in your professional life. I like focusing on both my professional and personal lives, but I don't mix them. It's a decision I have made.'

Kumar Mangalam Birla, chairman of the Aditya Birla Group and Shobhana's nephew, vouches for this—'I was once in a spot of trouble and she extended her help, giving me invaluable advice which has really seen me through. She probably didn't realize it herself, but that nugget of advice saw me through a very bad time and had a very positive influence on me.' Whenever his mother, Rajashree Birla, visits Delhi, Shobhana always makes time in her packed schedule to meet her. 'This makes me believe that she has a great balance in terms of work and life outside work and family,' he says. 'I also see her as being a very dynamic person who obviously understands her business very well. I genuinely think she has made the family proud.'

## FOLLOWING HER HEART

As a young woman, Shobhana had never spoken of her secret ambition to work in the media, and it was not expected of her. Those close to her, though, knew there was little doubt where her heart lay. Raised in a house where dinner-table conversations were about business, politics and the freedom struggle, Shobhana had always enjoyed a ringside view to the family empire. Why did she choose the media, then, with her father's blessings?

'It's like a cause, where you have the power to mould public opinion and the responsibility of moulding it for the betterment of society. Unless you have a certain passion for this cause and unless you feel strongly about society, about the nation, you can't be in the business of publishing,' she says.

Shobhana started a meticulous critical appraisal of the *Hindustan Times* — 'sort of interfering on a daily basis'—to prove that her interest was long term. She would examine the paper and bounce ideas off her father, pointing out news items he had missed. She was also tasked with supervising the *Sunday* magazine of the *Hindustan Times* and her in-depth scrutiny revealed to her father that she was there to stay.

K.K. Birla was a responsible industrialist who was aware that the *Hindustan Times* was a leading publication in a position of strength because of its high circulation and impressive profit-making in the 1980s. Inducting his untrained young daughter into the business meant that she would have to be made aware of every 'nut and bolt in the warehouse'. And Shobhana praises his foresight—'That's how I started, being trained for six months in every department—circulation, advertising, production, et al.'

It couldn't have been easy for her. The staff at HT was used to having the bosses live in Kolkata and to suddenly have the youngest Birla among them, appraising their contributions, was not a welcome change. Shobhana was looked upon as an intruder and her comments and suggestions were largely ignored as coming from someone with a lot of time to spare. She remained focused and calm. Members of her inner circle recollect that she would attend every editorial and management meeting, noting every point meticulously, without uttering a syllable. It was only after the meetings were over and the information minutely processed, that she would present her suggestions to her father in private.

Years later, when Shobhana took over as the vice chairperson and executive director in 1999, those who had doubted her capabilities sat up and watched her take over proceedings with a practised flair.

'Changing mindset or work routine is very difficult; getting people to give up bad old habits and pick up good new habits is equally difficult,' says Raghav Bahl, legendary media entrepreneur and founder of Network18. 'Shobhana has done a fabulous job in picking up an organization which was pretty mired in legacy, which was seen as an old-world product.' He believes that Shobhana has been very successful in turning the *Hindustan Times* 'into a modern new-age product and I don't just mean in terms of design. I think she has done a fabulous job not just in design but also in mindset.'

By 2000, when K.K. Birla and Shobhana had been working together for over a decade, the father was ready to hand over to the daughter; he was convinced, finally, that the newspaper had to be profitable on its own, but was not approving of how that would be achieved. The use of innovative advertisements, for example, did not go down well with him, and neither did the use of colour but he came around, eventually.

From changing a paper that had always been acclaimed for its patriotic flavour—where the profit motive was only a secondary one – to reorient the company as a profitable, professional and consumer-focused business, was one of the toughest challenges Shobhana faced. Despite obvious signs of being the heir, it took years of unflagging allegiance and hard work before she found herself taking over a position of power at HT Media Ltd. She went from being director, to executive director, and then vice chairperson but took over as chairperson only after her father's passing.

## GENDER BENDER

Shobhana's journey is instructive, not just for the media but also for working women in India. And especially at the time that she began working, in the 80s, it was much harder for a woman to prove herself. A member of the conservative Marwari community myself, I know that women could be involved in charitable work, but being in business was a strict no-no.

'Despite hailing from a fairly conservative Marwari family, Shobhana has gone on to become the First Lady of Indian media. I deeply admire her for her intellectual sophistication,' says Tharoor, adding that she is a very powerful role model because 'both men and women can see the determination, drive, decision-making and leadership that Shobhana brought to the once male-dominated professional world of media. She can be soft-spoken and firm all in one go, and I think it is due to this unique balance that Shobhana stands out as an icon for modern India.'

Bahl adds, 'When you are born into an influential and industrial family, there are certain expectations that follow. You are expected to be someone who can carry success heavily on your shoulders. Despite being so successful, she doesn't flaunt it or boast about it. She had the ability to bootstrap an old-world organization, pick it up from that level and convert it into a modern-day venture. What could be more inspiring than that?'

Aiming early on to take the newspaper to the Indian youth, Shobhana wasted little time in getting on board maverick thinkers and spin doctors to give HT a makeover. At the same time, she started the process of digitisation to gain accessibility, at a time when television news and the Internet had set off a massive news explosion.

The newspaper was turned into a sleek, well-designed and attractive spread, without a shred of compromise on its editorial content. And Shobhana was also one of the first to experiment with the size of the paper, recognizing how young professionals often read on the go while commuting, and she introduced the now-famous Berliner concept, as reflected in the *Mint* publication.

'Till a few years ago, HT was known as a rather dowdy publication, famous mainly for its badly written matrimonial ads. Apart from the editorials, op-eds and a few prominent editors' work, most of the paper was unreadable. But Shobhana pulled off a magical transformation. HT, today, is the most attractive paper visually, it's been the first to introduce colour photographs into the mainstream, it has lively features and editing, great writing and feisty columns,' says Tharoor.

In another landmark move, subsequent to the change in governmental policy on foreign direct investment in Indian print media, Shobhana sold a 20 per cent stake in Hindustan Times Media to Henderson Global Investors.

Subhash Chandra, the media mogul behind India's first satellite television channel, Zee TV, says, 'Undoubtedly, the 20 per cent stake sell to Henderson Global Investors by *Hindustan Times* was one of the biggest moves made by a media house in our country. It helped HT as a brand to make their presence felt globally and allowed her to expand in markets outside of Delhi—to Mumbai and other cities. It was a huge move on the part of the Hindustan Times and opened up fresh new horizons for the brand.'

As the first—and the youngest—chief executive of a national newspaper, Shobhana had quite a challenge ahead of her, fighting stereotypes and chauvinistic attitudes. She gritted her teeth and came to work every day, day after day, doggedly focusing on what was assigned to her, or what she assigned to herself. Her consistency and staying power finally did break the camel's back, and her in-house critics gradually learnt to appreciate her commitment. Ever the pragmatist, Shobhana believes that gender differences actually help efficiency and productivity because men and women bring different skills to the table, and she tells me that she has found that once you prove yourself, people tend to judge you and your work less.

She concedes, too, that while the challenges might be fewer for women in the corporate world today, societal expectations do not make their job easy, 'because each woman has many other issues apart from her profession. At the end of the day, you don't cease to be a homemaker, and you don't cease to be a wife or a mother or a sister or a daughter, unlike a man, who can pretty much leave everything at home.'

A working woman who is also a mother, Shobhana is no stranger to the dilemma millions of working women face when it comes to calibrating their dreams against their realities. She tells me that the trick is to follow your dreams and be invested fully in them, in the long term and not just the short term. In her own mind and life, Shobhana has always been very clear that she had just as much a role to play in the household as at work. Between her and her husband, they run a very successful business and media conglomerate with an expansive political, business and social network. Shyam Bhartia is chairman and managing director of the Rs 14 billion pharmaceutical firm Jubilant Life Sciences Limited, and Shobhana considers him a 'true partner and rare companion' for all times.

## A TRANSFORMATIVE LEADER

Against all odds, Shobhana has shifted the character of the *Hindustan Times* from being a follower, to being a leader and innovator in the market. While most media organizations run on bureaucracy and hierarchy, she has incorporated international-standard practices, inspired by the *Washington Post*.

Unlike her father who was known for his hands-on approach as a manager, Shobhana's knack has always been to choose the best in any domain and to then let them take over. From weaning Raju Narisetti away from the *Wall Street Journal* to launch *Mint*, she hired not only the biggest names in journalism, but also brought on board a host of professionals. Each one of them brought in fresh ideas, new ways of thinking and a wealth of experience. It is this assuredness in her that has allowed her senior management to enjoy complete independence, responsibility, trust, freedom and a lot of empowerment.

Some of the senior journalists Shobhana inducted went on to become individual brands in themselves. From her, I understand that this was a well-thought-out strategy and not a serendipitous development—'It's always good to create icons and to create brands, because when you help create a brand, that brand's success is linked to your success because that brand is associated with you. This is a very common marketing practice across various platforms.'

One of the key lessons that this hybrid management model has imparted is to not just respect the role of professionals in the firm but also respect their authority. Narayan concurs—'Her strength as a leader is people skills. She is able to spot and acquire the best talent and gets the best out of her people.'

Early into her leadership role, Shobhana realized that her plans for HT would need fresh resources, and a large sum of funds. She capitalized on the growing popularity and readership and floated a very successful IPO in 2005, raising about Rs 400 crore; the funds helped roll out Shobhana's ambitious plans.

Tharoor says, 'Over the last few years we have seen HT hire some very unusual people and also seen them leave. We saw the successful hiring of an Indian American to take over *Mint*, and once established and functioning effectively, move on. In a similar vein, she now has an eminent South African journalist on her team. So Shobhana really believes in higher standards and is unafraid to tap into international waters for it.'

'Look at what she has done,' Bahl says. 'She has not only changed the old-world approach of the newspaper in design or writing style, but has transformed an old-world newspaper wholly into a modern-day newspaper. Then she made that very fine entry into business journalism with the *Mint*. I think *Mint* is an extraordinary product. Then she had the courage and the plan to enter the Mumbai market which was totally dominated by one media player then.' Bahl believes her 'incredible success' is richly deserved. 'I don't think she got managing the business of a newspaper sense in inheritance . . . she didn't make any random discontinuous changes to her inheritance. I think she has made very positive discontinuous changes to that.'

Shobhana has spearheaded all these moves and ensured that they were successfully carried out. She started the group's business daily, *Mint* produced through an exclusive content-sharing deal with the *Wall Street Journal* and has partnered with Virgin Asia to launch FM radio Fever 104 channel. To my mind, she has been a leader who has transcended all barriers and myths.

On her legendary foresight and vision, Chandra says, 'When it comes to testing new horizons, she has far excelled any other media company. She has displayed the uncanny ability to spot and exploit trends; she has also ventured into the digital space much before anyone else did. Soon after we came into the market, she launched Home TV, then entered the radio space and, of course, several other news portals. She has helped diversify her brand in a big way and as a leader, has been forging new opportunities and going all guns blazing.'

## ROLLING WITH THE PUNCHES

Shobhana, of course, had her own share of problems. Home TV, the television venture she launched in the 1990s with the help of leading television personality Karan Thapar, went belly up soon after. 'It's true that the returns did not come in as quickly as we had expected them to, but I think we should have stuck in there for a couple of years. If we had staying power, we would have had a great first-mover advantage and would have captured a larger chunk of the market,' she says.

Bahl has a slightly different take on this issue. 'On television, [Shobhana] wanted to enter the entertainment segment. She could have been a pioneer and could have picked up the strength of her media group; they are very solid news players. I would say that it was a wrong entry point. But despite having a wrong entry point, I believe she should have shown a little more resilience in staying there because as we all saw, the tide turned. She left it slightly early in the curve of entertainment TV. In a nutshell, the problem was not just that they entered too early but also, that they exited too early.'

Not one to pick at wounds, Shobhana, however, still seems a tad wary of entering the television space just yet. 'I can say on record that I am not launching a TV channel. I don't know what we might do in the future, but at this point, we are not getting into television. With regard to the completely independent business venture, we had an alliance with the *Wall Street Journal* only for content, but no equity,' she says.

If Home TV was a setback, HT's radio venture—Fever 104 FM— has emerged successful. Following a tie-up with Richard Branson's Virgin Radio, HT had made its foray in 2005. While the station stands to be No. 1 in Delhi today, it has also managed a strong foothold in metros like Kolkata, Bengaluru or Mumbai, with a significant reach and presence. And then there is the success of her pioneering FDI venture.

R.C. Bhargava, chairman of Maruti Suzuki, has known Shobhana since 1973–74. When he was chair of the Doon Public School Society, he requested her to join the board. 'She agreed to join as one of our directors with no hassles or airs. She carried her intelligence, grace and dedication with élan,' he says.

After she took charge of *Hindustan Times*, Shobhana brought about nothing less than a design revolution, seeking suggestions from the legendary Katharine Graham (who, like Shobhana, had the conviction to break away from tradition to take up the challenging leadership of the family-run *Washington Post*) and recruited an art director Graham recommended to redesign HT. 'Change with continuity; Content is king,' are her twin mantras.

But she has done more than that. Shobhana has changed the rules of the game.

The emergence of India's first and much-anticipated Luxury Conference, besides the HT Leadership Summit as important annual events in the global calendar stands testimony to her remarkable thought leadership. Shobhana says, '[These] events were very consciously created, looking at a certain positioning. They give an edge in terms of saying that here are the important issues: we'll frame the issues; we'll try and provide solutions and answers to them. So, it's a very natural extension of what the brand stands for.'

After the Home TV debacle, Shobhana took two major decisions, putting her grit to the test. The first was to launch HT in Mumbai—the stronghold of the ToI group from the very onset; the second, to reposition *Hindustan*— their Hindi daily, as the nation's first all-colour Hindi publication.

Never one to shy away from a fight, Shobhana took on rivals *Times of India* with the same fearlessness that she displays in her own company. *Hindustan Times* had been the capital's leading daily for decades, earning a lion's share of the ad revenue when media houses were looked upon as public service institutions. But with the onset of the commodification of newspapers in the late 1980s, *Times of India* began inching its way towards *Hindustan Times* in terms of circulation, readership and revenue, and the latter posted an operating loss for the first time ever in 2000. That was when Shobhana announced a sizeable investment to rejuvenate *Hindustan Times*; she confesses that while HT did not think of ToI as a competitor earlier, they do now, and are not complacent about it. Yet the major difference between the two, Shobhana points out, is that editors at HT are promoted as brands.

But Bahl believes it's no big deal. 'Isn't it an epic battle in the marketplace? While Shobhana has not yet won the market share that she would like to have, I think she has launched a very worthy product and market share will come.'

Chandra speaks of this remarkable quality of hers—'One of the greatest lessons I learnt from her, was that there is no substitute for hard work. Hailing from a legendary industrial family, she didn't have an inherent need to work. But she did. Putting in hours, days and years of persistent effort and enjoying it along the way, she has been a tremendous influence to those around her.'

Spending time with Shobhana, one appreciates her unfaltering composure and grace, which are perhaps a reflection of her philosophy of life. With every failure she confronts, she allows it to teach her a greater life lesson. 'You have to bounce back. Fortunately, god has been kind, and we have excelled in every venture other than Home TV,' she says. 'You can't shy away from failure; instead, you learn from failure and you come back stronger and you take that risk again.'

When I ask her about how far these risks have taken her, she is true to character and modest in her assessment. Though HT Mumbai is a spectacular success, Shobhana prefers to think of it as having met expectations. By all accounts, the Hindi newspaper *Hindustan* is clearly the fastest growing in its genre. 'I think you need to get into a business only if you have the stomach for it,' Shobhana adds. 'Business means ups and downs; it means successes and failures. There is no sure-shot recipe for success only. Endless companies wind up, they go belly up, and people go bankrupt, but you have to have the grit to stay in there.'

When asked about her online attempts that had been 'bleeding' for a while, she admits that even though it was a concern, a gestation period is inevitable and cannot be avoided. As for the radio business, the verdict may already be out, but Shobhana, not one to give up on optimism, still maintains a stoic silence. For all of the company's successes, Shobhana is quick to emphasize that the team—a mix of media and non-media experts and veterans—has played a key role.

In the turf war between editorial freedom and marketing demands, Shobhana has refrained from 'dumbing down' of content; the management does not interfere in editorial decisions at HT. A journalist at heart, she emphasizes that there is no 'linking our editorial integrity with our revenues'. The senior management further reiterates how there is no conflict possible because it is very clear that the editorial division is not linked in any way to the commercial division. I note that this is something rare, a harmonious marriage between editorial integrity and marketing needs, with a leader at the helm who has passion for journalism as well as the Birla DNA of keen business acumen.

Narayan says, 'Shobhana gives people enough room to be independent, a lot of empowerment, responsibility, trust and freedom without being overpowering at all. She has a perfect professional strategy of running a company in a professional manner because professional managers, whether they are in business or in editorial, enjoy a great deal of independence and empowerment. That's her style!'

The late Prime Minister Rajiv Gandhi had, when in office, initiated the policy for inducting non-academicians as chairs of national universities and he invited Shobhana to lead a college affiliated to Delhi University as the chairperson. Always seeking to structurally address the lack of skilled people, Shobhana continuously explored the possibility of institutionalising journalism and took the decision forward during her stint at Delhi University.

In 2006, the United Progressive Alliance, under the leadership of Sonia Gandhi, nominated Shobhana to the Rajya Sabha, a rare honour for the head of a media company. The nomination spoke volumes not just about Shobhana's accomplishments but also the respect she has fostered across fields. But her journey to the Rajya Sabha was not smooth—a public interest litigation was filed, questioning her political affiliations and credibility in being nominated to the Upper House under the four permissible disciplines of literature, social service, art and science. 'She is not even a journalist, only a media baron,' leading lawyer Prashant Bhushan had argued in court. But the Supreme Court didn't take very long to dismiss the PIL, declaring the scope of 'social service' as wide enough to recognize her function as one of the most eminent voices in journalism today—or as she is often called, a veritable 'paper tigress'.

During her political career, Shobhana served in various capacities such as member, Committee on Finance; member, Committee on Empowerment of Women; member, Committee on External Affairs, among others. She was quite vocal on the floor of the Rajya Sabha about a range of issues, from child marriage abolition (she played a seminal role behind the enactment of the Child Marriage Abolition Act in 2007) to achieving empowerment through education, and the eminent US–India Civil Nuclear Agreement.

'She has conducted herself in the House quite independently—and Shobhana's conduct was honourable,' says Bahl. 'She was an active parliamentarian and by virtue of the fact that she was also the editorial director of a mainstream daily, I think she brought a very different perspective to various issues.'

'She has done a six-year stint as an MP in the Rajya Sabha and been very active, unlike any other nominated MP who takes a back seat,' Narayan says.

## A STANDARD OF GRACE

Despite being at the helm of a giant media empire spread across India, Shobhana is a private person who shuns the limelight. In fact getting her to agree to this interview took a fair amount of work as she is known to give interviews rarely.

Shobhana's structured schedules and precise ways are now legendary. And as one is told, ad nauseam, the values we learn as children remain with us through life, the same is true for her. K.K. Birla was a stickler for punctuality. And in his introduction to Krishna Kumar Birla's *Brushes with History: An Autobiography* (2009), Vir Sanghvi says about Shobhana, 'If she is five minutes early for lunch with him [K.K. Birla], she will drive around the block till it is time.' Punctuality and time management are crucial to her juggling act of heading a media conglomerate and being a wife, mother and family member. Her view on the matter is crisp, 'When you accept that you cannot do all that you would like to do, getting one's priorities right is the obvious answer.'

Recipient of one of India's most respected awards, the Padma Shri, in 2005, the World Economic Forum, Davos named Shobhana the Global Leader of Tomorrow way back in 1996. She has featured on several *Forbes* listings: '15 to Watch in Asia' in 2008, Power List 2012, and richest Indians, and also Indian Express Power List 2012. In 2009, she received the Outstanding Women Leader Award among the host of other felicitations that have come her way. In 2018, she was named the world's 88th most powerful woman by *Forbes*.

Characteristically, Shobhana refuses to make much fuss over awards and recognitions—'The awards are important in the light that they help motivate the organization.' Her greatest award, I reckon, is the high recall of brand

*Hindustan Times*. It bears testimony to Shobhana's commitment, perseverance and vision. As we chat she says, candidly, 'It's not easy to foresee. It's a difficult call. Consumption habits have changed and brand loyalty is not what it used to be.'

In a world in which tweets move at the speed of light and the citizen journalist seldom needs to rely on the reporter, Shobhana realizes how the landscape has dramatically changed, 'Most of these tweets are made by ordinary citizens who are tweeting about an event or quickly uploading files on YouTube. Aren't they the media as well? The first few pictures that we got out of Mumbai when 26/11 happened were by citizens.'

She predicts the emergence of many more platforms that will allow and encourage news, and the newspaper will only be one of them. 'But what will actually help the newspaper is the credibility of its brand,' she says. 'So, in the future, consumers will opt for news from multiple sources, like their smartphones, and will not wait to read the HT or watch one of the known television channels, but when they want to rely on that information, when they want to see how credible the information is, when they want to analyse the information, then they will turn to a known brand, and therefore, brands like HT will thrive.'

Nonplussed, I ask, 'So, what's the way forward for HT and for the media industry as a whole?' Shobhana responds with conviction, 'I think the more and more we look at ourselves as being content providers, the better we'll be able to leverage content over multiple platforms depending on the consumption patterns of the target groups. So, I see a huge growth going forward . . . At the moment, we are still very much stuck in the whole groove of being a newspaper. I would like to see HT being thought of less as a newspaper in the years to come and more as a content provider. And that content can be leveraged in several ways through technology. Our USP is the integrity and credibility of our content.'

Along with the commitment to strengthen the brand, HT is as committed to the digital environment. With an enormous amount of resources being plugged into integrating and refurbishing their newsrooms to suit the changing climate, Shobhana's strategy to strengthen their websites and presence on social media platforms like Twitter and Facebook, has been gaining phenomenal strides over the last few years. Going by the way HT is poised for the future, it seems it is more than ready to welcome and embrace change.

Subhash Chandra has little doubt of the extent of influence Shobhana has had on her brand. He explains, 'If you asked me, I would say brand Zee is much bigger than Subhash Chandra will ever be. But Shobhana Bhartia and *Hindustan Times* have an interesting correlation between themselves and it would be difficult to gauge which excels the other. To the reader, *Hindustan Times*, the brand, might stand out in a distinct light. But in industry, political, bureaucratic or even business circles, Shobhana Bhartia often far outshines the very brand she has helped revive.'

In a sense, the families and associations she heralded from have played a significant part in her illustrious journey. Besides her own lineage, her husband Shyam Sunder Bhartia is the scion of another well-known business family, and the chairman and managing director of the Rs 14 billion pharmaceutical firm Jubilant Life Sciences Limited (a spin-off from the earlier chemicals venture Vam Organics) with interests in pharmaceuticals, speciality chemicals, fast food chains, oil and gas, aerospace and IT sectors.

And Shobhana's story is her own—that of a young woman stepping out of a traditional business family to prove her mettle as a true inheritor of its entrepreneurial DNA. I find it especially remarkable that she did not prepare for any of this at a prestigious foreign university, and yet she has repeatedly brought in a fresh and unique perspective to everything she does. Being a Birla has helped, of course, but it is Shobhana's own fortitude, feistiness and sharpness that have made her the changemaker she is.

Conversing with her and studying her life, I understand that true power cannot always be seen or quantified. Power lies in a vision, and the goals that one sets to realize the vision; it lies in the ability to delegate with conviction and trust; to accept success with humility, and failure with equanimity, but to learn from it; it lies in raising the bar higher but in knowing when to stop. It also lies in being able to embrace your femininity and grace, while leading from the front. Shobhana Bhartia epitomizes this power best every day as she moulds the opinions of the world's largest democracy.

# SANJIV GOENKA

*Padma Shri recipient,* **Shobhana Bhartia,** *chairperson and editorial director of* Hindustan Times, *has changed the way an entire nation reads its news. A witness and compatriot to this journey has been* **Sanjiv Goenka**, *the chairman of the RPG-Sanjiv Goenka Group, and the scion of the luminary Goenka lineage. In a free-wheeling chat, Goenka lays bare what went into the making of the 'First Lady of Indian Media' and how she continues to inspire him.*

### Please share your earliest memories of Shobhana.

I grew up in Calcutta, a city where the Birla name worked like magic. It represented everything that one can expect from a name—success, respect, idealism and tradition. Nevertheless, the Marwari ladies shunned the limelight. Both Birla bahus and Birla girls were known only for their involvement with charities but not with hardcore business. Therefore, Shobhana can almost be likened to a rebel in her breaking through the barrier to enter the erstwhile men-only business arena. Over the years that I have known her, I have seen her transform from a conservative Marwari young woman into a confident, capable leader; a leader who has the courage and conviction to hold her own against anyone and everyone.

### You were very fond of Shobhana's father, K.K. Birla, and have looked at him with a lot of respect. How do you think Shobhana has taken the legacy forward, which was shaped and nurtured by her father?

K.K. Birla's fame extended to a world which lay beyond the immediate periphery of business. He had qualities which rendered him eminently suitable to be a press lord. The value system that he was known for forms an essential part of Shobhana now. She takes care to develop the relationships that he built and nurtured. I also think she is quite candid in how she expresses herself, very much like her father, and, like him, is very clear in her thoughts. I would like to say here that I think of her as someone who has surpassed her father in the field of publishing in very many ways. The *Hindustan Times* is what it is today because of Shobhana.

## How would you describe her remarkable business acumen and leadership?

Shobhana is a change agent, who is constantly reinventing HT. There has been phenomenal growth in terms of what HT used to be and what it is.

Shobhana has brought about change in the organization, presentation, thought processes and the calibre of the people. She has introduced a system of meritocracy, which is no longer based on loyalties, but on capabilities and confidence. Her transformation of HT from a completely privately owned to a public listed media conglomerate, her response to both investors and readers, reveals her clear focus that it is her reader who is her constituency.

Shobhana is very much her own person. She has transformed what she inherited from her father into a strong and formidable national conglomerate and is creating a much more challenging legacy for the next generation. She is someone whom I deeply admire and respect.

## What do you think are some of the similarities and differences between the business styles of Shobhana and her father; and how has the Birla lineage influenced her?

While it has not been my privilege to work closely with K.K. *babu* in the business arena, I have heard people commend his style of operation, fairness in dealing with people and his transparency. Shobhana has inherited those legacies. To my mind, she has probably redefined the way people look at '*the* Birla'. Having said that, you can't take away upbringing from a person and the influence of your family and people around you. I believe her instincts were defined by the people around her. As the first-generation Birla woman to take the unconventional route from every point of view, she has done wonders.

## How would you evaluate Shobhana's leadership style vis-à-vis that of her contemporaries?

At the outset, I think that they all have different styles and yet are all extremely successful. I think Shobhana is somebody who is amazingly frank in her expression, clear in her thought and vision, and she is bold. Launching *Mint*, for instance, was a very forthright decision which has paid off successfully now. The way she has redesigned and reformatted the daily takes a substantial amount of vision and courage. I know how difficult it can be to transform any old organization.

## How much has Shobhana influenced or inspired you as a person?

In various ways. She is someone who is remarkably frank, very truthful and straightforward. To me, that is an important learning: how one can be straightforward without being offensive even in an unpleasant or adverse situation. I think the more I interact with her, the more I am inspired by her. She leads people of very significant stature and earns their respect, while remaining humble. She reaches out to you just as a person. She is not the publisher of HT when she meets you, she is just Shobhana. And it is always a pleasure to meet her and watch her grow from strength to strength. She has reached the zenith of a torch-bearing business without sacrificing the softness which comes with a great family title.

## What are the key messages for women from Shobhana's life and career?

Not only did she break away from the idea that Birla women don't work, but she has achieved phenomenal professional success. Shobhana is efficient and great at multitasking, managing her home, family and business with equal dedication. In fact, she is on top of everything and is there for everyone who is close to her. This apart, she is informed and up to date on most relevant things. I think this ability to grasp, to sort of weed out that which is unnecessary and retain the necessary is very important. Her memory is phenomenal and she has a remarkable talent for reinvention. She continues to be humane in the way she reacts to people and reaches out to them, the way she stands up for people.

To me, it is these human values that so completely inform her vision and her leadership, which are inspirational; and I think these are all great attributes. She possesses toughness without giving up grace, endless energy, a clear vision and faith.

# INDU
# JAIN

•

*Ma's strengths are her supreme confidence and courage of conviction. On the other hand, she is also childlike and uncomplicated, never afraid to ask questions. That's why she brings freshness into the home and workplace, placing everything in perspective.*

**—THE JAIN FAMILY**

•

*B*efore my appointment with Padma Bhushan recipient Indu Jain, I spent days, if not weeks, preparing to interview her. It was part of my process before meeting each woman achiever who is featured in this book. While I did my homework and honed my background research before every interview, I consciously kept an open mind.

A part of me expected to meet a driven media baroness, in the manner of the late and legendary Katharine Graham, publisher of the *Washington Post*. Here would be someone who walks into newsrooms to chat with reporters; who analyses consumption patterns and confers with senior editors and managers; who sets the agenda for government and society. Yet, I kept in mind one of the most important lessons I have learnt while writing this book—you only understand someone when you are allowed into their world, and can converse with them within their context.

Bennett, Coleman & Company, publisher of the *Times of India*, is one of the world's most powerful media groups. Apart from this flagship newspaper, which has the highest circulation of all English dailies in the world, the group also publishes the *Economic Times,* the financial daily with the highest circulation in India, and the second highest in the world. With 7000 employees and a turnover in excess of $700 million, it publishes twenty-nine niche magazines, partners with the *Huffington Post* in India, and owns thirty-two radio stations and television channels such as *Times Now*, *Zoom* and *ET Now*.

The chairperson of BCCL, the acronym by which the company is universally known, is seventy-eight-year-old Indu Jain, who is the matriarch overseeing an empire valued at over $4 billion.

In the maelstrom of adrenaline and chop-change that the media is, hers is a name synonymous with respect and the kind of power that cannot be calculated by circulation figures, rankings or revenue. She is regularly courted by India's rich and powerful, by politicians and business tycoons alike, all hoping to curry favour with the many newspaper, magazine, television, radio, Internet and regional media brands that come under her jurisdiction. Yet, no matter how much and how thoroughly one researches Indu Jain, one never knows quite what to expect until one meets her.

People who have spent time with her attest to coming away with an experience that is distinctly enlightening, uplifting almost. 'Indu's interests are spiritual,' says Shashi Tharoor, politician and author, who had a chance encounter with her years ago, which left a lasting impression. He tells me he was staying at the Times of India guest house in Mumbai, and had breakfast with Indu, who was on her way to a retreat; they spoke about spirituality for over an hour and a half. 'At her age, the tremendous desire to learn, the quest for knowledge beyond worldly concerns, was very much there. She obviously reads a lot, and so it was not an ignorant person's quest; it was a knowledgeable person's quest and I found that richly rewarding.'

I am on my own quest, and so this is something to which I am keenly looking forward. As I drive into the grounds of Indu's palatial two-storied bungalow in the heart of Lutyens' Delhi, I am enveloped by an overriding sense of calm and tranquillity. Waiting outside her office, I admire a sculpture, a replica of the feet—perhaps Lord Mahavira's—that adorn all Jain temples. When I am led inside her sprawling office on the ground floor—3000 square feet of space furnished and upholstered entirely in white—Indu, dressed in a spotless white sari, greets me with a beatific smile and a blessing. She is the epitome of serenity and her presence seems to draw me magnetically.

Even before we begin the interview, Indu makes it clear that she wants me to write about her life only through the lens of her spirituality—'I am frequently asked how I combine my spiritual and business lives. I think the answer is that my office is merely an extension of my spirituality and my desire to share my knowledge, happiness and love with others. Essentially, bringing synergy between the inner and outer worlds is true spirituality. People attract attention; I don't. That's why you won't find much written about me. I don't desire to be written about so much. If I wanted, it would have been so,' she says.

In a controlled and measured voice, Indu tells me that these days, she prefers to spend most of her time at ashrams or retreats with her guru, Sri Sri Ravi Shankar. She periodically comes home to this bungalow in Delhi, to spend time with her sons, Samir and Vineet, and her newborn granddaughter Urshila. They live in an adjoining bungalow with their families. 'I was born a seeker. I was very curious to explore,' says Indu, answering my question about the roots of her spirituality. The way she has lived her life is a testament to this conviction.

## THE TIMES FAMILY

Indu was born on 8 September 1936, to a Jain Agarwal family in Faizabad, Uttar Pradesh. She married Ashok Jain, whose family belonged to the prominent mercantile Sahu Jain community from Najibabad, Uttar Pradesh. The couple had three children—Samir, Nandita and Vineet. Ashok was the eldest son of Sahu Shanti Prasad Jain, who went on to run a business empire which consisted primarily of large cement, jute and sugar mills. Shanti Prasad became the owner and chairman of BCCL in 1948 when his father-in-law, Ram Kishan Dalmia, sold the firm to him. The family was based in Alipore, Kolkata, the city that was home to other illustrious business families such as the Goenkas, Birlas and Thapars.

Shanti Prasad, a legendary figure in the media, started the journey to making the *Times of India* the country's leading newspaper. While it took on Ramnath Goenka's *Indian Express* in the early days, it was in the 1950s that magazines including *Filmfare*, *Femina* and Hindi periodicals *Dharmayug* and *Parag* were launched, marking the beginning of the Jains' involvement and interest in the media business, which has never waned.

In 1969, due to a legal dispute, a Mumbai high court ruling asked for the board of Bennett Coleman to be disbanded and a new one constituted. The next seven years were considered the 'zero years' of the company, control being returned to the Jains only in August 1976. At that point, Ashok Jain took over BCCL and Shanti Prasad stepped down to devote himself to philanthropy and social work. Ashok, a dynamic science graduate from Presidency College, Calcutta, set to work, reviving his inheritance.

Tragedy struck in 1999, when Ashok—who had had a long history of heart ailments and had undergone three bypass surgeries—did not survive a heart transplant operation in Cleveland, USA. He was sixty-five when he passed away. The family business was now in the hands of Indu, who had to balance her grief, that of her children, and manage a complex media business of which she knew little. 'Entering the corporate world was like developing another aspect of my personality,' she says to me.

Conventional wisdom holds that a person's mettle is tested in times of adversity, which bring out either the best or the worst in each one. While writing this book, I have met women like Anu Aga and Rajashree Birla, who crafted new identities with strength and grace after the death of a loved one, their resilience withstanding grief and loss. So it was with Indu.

Through her hard work and unique social awareness, she took the Times Group to a new level, in India and abroad. Aided by her sons Samir, the ideas person, and Vineet, the implementer, the Times Group, under her leadership and guidance, diversified into many fields and became very profitable. To an outsider, the charting of this success by someone completely new to the industry seems inexplicable.

In 1987, Samir took charge of the company while Indu played a guiding role. She has been the silent force within the Times Group, ensuring that the responsibilities inherent in a powerful media empire are not neglected. She believes that the role of the media is one of great responsibility because it has the power to make or break people—'We, being the largest media group, take it very seriously that news should be delivered as news and not sensation and handle it with utmost care. The content has become more responsible and the media is being used as a tool to cause real and positive change in society. I think we are heading in the right direction.'

Talking about the different phases of the Indian media, Indu points out that in the beginning, every little development or incident was portrayed sensationally—'Although that can still be seen today, audiences have matured. Media should give positive suggestions. It should be like a friend, philosopher and guide to the rulers of the country.'

In a country as large and distinct as India, people's priorities, languages, tastes, and the issues they face, vary vastly. This diversity sets India apart from most developed nations, which tend to have homogeneous societies that allow for media penetration to be nearly total. The challenge in this country, Indu believes, 'is to be so comprehensive that you appeal to everybody while being responsible. So, while many things in the media in developed nations have been tried, tested and set in stone, our media will continue to experiment with new things for a long time [to] find the right note that resonates across all these different people, find stories and issues that matter to everybody. People are getting more and more interested now in how the country is being governed. In such a scenario, the media has a very critical role to play.'

Her own biggest achievement, Indu feels, 'is having great torchbearers and big-hearted people for all the departments of the Times Group and the great synergy they bring together in making the *Times of India* what it is today. Of course, the strong foundation has been laid by the two brothers [Samir and Vineet] with their infrangible togetherness.'

Her primary role has been to act as elder statesman and a mediator between the various power centres. Indeed, she is often referred to as Shri

Maa within BCCL—'I aim to lend my ears to everyone in order to support the group. To be called Shri Shri Maa will take a little more time.' She describes her role as chairperson as a peacemaker, easing conflicts at all levels, removing any friction that happens and resolving problems. 'Communication and a sense of camaraderie are important. For any relationship to progress, there needs to be detachment within the attachment,' she says.

Eminent designer and curator Rajeev Sethi, who has known Indu for four decades, says, 'She struck me as a serene and extremely sensitive person with a quicksilver mind—the mind and her eyes connected to her spirit.'

I begin to understand the importance of what he is saying when I ask Indu what her prime concerns are as chairperson of the group. Her answer is succinct and simple—'Bringing balance, synergy and respect for one another's performance.' To the hard-nosed, rather more cynical journalists, such a mission was bewildering at first.

The *Times of India*'s prominent writer and editor, Bachi Karkaria, in her book, *Behind the Times* (2010), writes of how when Indu Jain told the staff at her regularly convened meetings that she 'wanted a kinder, gentler, happier paper', they were all gravely sceptical, having been inured to reporting on 'doom and disaster'. The writer concedes later that over the years, '. . . from this has been distilled the positive approach to the daily dose of calamity—the emphasis on the spark of human goodness which elevates all tragedy. Readers have embraced this enthusiastically.'

Some of Indu Jain's most favoured causes have been environment, peace, education, and, most effective of all, *saha-bhagi*, or harnessing people power in government and municipal decision-making. She has been most successful in getting those with influence to support these causes. Another aspect of how her spiritual orientation has permeated a space that seems traditionally immune to this dimension is the Times Foundation, which is her creation. Under its aegis, a space has been created in the Mumbai offices of the Times of India for free classes to be held on anything from reiki and yoga to the Bhagvad Gita. In Delhi, after her daughter's untimely passing, Indu converted her bungalow on Tilak Marg to a centre of wellness for public use.

Be it the Times Foundation, the corporate social responsibility arm of BCCL, or various trusts and societies such as the Bharatiya Jnanpith Trust, Sahu Jain Charitable Society, Ram Charitable Trust, Sahu Jain Trust and SP Foundation—the underlying principle for each is to give back to society and change the lives of the have-nots. Indu says that the basic intention has always been to give people the opportunity to experience *anand* (happiness) in giving, more than receiving. The Times Relief Fund and the Community Services and Research Foundation both work under the aegis of the foundation as well. The group also instituted a number of awards, including the prestigious Jnanpith Awards, in the field of art and culture, along with the widely popular beauty pageant Miss India, Filmfare Awards for cinema and the Economic Times Awards for corporate excellence.

Sethi says, 'The concept of giving comes very naturally to her; it is not a ritual superstition, it is just sharing that helps you grow and I think that there is certainly more CSR. Indu is deeply pained by the sinking of the spiritual space, and I think the foundation tries to recapture that space. She is concerned about this and eager to communicate it in a way that can be shared, and, that, I think is good.'

The Times Foundation, which has been built up by Indu, works under the motto, Your mission is our mission. Its motive is clear—to give back, help those in need and make a difference to the world at large. The foundation ensures that every issue it supports gets the space and attention it deserves, even from the government, and is sustainable after the initial momentum it is given. Working towards setting it up and monitoring the foundation have been very fulfilling for her. The work undertaken by the Times Foundation has been critically acclaimed across the world. In 2016, President Pranab Mukherjee awarded Indu the Padma Bhushan, India's third-highest civilian award.

'A lot more needs to be done in the area of better and clean governance. It should allow only people with impeccable honesty and integrity to contest elections; caste and religion politics need to be checked; and the elections should be held by open, transparent funding. Good health facilities should be available to all strata of society, and be better spread across the country in order to take the pressure off larger states or cities,' Indu says.

For Indu, spirituality and corporate social responsibility go hand-in-hand, and she shares her experience of corporate philanthropy in the Indian context—'Corporations have been doing much more than is publicized. They are extremely shy of advertising it. Even media talks only about their earnings and growth but hardly speaks about their giving back. The *Economic Times* again has been the pioneer in celebrating corporate social responsibility through Social Impact Awards.'

## AND HER NEXT MISSION?

'Popularizing spirituality in each reader's home and creating respect for all the faiths is my yet-to-be achieved milestone.'

Now the penny drops for me, as it were, and I understand why Indu insisted on spirituality being the focus of our conversation—it is at the fulcrum of everything she does. There is, and can never be, any other way to understand her and her life.

## GOD IS FUN

If one takes an objective view of BCCL over the past two decades, its milestones are numerous—the group now has a bouquet of brands; has penetrated new markets, packaged news in a reader-friendly format, pioneered the popularity of Page 3, implemented an aggressive pricing strategy; and reinvented itself several times over to stay relevant and ahead in the game. In this context, I think Indu's biggest contribution has, perhaps, been infusing the Times Group with her unique spiritual awareness and social sensibilities.

The Times Group was among the first to publish an independent newspaper dedicated to spirituality—*The Speaking Tree*—and is today involved in countless philanthropic and social projects. 'Remember, god is fun,' says Indu cheekily. 'The *Speaking Tree* is primarily an idea that Samir fought for because he felt that people did not speak much about spirituality.' The two of them recognized that even though the media was averse to addressing the topic, there was a need for someone to do so.

It started out as a daily article on the edit page, covering philosophical topics in an approachable way. It was a pioneering thing to do for, as Karkaria points out in another book, *The Times of Ideas*, 'Newspapers have traditionally been the dominion of the rational and tangible, their stock-in-trade is the fate of nations, political and economic . . . lifestyle and entertainment . . . but these too were of the Here and Now. The *Times* decided that, to be a complete newspaper, it had to go beyond, and explore the inner core as well.'

Its placement on the edit page is not intended to 'strike at the root of editorial convention,' Karkaria clarifies. 'In fact, the layout of the paper draws from cosmic temple design: temporal sculptures on the outer periphery, and the idol in its sanctum sanctorum deep within. Care has been taken to nurture *The Speaking Tree* so that it does not become esoteric and arcane. It brings experts to explain the meaning of life, but in the scientific, empirical idiom of today.'

That single article at the base of the edit page transformed into a weekly Sunday newspaper. Now most newspapers devote some space to 'sacredness', an article, a reflection, an illuminating insight from a spiritual leader that offers hope and a pathway to inner freedom.

Apart from being an entrepreneur, Indu is a philanthropist, a champion of education and a passionate lover of art and culture. Currently the chairperson of the Bharatiya Jnanpith Trust, Indu supports the development and promotion of all major languages in India. Especially close to her heart is the work being done by Nitya-a-Nandita, a unique spiritual centre based in New Delhi. Dedicated to promoting education, self-development, alternative healing, holistic belief systems and female empowerment, the centre, in keeping with its central philosophy of promoting *Advaita*, the non-duality of *atman* and *brahman* or the absolute, seeks to revitalize Indian society. The one field that she has not participated in, even though she was keen to at one point, is politics. It was her daughter, Nandita, who dissuaded her, saying she could achieve far more and do a better job behind the scenes than in the forefront of politics. 'And she was right,' admits Indu.

When I remind her that in an address to a peace summit, she had once said, 'Give women a chance and non-violence will effortlessly be the religion of the new millennium'—she smilingly retorts, 'Since god has always chosen women to be of the highest stature and run the universe, so should the government.'

Indu is also the guiding force behind the Oneness Forum, which she launched in 2003; it works towards promoting unity in the world. The Mahavira-Mahatma award, which she instituted under the aegis of the forum, is her attempt to promote Mahatma Gandhi's principle of ahimsa (non-violence). Recipients of the award include Sri Sri Ravi Shankar, and Dr Daisaku Ikeda, president of Soka Gakkai International.

While she has been naturally drawn to spirituality and is a follower of Lord Mahavira since childhood, later in life she accepted Sri Sri Ravi Shankar as her guru. She explains that a guru is a dispeller of darkness and having a guru has made a difference to her own consciousness and perception.

'I have moved from one guru to another and have been a devout believer of each one at that very moment. Each time that I have met a new guru, it has transformed me as a person,' she says.

I ask her why anyone would need to follow a guru if, indeed, the aim of spirituality is to grow oneself.

'Does having a teacher make learning math simpler? Would you like to join a university without a professor? Make your life simpler, find a guru.'

Popularising Indian heritage and culture, especially among the youth, takes up a lot of Indu's energy. In order to remain centred and develop a holistic view of life, young people need to focus on nurturing their inner world along with acquiring skills that help them succeed in the material world, she thinks. 'In the ancient tradition of a *gurukul*, a guru pointed you in the right direction, both within yourself and in the world around you,' she says, reiterating the importance of having the right guru for guidance.

When I ask Indu if it is possible to balance the often conflicting demands of running a business and being spiritual, she explains to me that there is actually a strong connection between spirituality and modern management because every person needs to triumph over themselves before winning over the world. She believes that management skills need to be tempered with self-awareness, and self-love.

## THE PURSUIT OF HAPPINESS

The more popular branches of Hindu philosophy associate acquiring wealth with maya (illusion), and equate spirituality with abstinence and renunciation. Indu, however, believes that life cannot be lived on such black-and-white terms—'Do you think Krishna, who was so wealthy, was in *moh* and maya? If everything is *brahman*, what would you renounce? It is a synergy, a balance to welcome both into life. My knowledge, my love, my *anandam* are shared in my office too.'

As I listen to Indu discuss the semantics of spirituality in a modern context, I am curious to know what she thinks of where contemporary Indians are, in the cycle of spiritual evolution. With a booming economy, and flourishing globalization, the youth are at an interesting crossroads, in their inner and outer lives.

'Indian spirituality has a lot of depth to offer and it is finding an appeal in youngsters now. Spirituality should be simplified and modernized for the youth to be able to implement it in their everyday life. It should be live, interactive and fun-oriented. During any kind of disturbances, it is important to find your way back home, to the centre of the mind,' she says.

The connection between young people, and ancient philosophy is what inspired her to write the *Encyclopaedia of Indian Saints and Sages*, which explains little-known aspects of spiritual texts and how this knowledge can lead to a better life. She does this by documenting the lives and teachings of ninety saints from the pre-eleventh century to those living today. Apart from showcasing India's rich spiritual heritage, she hopes the book will enable the young to rediscover their roots and imbibe learning that is bound to enrich their lives dramatically. In the book's preface, she writes, 'It is the legacy of Indian saints and sages that represents the true identity of Indian ideology. I bequeath this book to the youth of our country so that they can know and understand the roots from where they have originated.'

Listening to Indu speak about her life and philosophy, I am reminded repeatedly of the lives of great spiritual leaders, many of whom I have closely studied. Buddha, Krishna, Mahavira were born into great wealth and power. However, restless and unhappy, they chose to seek inner peace and happiness through a voyage of self-discovery and selfless service to society. The journey, for most of them, was a rocky one, battling tremendous hardship and personal losses, and it is only after successfully overcoming them that they were able to achieve oneness with god or what Hindus refer to as nirvana. This is never easy to attain and many give up trying. Indu, though, delved deeper into her spiritual quest after facing personal tragedies.

Indu also emphasizes the need to truly absorb religion and spirituality in one's inner life, in order to understand their core messages of tolerance and unity, because that is what distinguishes the spiritual individual from the fanatic. '[The fanatic] does not practise and live the religion, they speak without belief or understanding. The one who sees oneness in all religions is spiritual.'

Deeply influenced by *Advaita* philosophy, she says that living in the present should be the basis of life, with no regret for the past or the future—'We spend a lot of time doing both and it is not essential at all towards having a fulfilling life. Life is what is now. If we take care of this, past and future are taken care of by themselves. I am not a person who dwells on past or future. I love to be here and now.'

Catapulted overnight from being a housewife to running a media empire, Indu is well acquainted with the challenges faced by women when they try to break into a male-dominated world. She knows how much harder they have to work and how often they have to prove themselves. Interestingly, ancient Hindu scriptures are very progressive and liberal, she explains to me, when it comes to the role of women, whom she considers the centres of power, with the capacity to bring sensitivity to the table as business strategists.

Indu cites the examples of the goddesses Durga, Kali and Saraswati to emphasize that this is exactly how women were portrayed in mythology, too—'Man has forgotten that he is powerful because of feminine Shakti. By default, he started to destroy all the power of women by curbing her growth and development in every field. Thus, he became very disorderly and is now failing to handle himself. Shiv is the *shav* [corpse] without Shakti.'

The feminist in Indu comes to the fore when she speaks about women's issues. She views the lack of empowerment—financial, academic—as the reason for the rise of atrocities against women in India and holds the view that women have always had the ability to take prominent roles in businesses. 'The challenge of balancing the traditional and modern is something that we can easily take in our stride,' she says.

The founder-president of FLO, the ladies' wing of industry body FICCI, Indu says she wanted to create an individual identity for women in the corporate world, not one dependent on the norms and guidelines set down by men—'I didn't like moving as the tail or assistant of a man. I didn't like the man's world. For me it should be a world of both man and woman.' To this end, in 2010, the Times Foundation donated Rs 1 crore to the National Women's Empowerment Mission which is being used to set up the Pratibha Academy to nurture and develop leadership qualities in women.

## THE ROAD TO REALIZATION

Surrounded by all the luxuries enormous wealth can possibly buy, Indu has, over the years, chosen to withdraw to a simpler life. With most of her time spent nowadays at ashrams and with gurus, she says she feels only love for all. On finding spiritual certainty, a sense of self-realisation, she quotes to me, 'The very nature of *Who am I* means one has to find the answer within oneself. There is only one phenomenon manifesting in various ways and that's what I am.'

Saying godhood is our birthright and every individual should understand their being (*atma*), Indu says at her age, what immediately appeals to her is simplicity and authenticity, adding, 'Somewhere along the way, I've learnt that there is no good reason to get annoyed. The idea that you can harm somebody and do good to yourself—foolish as it is, a lot of people follow it and I feel for their ignorance.'

Live in the present is her mantra, by which she means not having regret for the past or worrying about the future, but seeking oneself and looking within. Elaborating on this, Indu says that there might be no difference in making an absolute choice between 'being happy' and 'having a purpose' in life. 'I don't see the choice at all because the alternatives that seem different may just turn out to be the same.'

When it comes to spirituality, Indu believes herself to be a seeker, a doer and a contemplative person, all locked in one, '. . . and much more; ultimately at the climax greatest lover and beloved both.' She says, 'The aim of spirituality is the growth in one's inner and outer self. It means balanced growth. People have lost this growth. They spend time on their work, business and other things but hardly take care of their inner self.'

She also answers the biggest question of all: 'Does god exist? Or is each one of us a fragment of the higher power? Does the law of karma exist?' She says, 'Experience it yourself. Choose the path of your liking: if you are heart-oriented then *bhaktimarg* and if head-oriented then *gyanmarg* [the path of knowledge]. Be brave, dissolve your small "I" [*main*] and experience the collective "I". That's what you are and that's what god is.'

Meditation, which helped her overcome enormous setbacks and challenges in life, should be made compulsory for all, she says. She believes it provides the answers in our conflict-ridden society, adding that every part of her life is meditation—some of it is very active while some of it is passive. She believes in the need to meditate for clarity as this helps settle the mind and achieve calmness. It is then that one is able to perceive things clearly without any distortions. Perhaps, the highest attainment of human life is then achieved.

## BOUNDLESS IN FREEDOM

Indu Jain is many persons in one—a media mogul, a spiritualist, a humanist and a cultural icon. Her biggest success so far has been the ability to run her company the way she has, along with her ability to be a fearless, unapologetic woman who lives with conviction and confidence. She has created a social conscience within her company, and made herself the prime example of a successful matriarchal figure. And over the years, as chairperson of BCCL, Indu has received many prestigious awards such as the Indian Congress of Women's Lifetime Achievement Award. These, she says, mean very little to her—'I honour only the award which my inner being gives to me or my masters give to me; the rest are fulfilling peripherally.'

French philosopher-priest Pierre Teilhard de Chardin once said, *We are not human beings having a spiritual experience. We are spiritual beings having a human experience.* Making this experience as purposeful as possible is perhaps Indu's single greatest desire which, she says, is 'to nurture the highest in me, so that I can also enjoy the lowest of low and become the master of both sides of the coin.'

I ask her what she would do if she had three days off and she instantly retorts, 'Being myself, boundless in my freedom! But that's my plan for life anyway, not just three days.' And that is the message she sends out to the youth: 'Life is an incredible adventure and you should give it your best.'

Sethi, who has always been enchanted by her joie de vivre, says, 'She is like the Ganga as it comes out of Gangotri—turbulent and very youthful. I have seen a certain spark in her eye which is just the same as it was forty years ago. When she responds to something or sees something that moves her, you see it reflected in her entire being—her eyes light up and she smiles instinctively.'

The lengthy interview is coming to an end and as I thank her for sparing so much time, I can't help asking her how she looks upon her own career in contrasts—she wields power and influence, but philanthropy and compassion are important values for her. She smiles and replies that it is an interwoven chain and if even one link were missing it would mean that she wouldn't have experienced wholeness.

271

# THE JAIN FAMILY

*Indu Jain, chairperson of Bennett, Coleman & Company (BCCL), views her job as that of a custodian of responsibility. She helms a media house that attempts to appeal comprehensively to a diverse, polyglot audience without being partisan or purely driven by the profit motive. The family has rallied by her side in co-opting the spiritual dimension she brings to the workplace. This interview brings forth what they regard as crucial life lessons they have drawn from her.*

**What has been the nature of the influence that Indu has had as chairperson of BCCL? She combines a rare combination of attributes to helm a driven, successful media house.**

Ma's influence on the company's development is no different than that of a conscientious mother's influence on her children and other family members. She is an inspiration and the moving force behind the company's resilience, confidence, progressive vision and all-round development, which successfully marries business acumen and credibility with practical spiritual vision. Her role has been that of a nurturer, providing subtle, but strong, and often silent, guidance, propelling the organization onward, towards higher dimensions, and at the same time, helping it remain grounded and practical.

**The Times Foundation, which has won international acclaim, is something Indu has built. What does it do?**

Under Ma's guidance, the foundation is striving to fulfil its mission to persistently and collectively encourage impactful interventions in the fields of education, health, environment, women's empowerment, disaster relief and rehabilitation, advocacy, vocational skill training and spiritual wellness.

Ma's vision is for the foundation to be a catalyst for positive change by enabling agencies to work towards minimising disparities and establish an equitable society. The focus is on multi-stakeholder partnerships—bringing together large and small organizations and individuals—that can help generate constructive, solution-oriented agendas for a more humane and sustainable nation.

**Indu has said that there is no contradiction between her spiritual quest and being chairperson of BCCL. How do the two meet—one aims at self-knowledge and the greater good, the other has profit imperatives to keep in mind.**

Ma's spiritual vision and the group's business vision are not two separate entities that need to be blended. The two are seamless, for Ma strongly believes that there is no contradiction in business and spirituality so long the group maintains the highest credibility and commitment which seeps into daily life and the consciousness of every employee and stakeholder. We are all working together to realize both individual and collective dreams—of sustainable livelihoods, of evolving to higher planes of contentment and achievement, and of extending ourselves to participate in not only contributing to material development, but also enhancing, enriching and empowering the quest for self-knowledge that leads to holistic progress that benefits all.

**What have been some of the key life lessons you have learnt from the way she lives?**

Ma exudes a quiet confidence and faith that remain intact despite any kind of perceived setback, or even exuberance, whether in the personal or professional domains. This is a great attribute or quality that is an inspiration both to her personal and professional families. Importantly, this quality of remaining unfazed and staying full of optimism and hope is what gives us great stability and confidence to keep the faith in ourselves and the work we do by exploring our potential in the best ways possible, no matter the challenges we have to face along the way.

# MARY
# KOM

•

*She is simply incredible. I think [her achievements] would not have happened without a strong character and that will, that desire to do something big. She has been able to find solutions to all those challenges and obstacles. And she has done it beautifully and more convincingly than anyone else. And that is why the entire nation is proud of her achievements. I think a woman might be able to understand how big a challenge it is to have a baby and then go out and perform. Men would never understand that.*

**—SACHIN TENDULKAR**

•

*8* August 2012 was a sunny day in London. The city was alive with the Olympic Games and, at the Excel Exhibition Centre, history was being made moment by moment.

Time came to a standstill when two women entered the arena to participate in the Olympics' first-ever women's boxing tournament. The home crowd roared for Great Britain's Nicola Adams, but the louder cheers were reserved for five-time world champion M.C. Mary Kom, India's brightest, most extraordinary athlete. She lost, but was still given a standing ovation as she won bronze, for herself and her country. When I think of that day, I cannot help wondering if those in the audience knew of the long, arduous journey that brought Mary there.

The daughter of landless labourers from Manipur—tucked away in India's restive, neglected northeast—Mary was the mother of twins when she won that medal. While knocking down five world championships to dominate the boxing arena, she had also punched the living daylights out of every preconception under the sun about class, sports, India's northeast and womanhood. I would like to believe that on that day in London, the audience cheered for Mary because they understood what it meant for her to be standing inside that ring.

I first meet Mary Kom in December 2013 in Bengaluru, at the launch of her autobiography, *Unbreakable*.

Her youngest son, Prince, is six months old, and as she plays with him, she chats with her husband—who is her staunchest supporter—Onler Kom. Dressed in track pants, which she wears with the agile grace of a fighter, Mary apologizes to me for being distracted by Prince, who is a bit unwell. It is about a year after the Olympics and the crowds are still fascinated by her, which explains her security detail. As we begin speaking, I quickly realize that Mary is unmoved by her meteoric success—her relationships ground her firmly—and she needs coaxing to talk about her life because, as she explains in her own book, 'I am most articulate in the boxing ring. With my fists.'

## ON HER MARK

Born on 24 November 1982, Mary was the first child of daily wage agricultural workers; she was christened Mangte Chungneijang (*chung* means 'on top/above all', *nei* means 'wealth' and *jang*, 'agile'). Contributing to her family's meagre resources has been a lifelong concern for Mary who, while still in school, began helping her father, Mangte Tonpa Kom, with paddy cultivation, fishing, collecting firewood and producing charcoal, and her mother, Akham, with weaving shawls and the housework. It was a tough life, and Mary tells me that as she ploughed, or herded bullocks, or carried sacks of rice around, she remembers having to pull leeches off her limbs in the paddy fields and aiming at water snakes with stones.

Her father, Tonpa, tells me, 'She was my right hand and my closest companion at work. She was quite comfortable with a man's work. As the eldest child, she did most of the work at home, too. She enjoyed playing marbles and made money from her friends. In her free time, she re-threshed hay thrown away after harvest and sold the produce.'

Providing their children with access to education as a way out of their bleak reality was important to Mary's parents; she walked an hour from home each way every day to an English-medium school in Moirang, leaving only after her morning chores. Once her younger siblings started school, she looked out for them. Her brother Khupreng says, 'She would take care of us when we were still very small. People didn't dare mess with us if she was with us.'

Though so much was invested in her going to school, Mary always did better at sports than in the classroom. This was not unusual in Manipur, where several people used to get jobs under the sports quota; but even though Mary bagged first spot at most sporting events, it took her time to persuade her father that her future lay there. In 1999, she finally joined a facility of the Sports Authority of India (SAI) in Imphal, Manipur's capital; she also began high school there at Adimjati Government High School. Mary would wake at 4 a.m., cycle to SAI, and return at 8 a.m. before heading to school. The four trips back and forth from SAI meant Mary dropped out of school when she did not pass her Class X examinations, but she appeared for them later through the National Institute of Open Schooling.

The bigger problem for Mary was finding her true calling in sports, even though she loved everything about it. After two years spent shuttling between relatives' homes as she tried her hand at pole-vaulting, javelin-throwing and track-and-field events, she heard that women's boxing had already been introduced at the National Games. Something deep stirred in her. Her imagination had been fired when Dingko Singh, a Manipuri with

278

similar humble beginnings, won the gold medal for boxing at the Asian Games in 1998. Mary approached L. Ibomcha Singh, the best boxing coach at SAI, and pleaded with him to take her under his wing. He agreed and a few days later, Mary began her daily six-hour training. She tells me that her punches were too hard for the other girls and so she trained with the younger boys who were her height.

Most world-class boxers start training at the age of eleven or twelve. Mary was over seventeen when she started and I ask her if that led to any disadvantages. 'Yes, but I was lucky that my body is flexible. I learnt very quickly,' she says.

Once she had found her path, she laboured on as if possessed, even though she didn't have funds for the right shoes or equipment; Mary's monthly budget was Rs 50 from her parents who had to make great sacrifices even to make that sum possible. Nor did Mary have the requisite diet or dietary supplements. But what she had in plenty was a winner's will—her life had already trained her in resilience and perseverance.

At eighteen, a year after she began training, Mary won her first gold; most boxers take a decade to get to the top of their game but at the finals of her first state championship, Mary defeated one of her first female coaches from SAI. She went on to win five World Amateur Boxing championships and is the first Indian woman boxer to strike gold in the Asian Games (in Korea, 2014) and the only Indian woman to qualify for the 2012 Summer Olympics, winning the bronze in the flyweight (51 kg) category.

## GIRLS CAN'T FIGHT

I have never been able to view a boxing match on television without wincing and switching channels but meeting Mary helped me embrace a new idea. Women are typically not taught to acknowledge their latent aggression and it is fascinating to see how Mary has tapped into that side of herself, and then channelled it with technical finesse. In a culture that does not encourage young girls to be sporty, she has broken the rule twice—by becoming a sporting icon, and in a sport traditionally considered hyper-masculine.

Because boxing was taboo for women, when Mary won her first championship, she had not yet told her parents about her inclination for the sport. She was sure they would disapprove. The day after her win, her father was at Moirang and overheard some men talking of a newspaper article about a 'Maki Kom' who had won the state championship. There was an unclear, grainy photograph published along with the report. Tonpa didn't know of any Kom girl other than his daughter training at SAI but her name was Chungneijang. He had no idea that his daughter had switched to boxing and also changed her hard-to-pronounce name, which was further misprinted in this piece.

Suspicious, Tonpa sent his wife to Imphal to bring Mary home. As it happened, Akham ran into her daughter midway; Mary was coming home jubilant to much fanfare, but Tonpa wanted her to quit boxing. He worried no one would marry her if she was injured or bruised while competing and realized that her possible lack of resources and access to training would place her at a disadvantage. But, as he tells me, 'She was determined to continue boxing despite my disapproval. Later, when she convinced me, I promised her I would do anything to support her training and needs. There was a time I left home for weeks, stayed in the wilderness, ate a single meal a day and sold the few cattle that we had. Her mother would weave and tend to the kitchen garden, and sell produce in the market.'

Mary consoled them by convincing herself that the sports quota would get her a job with the government, which would allow her to buy her parents a car and a farm. For herself, she wanted a Pulsar motorbike. After she won her first championship, the Ministry of Sports awarded her Rs 9 lakh; with a part of that, she bought Tonpa a paddy field and set up funds for her siblings' education. She also bought herself a bike but chose a less masculine version, as her mother suggested.

Always a fighter, literally and figuratively, Mary had to navigate the politics of the competing state, central and other training facilities in Imphal so she could make her place in the sport of her choosing. Manipur's many boxing circles included SAI and the nexus between state-run Youth Affairs and Sports (YAS) and Manipur Amateur Boxing Association (MABA). SAI students were often dropped during selections and in 2000, to qualify for the state-level tournament, Mary, along with some others, joined YAS but returned to SAI later.

## DEFENDING HOME

It would not be an overstatement to say that one of Mary's biggest achievements has been the spotlight her successes have shone on Manipur, a state torn apart by insurgency and often in the news for conflict. Mary, who belongs to one of the six sub-tribes that form the Kom-Rem community, always talks about home with great fondness and appreciates the support her community has extended to her, from the early days of her career.

Her suitcase with money and her passport was stolen when she was travelling to Hisar for the selection rounds for the first Asian Women's Boxing Championship in 2001. Even though Mary was selected for the championship, she was ineligible to compete because she didn't have a passport. This incident shattered Mary and she writes in her autobiography that she even considered jumping off the train. This time, too, the Kom community came to her rescue. A relative rushed to the passport office in Guwahati and another helped speed up the paperwork. Mary's passport reached her in the nick of time and was delivered to her by the president of the Kom-Rem Students' Union in Delhi, Onler Kom.

Mary had met Onler in 2001, as an eighteen-year-old while training at the Nehru Stadium in Delhi. Nine years older than her, Onler was a law student and a sportsman. As a member of the community, he checked in on Mary to make sure she was doing okay and a friendship grew between them. Onler tells me, 'I found something very rare in her that I hadn't seen in any other woman. It was not like falling in love, but more like understanding her better—her background, her problems and her needs. I felt responsible for her, like a caregiver. She was already a world champion when I met her.'

In 2001, when Mary got her first chance for an international medal at the first World Women's Boxing Championships in Pennsylvania, USA, she didn't have the funds she needed. She told Onler of her concerns, and he called a meeting of the union to raise money. Through their efforts, two Manipuri members of Parliament donated a sum of Rs 8000. Mary's father had given her Rs 2000 and others pitched in with a little more.

While the media was blind to this rising sports star, it was the Kom-Rem Students' Union and other members of the community who gave a warm welcome to their international champion at the Delhi airport when she returned from a championship in China. Back in Imphal, she was 'greeted with garlands and drumbeats and dancing.'

In her autobiography, Mary talks about the severity of the internal conflicts in Manipur, and she was able to unite the people of her state with her win at the Olympics—the Nagas, Meiteis and Kukis of Manipur swept aside their political differences to pray collectively for her victory. The local radio aired people's appeals to the state electricity department for uninterrupted power supply so fans could watch the match live. Some people flocked to houses with generators. Seconds after she lost, the lights went out.

When she won the Olympics bronze, actor Amitabh Bachchan tweeted: 'Mother of two from Assam, creates moment of pride for India!' Mary had, indeed, done India proud but the praise was marred by the fact that she is actually from Manipur and even in her grandest moment, the ignorance about the northeast was upsetting. She has often talked about how Indians from the northeast are made to feel like 'the other' in the rest of the country. 'Yes, I have faced discrimination many times. But I am a fighter. I'm an Indian. Even if I look different, have a different facial structure and skin colour, I know I am an Indian and I'm proud to be one,' she says to me.

## A LIFE PARTNER

As Mary went from strength to strength in her career, her relationship with Onler also grew more significant. She remembers how Onler proposed to her on the phone without actually saying anything and then over tea one day, he repeated his most unromantic proposal by telling Mary he wanted to marry her to protect her career. As she heard him speak about how he would never hinder her ambition and would always support it, she was convinced she had found the right partner.

Mary, known for the fierce look she wore in the boxing ring, spent Rs 20,000 on her wedding gown—it was one of the biggest extravagances she had ever allowed herself. As a child, she had preferred gender-neutral clothes. She was always conscious of her 'boyish' looks and believed that feminine clothes didn't look good on her. Walking down the aisle in her graceful gown, she felt more the cynosure of all eyes than she ever had in any boxing ring, she tells me.

It is an incredible marriage and Onler has been the rock of professional, emotional and social support to Mary. He kept his own sporting ambitions on hold and decided to become Mary's manager and mentor, and it paid off— Mary did even better after she got married. A month after their wedding, the couple returned to Imphal where the government had allotted Mary a house at the National Games Village. However, she refused to accept the job of a police constable offered to her because she believed she deserved better. Later that year, Mary won another gold at the third World Women's Boxing Championship in Russia. The government now offered her the post of a sub-inspector, which she accepted.

When she travelled to Delhi for her fourth championship, in 2006, her entire family was present to cheer her on. Winning gold once again, she had a World Championship hat-trick and was christened the queen of boxing. This happy streak was broken when, two days after Christmas that year, the couple learnt that Onler's father, who had gone out to refill coal for the oven in the evening, had been kidnapped by insurgents. Late that night, villagers found his dead body. (Many questions about his murder still remain unanswered.)

An inconsolable Onler wanted to avenge his father's death and even considered joining the insurgency, and Mary was so anguished at the thought that her popularity had drawn attention to him that she considered giving up her career. Onler tells me, 'Mary decided to stay at home as a housewife. It took over six months for me to convince her not to.'

Through this turmoil, Mary had been troubled by nausea that she attributed to the emotional trauma but she soon realized it was actually morning sickness. Her pregnancy cured Onler of his need to seek revenge for his father's murder. And when they learnt that they were having twins, Onler considered it a sign because his father had also been one of a pair of twins. On 5 August 2007, Mary gave birth to identical boys, Rechungvar and Khupneivar.

## MOTHERHOOD – THE END OF A CAREER?

The year she spent recovering and nursing her children, there was, serendipitously, no major championship. When she returned to her first training camp after childbirth, she was weak, nauseous and suffered from many aches and pains. The camp, which would lead to the selections for the fourth Asian Women's Championships, was held in Hisar. Mary was miserable away from her children and angry because her body wasn't cooperating. But even so, after a two-year hiatus and one training camp, Mary went on to win gold.

It is not easy to see a loved one play a sport such as boxing, which is rough-and-tumble, and I ask Onler how he feels when he watches Mary in the ring—'It is something unusual to see a girl getting punched. Sometimes she would get injuries and cut marks. It's never easy for a husband to watch his wife being hit. When I see her fall, I cry inside. But then, you give a push to your heart and say, "*Chalo*, this is a sport; you give sometimes and you get sometimes."'

A year later, though, Mary had to face the dilemma between motherhood and career. She was training at the SAI centre in Patiala for the Asian Women's Cup in Haikou, China. Back home in Imphal, Onler took the twins to the doctor for a routine check-up because Rechungvar had a cold. But soon, they discovered that Khupneivar had a congenital heart disease. Mary's face contorts with pain when she talks about that time. Her son needed surgery and Onler brought him to Chandigarh for treatment. Mary did not want to travel to China but Onler persuaded her to go. Even as her heart broke for her little son, Mary won gold and rushed back immediately after to be at the surgery.

I am both touched and inspired by the devotion Mary and Onler share, for one another and their family. When Mary is away, Onler's routine as a stay-at-home dad is hectic—'I am up by 5.30 a.m. to feed the kids and send them to school. I know how hard it is to be with two babies sleeping on either side of the bed when their mother is away, to wake up in the middle of the night and feed them milk. It's one of the hardest things I've faced.'

## FLOAT LIKE A BUTTERFLY . . .

Mary is slight and looks almost fragile and it's difficult to imagine how such incredible strength is packed into such a small frame. This is not uncommon, I learn, as we speak. Her first coach Ibomcha Singh said she was too small for boxing. He took her on only because she wouldn't return with no for an answer. Most people are astonished to watch her defeat opponents far taller and stronger than her. She has compared herself to David taking on the Goliaths—and rightly so.

And more than her physical resilience, Mary's career has advanced because of her ferocious determination and ambition. She was never shy of aiming for the Olympics even though she was probably past the peak of her abilities by the time boxing was finally declared an official Olympic sport. The AIBA had lobbied for years to include it in vain and her heart sank when she heard women's boxing wouldn't be part of the Athens Games and, again, when it was excluded from Beijing. Mary knew time was against her but chose to believe in her dream.

When she finally made it there, there were more challenges. Even though Mary was a five-time champion in the 45 kg, 46 kg and 48 kg categories, she had to fight well above her weight in the 51 kg (flyweight) event. It was the lowest admitted weight category for that year. Mary weighed in at a shade under 51 and had a petite 5-foot-2-inch frame. But she more than compensated with her lithe footwork. When she returned home with a bronze, Mary captured India's imagination and made the nation realize that it could master sports other than cricket. And in a market that is limited by its worship of cricketers, she has become a coveted brand for sponsors.

This is now, and it's easy to gloss over Mary's hard-fought journey to the arc lights. She won gold at the World Boxing Championships six times in a row but her achievements only featured on the back pages of newspapers the first five times. Though she had received the Arjuna Award in 2003 and the Padma Shri in 2006, when, in 2007, her name was submitted for the Rajiv Gandhi Khel Ratna Award, the highest honour the Indian government gives a sportsperson, former Olympic athlete Milkha Singh had never heard of her and struck her off. It finally came her way in 2009. As the world began to recognize Mary as the incredible sportswoman that she is, the Indian government and media too awoke to her fearless skills, both inside and outside the ring. In 2016, Mary was nominated by President Pranab Mukherjee as a member of the Rajya Sabha, the upper house of Indian Parliament. In 2017, Mary and Akhil Kumar were nominated as National Observers for boxing. Mary confirmed the nation's trust in her by winning a historic sixth gold at the World Boxing Championships, making her the only woman in the world to have done so. After her sixth world title, the Government of Manipur conferred the title "Meethoi Leima" (loosely translated as great or exceptional lady) on her in an elaborate felicitation ceremony organized at Khuman Lampak Sports Complex in Imphal in 2018 and declared that the stretch of road leading to the Games Village in Imphal West district, where Kom currently resides, would be named 'MC Mary Kom Road'.

But writing history didn't stop there. In 2018, Mary won India's first Commonwealth Games boxing gold, igniting newfound passion in an entire generation of struggling sportspersons and the belief that anything was possible with will, hustle, and consistency.

The government has also now allocated three acres for Mary to fulfil a long-time dream of hers—the Mary Kom Boxing Academy. In *Unbreakable*, she writes, 'I have proven that women can achieve as much as men can, and I have shown that boxing can be as engrossing as cricket for Indians. Today, there is a marked improvement in facilities for other sports. I hope that my academy will prove to be another step towards bringing boxing out of the sidelines.'

The academy trains underprivileged children free of cost because, as Mary tells me, 'I'm from a poor family. Many of my students are from a similar background. I just want to help them and support them even if all of them won't be champions. I do have a dream of finding the next Mary Kom.'

She has hired a full-time coach for the academy and trains talented students herself when she can. Onler, who helps her run the institution, tells me, 'I once asked Mary what she will do when she retires after four or five years and she replied, "I will die as a boxer."' That said, Mary had decided to retire after the 2016 Olympics in Rio, because she believes her body will eventually not be able to sustain the rigour boxing demands. She wants to give her children more time, and give back through her work at the academy but, ever the dreamer and fighter, she wants to win an Olympic gold before she hangs her gloves up for the last time. As of now, she has her sights set on gold at the 2020 Tokyo Olympics.

When she was a child, Mary loved watching Jackie Chan's films and was also deeply inspired by the legendary boxer Muhammad Ali, who overcame insurmountable odds. But she never would have guessed that her own life would be the stuff of dreams and that she herself would 'float like a butterfly and sting like a bee'.

It was only fitting, therefore, that Bollywood caught on to the deeply inspirational narrative of her life. The film *Mary Kom*, produced by Sanjay Leela Bhansali and directed by writer-director Omung Kumar, despite its overt dramatisation of fact, has ensured that her story lives far beyond her victory.

Mary is currently Puma's training ambassador to promote women's fitness sportswear across India. (Until now, Puma had a single brand ambassador devoted to all clothing lines, Virat Kohli.) Mary works tirelessly to promote the importance of fitness and sports, recently flagging off the 2019 Standard Chartered Mumbai Marathon to support a variety of causes and running as a lifestyle.

Every time I've seen Mary in the ring, read about her, met her, I have been struck over and again by her authenticity and genuineness. Her coach, Charles Atkinson, says Mary's biggest asset is her integrity. 'She will always give you a straight and honest answer, and her integrity is beyond question. When I first met Mary, she was all about aggression and all-out aggression. She is aggressive in the boxing ring, nurturing with her children, 'masculine' in her choice of career, 'feminine' in her love for fashion and shopping, a star all over the world, and a wife and mother at home.'

'When I was getting married, everyone cautioned me against it. Afterwards, they all said that I would lose steam and ambition. When I didn't, they made hurtful remarks about my in-laws: "Look at them. With Mary as their daughter-in-law, their fortune has changed." . . . Then, when the babies arrived, they said, this is the end,' Mary writes in *Unbreakable*.

None of these hurtful comments has ever stopped her. Nothing has ever stopped her. Mary has challenged life to a duel and won every time. She truly is the last woman standing.

# PRIYANKA CHOPRA

*Priyanka Chopra and Mary Kom are a power pair. Both are determined women who work hard to stay at the top, where they have gotten through grit and grace. Both are fun, ebullient women who combine feminine strength with softness. Both command respect and admiration from millions. Priyanka Chopra talks about playing the role of the Olympian boxer—the challenges, the pleasures and why she chose to share Mary's story with the world.*

**You are known to play strong women on screen, to critical acclaim. What made you choose to play Mary Kom?**

Quite simply, the thought that her story had to be shared with the world. She is such an inspiration to every woman out there who is looking to chase a dream, no matter how unconventional it may be. She is a living, breathing example of fighting the odds to make your dreams come alive. She is a boxer, mother, daughter, wife, homemaker, fighter, and, above all else, a woman.

**You have been reported to always 'work' on the character you play in your movies. How different was your training to emulate a living sports legend?**

It's no secret that playing Mary Kom has been one of the toughest roles of my career. The fact that the film is based on the life of a living legend who is still active and on top of the game in her chosen profession, made my job that much more difficult. It was a double whammy in many ways, taking everything I had, both emotionally and physically. The physical training coupled with the boxing training (I had to learn to fight like Mary) was supremely exhausting. Sometimes, it got so much that I felt like I was training to qualify for our Olympic team! Getting into the mind and emotions of Mary Kom was also such an amazing challenge.

**Coming from a poor family, Mary struggled to educate her siblings. Her success as a world champion is a testament to her determination, perseverance and drive to succeed. You have**

**met her on a number of occasions. What is it like to spend time with her?**

Mary is pretty much a what-you-see-is-what-you-get kind of person. She is the person you read about. She is very clear about what she wants out of life and is not afraid of any hard work in making it happen. And she also has a huge advantage in the form of her husband, Onler. Not to take anything away from Mary, but Onler is, for me, the poster boy of what a loving, supportive husband can be. He has given her the space and the emotional backing to go out and make her dreams come true. That is so amazing, especially in a country like India, where that role is usually expected of the woman. They are an amazing couple and I think the relationship itself has helped Mary in so many ways.

**In a very basic sense, Mary Kom may be likened to you. Coming from a non-sports background and having no godfathers in the chosen line of work, she too managed to make her mark the hard way. What would you say are the traits that are most common between Mary and you?**

From my first-hand interactions with Mary, this is what I think are the similarities: We both believe that there is no substitute for hard work to make your dreams come true. We are also determined and very focused in achieving those dreams. Family means everything and we are super grateful for everything that we have been given.

**What trait of Mary's do you wish to have?**

Her ability to not only be a world champion sportsperson but also a gold medallist mother and wife. I think her work-life balance is pretty amazing. I love what I do and, therefore, I can never say no to doing more, which leaves me with no time for myself. Hopefully, when I decide to get married and settle down, I can find a way to juggle both as successfully as she does.

# SANIA
# MIRZA

*Just like me, Sania is a young professional player, baring her heart. I have always been honest in my opinions, too. If a lot of people don't like it, they need to understand that we work in a certain way. It is not easy to censor yourself all the time or only say the things people want to hear. You have to be yourself. You make mistakes, learn from them and become a better person, a better player.*

**—YUVRAJ SINGH**

The first time Sania Mirza picked up a tennis racquet was as a six-year-old in 1993. I ask her what she felt like in that moment and she instantly retorts – 'Tiny.'

Twenty-six years on, the ace tennis star with several incredible achievements and a Padma Bhushan to her credit, feels anything but tiny, both on and off the court. That was a proud day when she became the first Indian woman to enter the top thirty of the Women's Tennis Association rankings. And now she has been ranked No. 1 in the world in doubles (her most successful partner has been Swiss Martina Hingis), has won back-to-back Grand Slam titles and has remained the top-ranked female player of the country for over a decade.

In a country obsessed with cricket and with few women sports stars, Sania crossed the $4 million mark in net worth in 2014. At an age when most tennis players retire, she has given her career a fresh lease of life by turning her focus entirely to the doubles, and her partnership with former world No. 1 Martina is paying off handsomely.

It is possibly her never-say-die spirit that has also reflected in her soaring endorsements with many top brands. She is the richest female sportsperson in the country, but more importantly she is the face of inspiration for those who look ahead to a brilliant career.

Sania is an icon—she has broken the taboo around professional sports for young Indian girls, especially, and compelled the nation to switch the sports channel on to watch something other than cricket matches. And more than any of this, there is Sania's feisty spirit—her courage, optimism and ability to maintain grace under fire that never cease being admirable. For all these reasons, I preserved a space for Sania in this book.

We are to meet at the Mirzas' beautiful bungalow in Jubilee Hills, Hyderabad, where they moved when Sania was seventeen. I am shown into the drawing room of the two-storied residence that Sania shares with her mother Nasima, father Imran and younger sister Anam. In a few minutes, Sania walks in, dressed in a gorgeous Tarun Tahiliani *anarkali*; she gathers all the energy of the room around her.

'No, this is not the way I normally dress at home,' she says, before I ask. 'I have to go out after the interview and decided to save time.'

Gregarious and friendly, Sania can pass off for any other woman her age, but within five minutes of talking to her, I am aware of a discernible steeliness that can only come from breaking as many barriers as she has. 'I have friends who are still wondering what they want to do with their lives. Here I am, talking about what I want to do as my second career. Life has been extremely eventful and full for someone my age,' she says.

## LITTLE CHAMPION

Sania was born in Mumbai on 15 November 1986; her father, Imran, was a businessman who dabbled in journalism and edited a sports magazine called *Sportscall* in the early-80s. He grew up in Mumbai but later moved to Hyderabad, a city to which his family belonged. At six, she was walking past a tennis court when her mother, Nasima, casually asked her if she wanted to play. Without a clue about what that meant, Sania said yes. Nasima took her little daughter to the courts the next day; the trainer was not sure she was old enough to play but Nasima would not hear of it. Three weeks later, the trainer told Imran that Sania had a rare talent for the game. The proud father tells me—'When I first watched her play, I could see that there was something very special in her sense of the ball and timing.'

That talent may well be genetic—Sania's grandfather, Mohammed Zaffer Mirza, played club cricket in Middlesex in England; Ghulam Ahmed, former India test captain, was a relation and Zaffer Mirza's childhood friend; Asif Iqbal, who captained Kent CCC and the Pakistani team, was also a relation who started his cricketing career playing Ranji Trophy for Hyderabad; and Imran, too, had played some serious club cricket and was a respected sports journalist. Sania even jokes that had she been a boy, she'd have been a professional cricketer.

Not much taller than the net when she played her first tournament, Sania defeated a sixteen-year-old national-level player and left the audience spellbound. At nine, she travelled to Bengaluru for her first outstation tournament; Imran remembers that though Sania lost in the finals, a woman took her autograph and told her she was going to win Wimbledon someday.

'When I was twelve, I won the nationals under-fourteen and under-sixteen in Delhi and I got my first sponsorship with Adidas. That's when I decided that I wanted to be a professional tennis player. In my head, that was the turning point,' says Sania to me and I can hear the determination in her voice, even all these years later.

Imran has been more than just Sania's dad—he is her mentor, coach and manager; she makes no decisions, personal or professional, without his participation. However, the Mirzas have never burdened Sania with their expectations or goals.

An alumna of Nasr Girls School in Hyderabad, Sania says, 'My parents were not pushy even though they wanted me to play at the highest levels. I loved school and was a very good student, even though I travelled seven months a year. I didn't want to miss school or matches—that was the biggest conflict. I was always the one who wanted to go practice, and it helps to know that this career was entirely my own decision. I was at the gym for seven to eight hours a day, after which I would come home and do homework. I finished my schooling, took my boards and joined university.'

Sania would have completed her BA in Psychology but when her Wimbledon Grand Slam match clashed with her second-year final examination, she had to drop out. In 2008, her illustrious sports career earned her an honorary doctorate from the MGR Educational and Research Institute University.

## IT TAKES A FAMILY

The Mirzas did not just invest emotionally in their daughter and her career, but financially, too—every penny they could spare was diverted towards her ambitions. This was necessary because unlike cricket or hockey, where sportspersons are partially supported by federations, a tennis player has to fund his/her own game entirely.

'It's a gamble. Not everyone can raise the amount needed. You have to be very lucky to have that. When you are playing the juniors you don't make any money, but you travel about thirty weeks a year. When you play in junior Wimbledon you don't make anything. You invest a lot of money without any guarantee of a return,' Sania says, and tells me that she is immensely grateful to her parents for making it possible for her to play.

Among the first challenges for the Mirzas was finding sponsors; Imran chose tournaments with this criterion in mind. 'We needed to balance her ability to win a tournament with the names that would impress sponsors,' he says, adding that normally a tennis player's career lasts until they're in their mid-twenties to early-thirties and if the funds get delayed by even a year, it could be too late.

Imran, who coached her when she was a child, says, 'She was aggressive in her game despite her coaches trying to hold it back. While she wouldn't win matches due to her lack of consistency, I knew her aggression would take her places. Before a match I might give her tips on how to handle her opponent's forehand or backhand, deal with his or her footwork. That's all the coaching she needs.' He still coaches her though over the years Sania has worked with professional coaches.

At thirteen, Sania travelled to the US for her first international tournament but didn't win many matches. Going ahead, at Wimbledon she was scheduled to play against some of the opponents who had defeated her and Imran worried about that. 'I need six months,' she told him. And sure enough, she defeated each of those players at Wimbledon. Ace cricketer Yuvraj Singh, who calls Sania his friend and adviser, tells me why he is awestruck by her—'Unlike many aspiring tennis players who would only dream of winning Wimbledon, Sania went ahead and did it.'

Her first time at Wimbledon, at the junior level in 2001, she was the first Indian woman in fifty years to be there. The next year, partnering with Leander Paes, Sania won a bronze medal for India at the Asian Games in Busan. At fifteen, she was then the youngest participant to win.

Everything changed in 2003. At the Wimbledon girls' doubles, partnering with Alisa Kleybanova, Sania struck gold. At sixteen, she became the youngest and first-ever Indian girl to have won a Grand Slam title. To me, she says, 'I was in disbelief. After that, all hell broke loose. I became famous overnight. My dad was in India and he would tell me that reporters were parked outside our house. When I came back there were hundreds of people waiting at the airport. That was my first taste of stardom and I was a little overwhelmed.'

## TURNING PROFESSIONAL

Early in Sania's career, advertising and theatre guru Alyque Padamsee had predicted the sweep of *Sania mania*. In 2005, it had already begun. When Sania entered the finals of the AP Tourism Hyderabad Open, the stadium in her home town was packed to capacity and the crowd was delirious. She won the match and the tournament, securing her first WTA title. Such adulation is usually reserved for cricketers in India but as a young tennis player, Sania changed that. She was named 2005 WTA Newcomer of the Year and featured on the cover of *Time* as one of the '50 Heroes of Asia.' In 2005 Sania soared from number 300 to thirty-one and then twenty-seven in 2007. She made it to the semi-finals of the Hobart WTA tournaments, the second round of the Australian Open, finished eighth in the US Open Series and won four doubles titles. Her best singles result ever in a Grand Slam was reaching the pre-quarter final in 2005 in the US Open where she lost to the ultimate winner Maria Sharapova.

What gives Sania an edge over others? Her most important strength, Imran tells me, lies in her mind. She does not work herself up thinking about a match, and doesn't get intimidated by the opponent's ranking or reputation. Sania tells me, 'If I am at an exhibition or gallery opening I won't be talking to myself. When I am on the tennis court, I don't hold back. There are so many emotions involved in a two-hour tennis match. There's frustration, happiness, sadness, you miss a ball and you are annoyed; you win a point and you cheer yourself up. The tennis court is where I am completely myself. I don't care how I look or behave.'

Sania has some incredible physical advantages—her inimitable forehand, the force with which she hits the ball and her energy on court have often been praised. She is also double-jointed, which means she is more flexible. Her kryptonite, however, are injuries—she is very prone to them and had three surgeries by the time she was twenty-two.

A bad year hit her in 2008—Sania was plagued by a slew of injuries and had to withdraw from several matches including the French Open and the US Open, but she participated in the Beijing Olympics. When she injured her wrist, Sania thought her career was over—'I couldn't comb my hair or pick up a fork. I was in serious depression, thinking my career is over. I tried to do anything but sit in my room all day and cry. It's the worst feeling in the world when you have to sacrifice the things you love.' Her anguish was understandable, considering she had defeated three top players—Martina Hingis, Svetlana Kuznetsova and Nadia Petrova—in 2006. 'Every time I have been hurt, I have faced a crisis. As tennis players or as athletes you have to learn to trust your body again. For the last seven to eight years I don't remember waking up in the morning without pain.

My body didn't feel twenty-nine. It felt like forty because of the surgeries and the injuries I have put it through. Fortunately, all my injuries have been joint-related and I've never had a muscle tear.'

A friend who stood by her at the time was Singh, who only has kind words for Sania—'Whatever I shared with her was out of my personal experience and I always thought if it helps her, it will be great for her to come back and play. In fact, Sania was the second or third person to call me when I was battling cancer and, as a friend, she kept in touch with me throughout my recovery. I think we will always have that bond for each other's health because as players, you want to help each other out.'

In 2009, Sania bounced right back with a Grand Slam title for mixed doubles with Mahesh Bhupathi at the Australian Open.

## THE SPOTLIGHT AND ITS SHADOW

With her energy and confidence, Sania became a shining example of new India and proved that success was merit above gender and identity. Singh says, 'I remember meeting Sania in Mumbai as a young, vibrant sportsperson who had a spark on her face. In women's tennis, we needed someone to represent India on the international stage and Sania did exactly that. She became the face of young, successful women tennis players.'

In 2004, she was conferred the Arjuna Award and two years later, the Padma Shri. Young, attractive and at the top of her game, Sania became a brand and was flooded with endorsement offers and sponsorship deals. She was the most-searched celebrity in India on Google, and when former US President George W. Bush visited India in 2005, he called Hyderabad 'the city of Sania Mirza.'

By 2015, Sania had returned as a superstar, the only shining light of Indian tennis. She won two Grand Slam women's doubles titles – the US Open and Wimbledon—partnering Hingis on both occasions. And, for the first time in her career, she reached the absolute pinnacle by ending No. 1 in the WTA rankings.

In fact, 2015 has acknowledged Sania for what she really is—a sporting superstar on the international arena.

Sania was also given India's highest sporting honour, the Rajiv Gandhi Khel Ratna Award, by President Pranab Mukherjee at a function at Rashtrapati

Bhavan in 2015, and the Padma Bhushan, India's third highest civilian honour, for her contribution to sports in India in 2016.

Fame, though, is a double-edged sword. 'I grew up in the limelight and people have seen me evolve from a chubby girl whose face was full of pimples to what I am now,' she says. The media could never get enough of her and coverage of Sania shifted from the sports pages to Page 3.

An honest, fearless girl, Sania says it like it is and that made her easy game for the tabloid media. She had been propelled into the limelight long before she could learn to be tactful, and every move she made was analysed and critiqued. Her innocent remarks often made headlines. Her bright, funky T-shirts with bold one-liners printed on them became a national talking point.

A cleric with the Sunni Ulema Board issued a fatwa against Sania and commented on her 'indecent dressing' on court. Sania's parents made a public statement supporting her, and she, too, asked everyone to focus on her game and not the length of her skirts.

The incidents continued, and there was a buzz that Sania even considered quitting tennis at one point, but her love for the game would not let her.

Sania, wiser now, says, 'In this part of the world, people are very quick to point fingers at others, regardless of what they are doing or not doing. The media makes of our statements what it will, conveniently ignoring our clarifications.'

In 2019, Sania Mirza featured as the only Indian woman athlete on the ESPN World Fame 100 list, an annual list of the most famous athletes on the planet. There were only three women in the lists—Serena Williams (17), Maria Sharapova (37), and Sania Mirza (93). As of January 2019, a Sania Mirza biopic was being produced by Ronnie Screwvala's production house RSVP, with a message for little girls all over the world that they could do whatever they put their minds to.

## LOVE MATCH

In 2010, Sania met Pakistani cricketer Shoaib Malik in Hobart, Australia, where both of them were playing. While Sania thought they met at a restaurant because destiny planned it, she later learnt that Shoaib had actually set it up after a teammate told him that she would be there. Within months of meeting each other, the couple knew they wanted to spend their lives together. Shoaib met

Sania's family in Dubai and requested his parents to meet the Mirzas formally with a marriage proposal. Unfortunately for them, the media, with its daily search for controversy, turned their relationship into a battleground between the two nations—in the Indian press, it became 'our' superstar marrying into 'their' culture. Imran says, 'For any parent, a daughter's marriage is very special. But my feelings were mixed amid all the media hue and cry.'

Despite the many honours Sania brought the nation, her loyalty was questioned in this chauvinistic tone. She was asked whether she would change her nationality and who she would cheer for in an India-Pakistan cricket match. Sania remained calm and rational and said, several times, 'I cheer for India, but hope that Shoaib scores a century. We are getting married, not making any political statement on (Indo-Pak) relations.'

Sania tells me, 'We met, fell in love and wanted to spend our lives together and it was really as simple as that. People used to ask me whether I considered the fact that he was from Pakistan. It never struck me or him that we were from countries that didn't get along. That was just not how we were brought up.'

The couple married in April 2010; both their nikah in Hyderabad and the *walima* in Lahore were covered by a media blitzkrieg. Sania wore her mother's wedding *sari*, and looked resplendent despite having to constantly defend herself and her new husband. Even now, when she has continued to play for India and not relinquished her nationality or her home, the controversy has not been put to rest. When she was made brand ambassador of the state of Telangana, certain right-wing politicians raised objections because she was married to a Pakistani. Again, Sania had to defend herself, saying she was 'born an Indian, will remain an Indian and die an Indian.'

The couple has set up house in Dubai—a neutral venue and close enough to both their home countries. Ask her what she admires about Shoaib and pat comes the reply, 'He is extremely patient. If we have fights, nine out of ten times, they are started by me, and he barely argues. Being married to someone who understands the pressures that go with playing sports really helps. When you lose a match you don't have to explain things to the other person. They know that they just need to back off and stay away for a couple of hours.'

I realize that spending time together at home is not the norm for this couple. 'When I don't travel for myself I travel with him. It's easier for me to accompany him as mine is an individual sport but his is a team sport, which means he gets little room to manoeuvre,' says Sania.

When not on tour, Sania prefers to stay at home, laze, watch movies and surf the Internet; music, especially popular Bollywood numbers, is a passion. She enjoys swimming and never misses her daily prayers and reading of the Quran. And, as a young woman who loves fashion, she owns more than 300 pairs of shoes. Singh describes Sania as 'headstrong, and more like a boy,' and tells me that her one quirk is an irrational love for Chinese food—'What she eats in one meal, I cannot eat in a week! And she is a big bully, who is always in good spirits.'

An injury Sania sustained in 2017 forced her to spend 2018 on rest and recovery. As luck would have it, she was also pregnant with her and Shoaib's first child, who was born in October 2018. True to their progressive mindset, they named him Izhaan Mirza-Malik, keeping both the cultures they came from in mind. And such is her commitment to her sport that Sania was back to the grind within three months of giving birth, working to get back to her fitness schedule.

Sania talks to her younger sister Anam, a basketball player-turned-journalist, every day for an hour, even if she is on tour. 'We have a difference of eight years between us and weren't so close before. But now I believe I can relate to her and we've really bonded over the past few years,' says Anam.

## DOUBLES DESTINY

When Sania slipped out of the top 100, there were media reports that she had slacked off but the truth was that Sania switched lanes and began focusing on the doubles circuit. The well-timed decision has paid off—she has managed to seal her position in the top five for doubles, winning thirty-six WTA doubles titles in her career with as many as twelve different partners.

One of the things to admire about the manner in which she conducts herself professionally is her forthrightness and dignity. Sania did not qualify automatically for the 2012 London Olympics because she was not in the top ten, and had to wait for a wild card entry. When it did happen, Sania was embroiled in a controversy that, once again, was not of her own making; it involved the allocation of a partner to Leander Paes alongside whom both Mahesh Bhupathi and Rohan Bopanna refused to play. The All India Tennis

Association allowed Paes to choose his partner for the mixed doubles – Sania was expected to step up. She had just won the French Open in partnership with Bhupathi and did not appreciate being made a pawn in this controversy. She released a written statement: 'While I feel honoured and privileged to have been chosen to partner Leander Paes, the manner and timing of the announcement reeks of male chauvinism.'

Leander and Sania finally did represent India at the 2012 Olympics, but lost in the quarter-finals.

The next year, Sania did consider missing the Asian Games to improve her doubles rankings, as the tournament isn't recognized by the WTA. Instead, she ended up captaining the Indian tennis squad and won two medals. Under her guidance, the team won a total of five medals of a possible seven. This success came after another Grand Slam victory—the US Open.

'She loves to defy the odds. If she is entering the court with Serena Williams then she is not going to be enamoured of Serena and will believe that she can beat her. Whether she does or not is beside the point, but the belief stays with her,' says Imran about Sania's optimism and determination.

Sania says, 'Everyone is beatable. I played Hingis in Kolkata for the first time in a semi-final before 5000 people. She played an outstanding match. I came off court, knowing there was nothing I could have done differently. But three days later, we went to Korea where I beat her. Six months later, we played in America and I won again. She retired two months after that. You can't be judged based on one or two matches.'

Eventually, Sania and Hingis partnered as a doubles team and went on to win a number of tournaments, propelling them to No. 1 in WTA doubles rankings in 2015. The feather in this team's cap, however, will probably always be the 2015 Doubles Wimbledon win, which became Sania's first Grand Slam Doubles win. They split in August of 2016 after a string of poor performances.

Sania's biggest dream is still in the making, though; she began building the Sania Mirza Tennis Academy in Murtuzaguda, Hyderabad, in 2013. As I am shown around the magnificent academy, I can see why she is excited—'The academy is the biggest contribution that I am going to make.' Spread over an extensive area, it has nine plexi-paved tennis courts and three clay courts of Grand Slam standards. It also provides access to international coaches.

'I don't have support from the government—it's all my own investment, including the land. I am going to make this dream come true on my own.'

Imran, who is at the academy full-time, says, 'We are setting up the academy so we can give back to the country what we have earned in the last twenty years.'

Sania makes it a point to play with the younger players here whenever she is in Hyderabad. If anyone shows promise, they are groomed by the tennis ace herself. She tells me, 'One of our main goals is to try and get kids from rural areas because people have this misconception that tennis is only for the elite, like golf.'

In her bid to contribute to the sport she loves, Sania is now one of the four vice presidents of the Indian Tennis Players Association (ITPA).

'It's very easy for me to say that I have fame, I have money, I have a perfect husband, so I could easily not work hard any more. The average tennis career is very short. After three surgeries I could have said that. But I like to fight back hardest when people think that I am out for good. It's this spirit that kept me going right from the start,' Sania says to me, when I ask her how she stays motivated.

The greatest testimonial of what she inspires comes from her younger sister Anam—'She taught me to believe in myself, no matter who I'm up against, no matter if the whole country is against me.' And when Anam got engaged mid-September to Akbar Rasheed, Sania was by her side, providing all support.

Bold, honest and outspoken, Sania is an Indian woman of the twenty-first century—'If I were not a celebrity, I would behave the exact same way I am behaving today. Maybe that works against me. But I am not going to change that. I have always been true to myself and my family, and I don't ever want to be any other way.'

# MAHESH BHUPATHI

*Sania Mirza became India's first woman player to pick up a Grand Slam title when she won the Australian Open in 2009 with compatriot* **Mahesh Bhupathi**, *regarded as one of the best doubles players in the world who has partnered some leading names. Sania is someone he has known from her childhood and the rapport they share on court and off has helped them win many a Grand Slam title. Bhupathi offers his perceptions on all that enables them to win when they partner each other and Sania's supreme strengths: her forehand, which serves as 'a weapon', and her own mental toughness and individualistic personality that have seen her through many a controversy.*

**How did your association with Sania begin, and how would you describe her?**

Sania always had a tremendous amount of talent. We, as a family, have been associated with the Mirzas for a long time. She had a short stint at my dad's tennis academy, and then, we started managing her when she was fifteen. I was present when she won her junior Wimbledon doubles title. There was no doubt in anybody's mind that she was talented and she has been very fortunate to have been able to make the most of it.

Sania has a very strong personality. One has to be very strong mentally to reach the level in sports that she has; one has to be able to deal with both success and failure. At the same time, the fact that she has been through much controversy in her short professional career has made her stronger and more rounded [as an individual].

**You and Sania partnered consistently between 2007 and 2012. What does she bring to the court as a doubles partner? Are some players, like the two of you, inclined towards doubles?**

Playing singles or doubles depends on your individual capabilities and ability to handle both games. Most top women players play singles and doubles except Serena [Williams] and Maria [Sharapova]. Most of the time, one has to find a partner who can complement one's own style in doubles. In Sania's case, there is a solidity in her ground strokes and she understands the angles and the intricacies of playing doubles. She needs someone who can complement her and make use of her strength when putting the ball over the net. For me personally, I am able to complement her and finish off the point at the net when she is picking up big strokes. While Sania had a successful singles career, she had an even more successful one playing doubles.

**How important is temperament and understanding between partners? How would you compare Sania with some of the partners you have played with in the past?**

Doubles and singles are different disciplines. They have different intricacies, different courts, and different angles. It is tough to compare partners and I have been blessed to play with many world-class players. But Sania was also a friend, so it made it more enjoyable and definitely precious to win two Grand Slams with her.

**As an international athlete such as yourself, what level of preparedness and finesse in the game is required to reach the top?**

There are no shortcuts, especially when you are trying to become the best player in the world. The level of preparedness, it has to be better than everybody else in the world otherwise you are not going to be at the top. You need to make that extra time to practise, to prepare, and to become rough and tough in matches, and to do more than what everybody else is doing.

**Sania and you together won the Grand Slam. As a senior, how do you see her having improved her performance over the years?**

She's winning consistently and has been on tour for ten years now. She started touring very young, winning her first tour in Hyderabad at the age of seventeen. She deserves much credit for performing consistently day in and day out.

Sania works very hard. Making a comeback after three surgeries is extremely challenging. She has evolved as she has had to make adjustments to her game as required by the injuries. She deserves to be commended for that.

**Sania was recently awarded the Rajiv Gandhi Khel Ratna Award and the Padma Bhushan. What are the qualities in Sania that make her a role model for young sportspersons?**

Sania, in general, is a world-beater. She has come up through a lot of trials and tribulations by the media, and fought through everything, personally and professionally. She has created a big movement for girls to want to become champions in all sports, and she has shown the world that it can be done from any perspective, and girls around the country are rallying to try and become professionals in sports.

I admire Sania's mental toughness, to be honest. She is able to understand the complexities of becoming a superstar, and she works towards it daily, faultlessly. She has single-minded focus, and in today's world that's the only way to achieve great things.

**What do you think is the way forward for her?**

About the future, only she can tell. She is among the top ten in the world and as long as she wants to play, she is going to be competitive at that level.

# SAINA NEHWAL

•

*Comparatively it is easy to reach the top but extremely difficult to remain there because of the pressure. Only the toughest can survive at that level and Saina has done that commendably well. This shows her mental toughness and also her never-say-die attitude. She has set extremely high standards for the players of the next generation.*

**—PRAKASH PADUKONE**

•

Sportspersons are defined by the sport they play. And when they succeed, they gain much from the sport—fame, wealth and glory. Very few, though, have the ability or get the chance to give back to their sport. Saina Nehwal could, and did.

In India, badminton, like any other sport that isn't cricket, was not given too much importance; in fact, it was seen as a game played by families, on picnics. On 22 October 2012 Saina changed that, when the badminton champion trumped Dhoni's men in headlines across the country. The then concurrent 4–1 series victory by India's cricket team against Sri Lanka was relegated to the inside pages, while Saina, with her Olympic bronze, dazzled on front pages. She managed to make badminton a serious sport, and a fashionable one.

At Hyderabad's Gopichand Academy, registrations soar, and coaches believe that even fifty branches will not meet the demand for badminton coaching. 'Saina has played a very big part in popularising badminton in India, and it has become a major sport in the country, thanks to her stellar performance at the world level,' says legendary badminton champion, Prakash Padukone.

At the time of this writing, Saina was back as world No. 1, wresting the spot from Spain's Carolina Marin and was conferred the Padma Bhushan at the 2016 Republic Day honours. She had climbed to the top spot earlier, displacing Olympic gold medallist Li Xuerui, but had fallen to second spot as Marin had moved ahead. Then, even as Saina lost in the final of the 2015 BWF World Championship to Marin, the Indian nevertheless made it to the top spot in the BWF rankings, the first Indian woman ever to do so.

Each time she plays, she carries the dreams and hopes of a nation with her, but wears them lightly. A fighter on court and an introvert off it, Saina has a spine of steel; a determined, intelligent young woman who keeps her eyes on her target at all times. She has not only survived the maelstrom of fame, but also managed to stay unscathed by it. This is proven to me when I enter the Nehwal home in Hyderabad; there is no bluster to it at all, and pride of place in the modest house is given to a cabinet that showcases Saina's medals. The bronze, silver and gold wins echo the journey that Saina's taken herself and her family on. And I feel privileged to talk about it with them.

## GOD'S OWN CHILD

Saina, second daughter of Harvir Singh Nehwal and Usha Rani, was born on 17 March 1990. While her parents were thrilled that she was born a girl, Saina's extended family were not pleased. Saina's grandmother, too, subscribed to this philosophy and was devastated by the news of a second granddaughter.

This meant that Saina's parents—untouched by gender biases—have always been especially supportive of their young daughter. Her mother's nickname for Saina was Steffi, after Steffi Graf.

An energetic child, Saina was always up to mischief, which led to several mishaps. Usha tells me that four-year-old Saina cut her finger deeply while playing, but did not cry, which led her mother to understand that her daughter was a tough girl, and a fighter. The family—Saina's older sister, Abu, included—spent a lot of time at the faculty club in the Haryana Agricultural University, where Harvir and Usha played badminton. They were a formidable pair who won tournaments. Harvir tells me that, uncannily, the first time Saina stepped on to a court, she laughed with indescribable delight.

In 1998 Harvir was offered the post of principal scientist at the Indian Council of Agricultural Research (ICAR). The post meant that he would move from the state to national cadre, but it also meant that the family would have to move to Hyderabad. The decision to shift base was a tough one and was finally taken by Usha. Saina believes it was fate. Once they settled into their new lives, Harvir was keen that Saina should not be lonely and he signed her up for karate classes. She did exceptionally well, reaching the brown belt category, but her tryst with the game ended after a mishap. And Saina was back to her routine of school, home and no friends.

Around that time, Saina accompanied her father on a visit to the Lal Bahadur Stadium in Hyderabad; he was considering hiring it for a tournament. While her father was making his inquiries, Saina was rifling through badminton racquets and playing with them and she was spotted by P.S.S. Nani Prasad Rao, a noted badminton coach. Impressed with the way she held the racquet, he suggested coaching her over the summer. Saina's badminton-loving parents needed no convincing and the path opened up for Saina.

While she confesses to being 'daddy's girl', Saina inherited her love and passion for badminton from her mother. Usha was the better player of the couple, working her way into district-level tournaments and she even played in the early days when she was pregnant with Saina. Clearly, her unborn child absorbed that dedication to the game. 'My mother was a player, she understood the game and she used to say to me, "I'll make you an Olympic champion,"' says Saina.

Saina tells me that it was this belief that nudged her to dream big—'I was very focused and you cannot focus like that without someone to help you. My mom was that person. She was really into the sport and would not let my focus shift. I was studying or playing and studying or playing. When I used to play badly in these games she used to scold me.'

Usha could be tough, but she was Saina's support system in every way. When her daughter's legs ached from rigorous training, Usha would offer massages. And yet, whenever Usha thought Saina had not played well, she ticked her off. Saina tells me that while her father inspired her to play, it was her mother from whom she learnt the art of winning and losing. One time, after she played an under-ten tournament poorly, her mother slapped her as she came off court. Saina's peers laughed but she remembers telling them that her mother had done that for her betterment.

It is incredible to me that Saina was able to view the situation constructively at such a young age; clearly, she knew she had much to achieve. Her coach and badminton ace, Pullela Gopichand, explains what drives her—'Saina's biggest asset is her unrelenting patience. When she came to me, she did not have a naturally perfect game. But, right from the beginning it was clear to her that the only thing that she needed to win a game was a combination of dedication and hard work. And so, she would patiently just keep at it with power and grit.'

The collateral damage of all of this, unfortunately, was Saina's academic career, which hit her hard because she was a brilliant student. She was forced to skip her first year intermediate examination as it clashed with the Melbourne Commonwealth Games and, later, she missed her supplementary exams, too, because she was in the Philippines. Eventually, Saina and her family came to terms with the fact that she was going to have to give up academics altogether.

## MAKING IT HAPPEN

Harvir Singh believes that it was his daughter's fortune that brought the family to Hyderabad. His work as a scientist was not lucrative enough to support her though, but no sacrifice daunted him if it would help Saina get closer to the top. He had to dip into his provident fund six times, even at a time when Saina's potential was not clear to them. He turned down several career promotions because it would mean that they had to leave Hyderabad. Keeping his daughter's badminton dream in mind, he chose to remain in the same post until retirement.

'Once I realized the potential in Saina, I completely devoted myself to ensure she becomes an international-level player. She was just focusing on her game. There were no movies, meals out, parties, etc.—nothing that would have distracted her. The paucity of funds was the only hindrance to giving her the best training and equipment, but we managed to cross that hurdle too,' he says to me.

I am touched to learn that Saina was never told about these decisions because her parents did not want her to feel conflicted; she was only given the good news, always. She did not even know how much her racquets cost.

Fellow badminton player and now life partner Parupalli Kashyap—who also trained at Gopichand Academy—tells me that Saina's parents had a deep knowledge and love for the sport; they mentored and groomed her to be an ace player—'Saina's mother played at the state level, so she knew what Saina needed when she was young and just a beginner. Her father played at the national level and, hence, he was able to help Saina as she grew older and started playing nationally.'

Within the first year of starting to play, Saina began to show indications of her enormous talent. She tells me that she lived with dark circles under her eyes—unlike her peers—because she constantly worried about turning professional. And, yet, coach Vimal Kumar tells me that he remembers seeing a 'bubbly' ten-year-old Saina playing amazingly well across age categories—'She was quite a focused and intense girl. The physical rigours she endured were tremendous, compared to many others. These points gave her that mental edge to move forward.'

Saina won the National Junior Badminton Championship in 2004; at fourteen, she was the surprise of that tournament. It was a stunning win, and she kept getting better, building on her strengths. 'The best thing about Saina's game is her consistency. She doesn't stagnate or cower. She plays with aggression and attempts to improve her techniques with every game,' says Gopichand. Saina defended her title the year after and was ready to enter the next level.

The seniors' world was more competitive, and Aparna Popat was still the great Indian hope. In 2005, Saina reached the final of the Senior National Championships, losing to Popat in the title match. Even so, she was firmly on India's radar. The Asian Satellite Tournament and the Uber Cup in 2006 followed, with her becoming a firm fixture in the national squad. The Commonwealth Games 2006—the big fish, as it were—were around the corner, and Saina was not too sure of how she might fare. But determination can beget luck.

Popat lost a crucial match to a British player at the Commonwealth Games and was injured. Coach Kumar tells me that when it happened, Saina was seated next to him. 'And she said to me, "If you give me an opportunity, I feel I can beat this [British] girl." She was sixteen at the time. I looked at her and knew she was not arrogant because she firmly believed that she could beat that player. I put this forward to other coaches and despite them feeling that she was too young, we fielded her. Saina won all matches including against Singapore and rose to world No. 6.'

Saina was a totally different player compared to her opponents; she was aggressive, and blended power with excellent technique. This often made her opponents look helpless. Kumar tells me how Saina even surprised Indonesian coaches with her determination and focus—'I remember coaching her for the 2006 Commonwealth Games. She would always keep very aloof. She woke early, did her stretches and waited for us at the training centre.' That year Saina won gold at the Philippines Open and the title match at the Junior World Cup in Seoul. She was now Popat's contemporary, and India sat up and took notice.

Saina calls 2007 'the year of the tears'. Naysayers and critics dismissed her success and questioned her talent. Saina's parents stood by her, helping her understand the vagaries of winning and losing. With the family's encouragement, however, Saina was able to treat the dip as a learning curve, and the year became the fulcrum of her career.

Arjuna Award recipient and ace badminton player Kashyap analyses the qualities that have contributed to Saina's rise—'Her hard work, dedication and her ability to push herself every single day to get better at her game are solely responsible for her success graph. She may not be as skilful as compared to other players, but she has an unbelievable mental strength, which reflects in her game. Her concentration and determination on court are two of her biggest strengths.'

From 2008 to 2010, Saina went from win to win, and no one could cast aspersions on her again. In 2008, Saina was ranked at twenty-three, and though she missed winning a medal at the Beijing Olympics, spectators and critics agreed that hers had been one of the best badminton matches by an Indian at any Olympics. A few months later, Saina won the prestigious Chinese Taipei Open and by the end of the year, made her way into the top ten.

## ON TOP OF THE WORLD

In early 2009, Saina was world No. 9. She was the first Indian woman to win the Indonesian Super Series, and won at the Indian Open Grand Prix. The next year—which she calls her best yet—Saina won the Indian Open, Singapore Open, Indonesian Open and Hong Kong Open. At the Commonwealth Games in Delhi, Saina won the gold, and scaled up to world No. 2. And she repeated this feat in 2018, making her the only Indian singles player who has won two gold medals at the Commonwealth Games.

P.V. Sindhu, who trained alongside Saina, shares, 'I learnt certain technicalities of the game by watching Saina, who continues to inspire me. I work hard because she does, and I want to be as successful, sincere and committed as her.'

In 2012, Saina won the bronze medal at the London Olympics, when her opponent Wang Xin forfeited the game while leading. She tells me that people wondered whether her opponent's injury and subsequent withdrawal from the game made her happy, because it meant an Olympic win for her. But Saina couldn't imagine why they say that—'I am a very relaxed and cool person on court. When [Wang Xin] fell I was not thinking about the medal, I was thinking what happened to her.'

That said, the win did catapult Saina into the eye of the storm; she won praise from legendary cricketer Sachin Tendulkar, who even gifted her a BMW on behalf of the company. Batsman Yuvraj Singh tweeted—'Saina, you beauty. I'm sure like me every Indian is proud of you.'

Ask Harvir about the Olympic win and he says that it did not make Saina complacent; she trained her eye on the Denmark Super Series and went on to win it.

Saina's achievements make a long roster at the time of this writing, and shifts between the No. 1 and 2 slots. When I discuss that with Kashyap, he says, 'Saina is extremely focused and goal-oriented. She strives to get better and fitter, especially after the slew of injuries. On court, you will never see Saina wasting her time or taking it easy. Despite being senior to her, there is a lot that I can learn from her. Her primary strength is her consistency—she brings her 100 per cent every day and that makes her an ace international player.'

For her part, Saina tells me, 'You have to be hard if you want to be good. Especially in India, nobody did so well in badminton. It's a very difficult sport. The rallies are very fast, and there is a lot of strain on your legs. I have not seen a girl from India as physically strong [as the Chinese]. I changed all of that and showed Indians that we can beat the Chinese and any other players.'

In 2009, Saina was given the Arjuna Award following her winning the Indonesian Open Super series title. She had also won the Chinese Taipei Grand Prix gold. It was one huge step for her as she accepted the award from President Pratibha Patil.

In the wake of her great success she even benefited her coach Gopichand. Gopichand was given the Dronacharya Award, India's top honour for sports coaches. After the award ceremony, Saina, then nineteen, dedicated it to her parents and her coach. She said it would motivate her to go for gold at the London Olympics in 2012.

Her march remained relentless, and in the very next year she was conferred both the Padma Shri and the Rajiv Gandhi Khel Ratna Awards. The Padma Shri came barely four months after the Arjuna Award. It carries a medal, a scroll of honour and a cash prize of Rs 5 lakh. The Khel Ratna, India's highest sporting honour, comprises a bronze statuette, a citation and a cash prize of Rs 7.5 lakh. She missed the opportunity, though, to personally collect the prize from President Patil that August 29 morning, because she was in Paris fighting at the World Championships. She lost in the quarter-finals. In 2016, the Government of India conferred the Padma Bhushan on Saina Nehwal.

None of these came a day too soon.

## DOING THE MATH

Parents whose children dream of glory in a sport know that the biggest challenge is organising funds. While it was a challenge for Harvir, too, he was determined to support his daughter in her chase towards her dream and Saina's determination was the motivation for him. He says, 'Saina has faith in her game and is a disciplined sportsperson. A non-demanding daughter, she is completely dedicated to badminton.'

Until 2003, the Sports Authority of India paid Saina a small monthly honorarium. Even as her parents made the sacrifices they did, in 2005, the Mittal Champions Trust chose to sponsor Saina, which would allow her to participate in any tournament she chose for the next four years. In 2007, the trust gave her an additional lump sum, which went a long way. At the same time, Saina was being offered a variety of endorsements. She signed a deal with Rhiti Sports Management for a huge amount, which was unprecedented in Indian sports except for cricket. The ties with Rhiti Sports Management were however short-lived, and she soon moved on to KWAN entertainment and marketing solutions.

While she enjoys the bells and whistles of promotions, and meeting other sponsorship and brand requirements, Saina tells me she is not too fond of being on shoots but understands that it is an important piece of the bigger picture. I am impressed by her pragmatism. In the age of instant stardom, it is easy to get wooed by glamour, but Saina quips that to her it is the game that is glamorous. And it is interesting to note that despite her nonchalance, Saina has made India fall in love with badminton.

Coach Kumar says, 'The profile of the game has really gone up because of her. As an Indian girl who has achieved so much, she is a great example. After [former athlete] P.T. Usha, Saina has become a real role model.'

## OFF THE COURT

Saina tells me people always point out to her that she is a tigress on court but silent off it. There was a time when her seniors complained that she showed them no respect. The truth is that Saina is an introvert who comes alive as she plays, and is steadied by her routine. She starts her day at 6 a.m., with a hearty breakfast. After rigorous training and practice sessions at the

Gopichand Academy for four hours, she has lunch and takes a short siesta before getting back to work for three hours. After dinner, she listens to Bollywood music, or watches others' games on television. In between her routine, Saina makes time to hit her personal gym at home and practise yoga, which helps her concentrate.

That said, as tough as she is on court, Saina is a normal woman off of it, with a love for ice cream and shopping. She has no time for a social life, and confesses to me that when she travels, she often feels quite scared when she wakes up at night, without her parents close by.

Saina tells me that she'd have never progressed without her coaches, or the unflinching support of her parents. She was initially trained by the esteemed coach Nani Singh and was then spotted by the famous S.M. Arif, the Hyderabadi legend of badminton. After she became national junior champion, Gopichand, took the initiative to nurture her talent.

He tells me, 'Saina is not a natural player, but she is a terrific student [of the game]. If you teach her a particular game play, she will practise it till she has got it perfectly, and then use the stroke at a critical juncture in the game, such as when it is tied at twenty.'

As a special stint, Atik Jouhari, the Indonesian badminton legend, coached Saina in 2009–10. This stint, she says, was very important as it polished her game and she worked really hard on her technique. In August 2014, Saina moved to the Prakash Padukone Academy, shifting base from Hyderabad to Bengaluru after the World Championships, to train under coach Vimal Kumar. 'She wants to be the top player in the world and she is a very demanding girl. She will ask you straight questions. She wants to know that I am putting in the effort,' says Kumar.

Saina acknowledges that she has only a few years of the game left but that doesn't scare her. She also talks about the importance of infrastructure in the country; the current scenario requires serious attention and there is a need to include foreign coaches for training. True to her calling, she intends to set up her own badminton academy to further her legacy. She tells me, 'I got an offer from Haryana to [open] the academy there, and from Bengaluru. I will do it someday for sure.'

I ask her why she wants to set up an academy and she is quick to rationalize—'The area to look into here is the infrastructure of the game. Getting more coaches from abroad is crucial—coaches who can give full time to the game, who can be there from 4.30 in the morning till night, training kids in each and every part of the country. My dream is to have 300 to 400 players or even 1000 players of the same level, and then it will be the same as China. I am not asking to change it suddenly, but why not begin it now so that in the future we can see the change?'

It is easier for me to understand Saina's passion for founding an academy in this context. Right now, however, her game is her priority and she is willing to wait for the opportune moment to start investing her time in an academy.

Kashyap tells me that Saina is very open to learning and discussing her training or the game—'There is a lot that one can learn from Saina, one being her never-say-die attitude while training and in tournaments. She pushes and inspires all of us to train hard and play harder.' Saina's ambitious outlook clubbed with her zeal to encourage and push other players to improve their games reminds me of Sindhu's words, 'I consider Saina to be a terrific player who not just practises with me but also discusses my game after I am back from a tournament.'

If you think about Saina's life—the odds that were stacked against her by her own family when she was born, the fact that her parents struggled to meet the financial demands of her ambitions and the cricket-obsessed mindset of India—she could have been the average Indian girl from her socio-economic strata, who goes through school and college, is asked to marry a suitable boy and buries her dreams in the minutiae of day-to-day life. But she hasn't, and her parents didn't let her, even if she ever thought of giving up.

Harvir tells me that his biggest contribution as a father was to bring Saina to a badminton court when she was a little above eight years old. In less than a decade, she has brought recognition to India in one of its least regarded games and is one of the few women players globally—and the only one from India—who has been able to challenge the domination of the Chinese in badminton. When I ask her why Saina is the new icon of India's youth, Sindhu says, 'She has proved it to the world that no one is unbeatable in this sport any more by repeatedly getting everything right on the day she plays against any star opponent.'

As a hat tip to her courage, a biopic titled *Saina* is being directed by Amol Gupte, with actress Shraddha Kapoor playing the title role.

## FAME AND FORTUNE

Years of struggle and determination have brought Saina many laurels. And according to Pullela Gopichand, the team of Saina and P.V. Sindhu could bring home many more medals for Indian badminton. Saina remains thoroughly committed to securing a medal at the Tokyo Olympics 2020.

When Saina finished runner-up to Marin at the All-England Badminton Championship in Birmingham in March, one of the premier championships in the world of badminton, she was given a cash award of Rs 25 lakh by the government. Saina became the third Indian and first woman from the country to reach the final of the prestigious tournament, Prakash Padukone and Pullela Gopichand having won the men's singles title of the tournament in 1980 and 2001, respectively.

Not only was this stellar recognition of her efforts, but the money has gone a long way in shaping her career and the country's pride associated with it.

It has been a long journey from Hisar to the elite of the world, a journey that has been dotted with incredible tales of heroics by the youngster, and a story that has all the ingredients of a potboiler movie script. Today she is one of the highest paid athletes of India (outside cricket) and has a fan following that rivals that of cricketers. More importantly, she has become the role model for millions of girls aspiring for empowerment.

Today the country waits eagerly to see her as one of the Olympic greats, hopefully with a gold medal. But till then it will be hard work all the way for Saina.

# SACHIN TENDULKAR

*Those who occupy the top rung know what the climb entails. **Sachin Tendulkar** is an icon in everyone's eyes; **Saina Nehwal** is the first Indian woman to become world No. 1 in badminton. The cricket legend, who remains an unobtrusive mentor to her, says that high achievers like her think and execute differently. They do not look at problems as roadblocks, but as spurs to solutions. The two world-class sportspersons also have a deep love for the game they play, a passion that powers all those endless hours of practice on the path to perfection. Tendulkar talks about Saina's win and the need for humility when the honours come in.*

**Saina was the world No. 1 this year in badminton. You must know only too well how it feels to be at the top.**

It does feel very nice to be at the top and it's a proud moment for all of us that Saina was No. 1. Getting there requires great sacrifice—you spend less time with family and friends—hard work and discipline. It means chasing one's dream to the exclusion of everything else to achieve this feat. Saina would have done all this to reach where she is today.

**In day-to-day terms, what do you think working towards such an achievement entails for Saina?**

I know—and Saina would, too—how difficult and physically taxing it is at the highest level. Any sportsperson wishing to excel has to be passionate about the sport and has to be prepared to go the extra mile. And I can say this from experience: I never looked at my watch when I was practising—I was out on the field until I felt satisfied in my heart. So it was not about how many deliveries I faced. Likewise, for Saina, I am sure she was not counting how many shuttles she hit every day, but what it took to feel satisfied with her session of practice. This apart, [Pullela] Gopichand took a lot of interest in working with her and bringing her game up to a different level.

**How does one continue to stay at the top?**

The guys who are at the top are invariably the ones who work the hardest. They think differently, they execute their plans differently.

We tend to overestimate problems and underestimate our ability to solve those problems. But the moment we learn to start flipping those two viewpoints and shifting the focus to finding solutions, we find a way. And that's when success comes.

Getting to the top is always tough for any sportsman, regardless of experience or skill at the game. When we accept this truth, the pressure is off because we know then that there is no shortcut to success. Both Saina and I have a capacity for hard work. And to stay at the No. 1 position takes plenty of hard work. It will test one's commitment and one's character. Saina has passed all those tests so far or else it would not have been possible for her to become world No. 1. The question is, can there be a repeat performance every now and again?

### Do you think Saina can repeat her success?

Yes, of course. From whatever interactions we have had, and from whatever I have seen of her game, she comes across as a balanced person and humble, and to me, that is really important. The better you play and the more accolades you get, the more humble you have to be, I think. I see that in her because I think her family, too, is like that. It is important to celebrate victories, but not to get carried away. Also, it's equally important to not lose heart in the face of defeat. And the family plays a major role in this.

### You gifted Saina a BMW. Why did you specifically choose her for the felicitation?

I just handed over the keys to her; it was not a gift from me per se. My contribution was to get a good deal for BMW, being the company's brand ambassador; the brand wished to gift her for her stellar performance. It feels good to see a fellow sportsman being appreciated like this as it is equally important that sports personalities other than cricketers also get appreciated and rewarded for their great performances and I am extremely happy that happened and I wanted to be there for it.

### Saina's parents have absolutely stood by her through all the ups and downs in her career. How important would you say the support of family is?

This is extremely important. We always look to our loved ones for support and their response to our careers. If that response is not positive and helpful, it has a negative impact on us. I am sure that without their support it would not have been possible for Saina either to reach the top.

I used to exchange messages with both Saina and her family, and I always told them that they must continue to support her because this was helping her, and the whole country was looking forward to her success.

**You were the only mentor Saina has had, apart from her coaches. What was that relationship like?**

I don't think I have guided her in badminton. I have always appreciated her performance—that is all we can do. I am not an expert to tell her what to do in her sport, but as a well-wisher, and above all, as an Indian, I have supported her consistently—regardless of whether she wins or loses. That is enormously encouraging for a sportsman. I have experienced it myself and I would want to extend that to her.

**Saina, who hails from a small town in Haryana, started out playing badminton quite by chance, and success followed. What do you think lies at the root of her achievements?**

If there is passion for the sport, the results will follow. Actions follow thoughts. If one is thinking right, the right things will happen. Saina's success is a sure example of that. When I was in school, I, too, started out with a different sport: martial arts. It was the craze then. After watching Bruce Lee movies we all wanted to learn it. But luckily, I found the cricket bat and stopped pursuing the nunchaku. And it worked out for me.

**What does Saina's success mean in a larger context for India?**

Achievements such as Saina's will always be celebrated. People will be talking about her career even twenty-five years from now.

Her contribution to badminton lies in the fact that she has been able to inspire many youngsters to pick up the racquet and want to be the next Saina.

She has raised the bar in terms of taking the sport to the next level and inspiring young people. I think this is similar to what Sania has done for tennis.

**Is there any piece of advice you have for Saina Nehwal?**

Stay the way you are, don't let that passion die out. Continue to be in love with the sport.

# ACKNOWLEDGEMENTS

To the sixteen women for inviting me into their lives and believing in me.

To the hundred contributors for sharing their time and thoughts.

To my family for their unconditional love and trust.

To my friends for being the support system and strength.

To Deepak Parekh for facilitating the progress of the book.

To Penguin Random House for publishing my book.

# CONTRIBUTORS

**Ajay Banga** on Indra Nooyi

**Ajay Piramal** on Swati Piramal

**Akash Ambani** on Nita Ambani

**Anam Mirza** on Sania Mirza

**Anand Mahindra** on Swati Piramal

**Ananya Goenka** on Nita Ambani

**Anil Agarwal** on Zia Mody

**Anupama Chopra** on Priyanka Chopra

# CONTRIBUTORS

*Anuradha Mahindra* on Nita Ambani

*Azim Premji* on Yasmeen Premji

*Bahram Vakil* on Zia Mody

*Bandana Tewari* on Anamika Khanna

*Chanda Kochhar* on Indra Nooyi

*Charles Atkinson* on Mary Kom

*Cyril Shroff* on Zia Mody and Swati Piramal

*D. Shivakumar* on Indra Nooyi

*Deepak Parekh* on Kiran Mazumdar-Shaw and Zia Mody

*Devi Prasad Shetty* on Kiran Mazumdar-Shaw

*Dilip Shanghvi* on Swati Piramal

*Gita Piramal* on Rajashree Birla, Yasmeen Premji and Zia Mody

*Harvir Singh Nehwal* on Saina Nehwal

*Hasit Joshipura* on Swati Piramal and Kiran Mazumdar-Shaw

*Imran Mirza* on Sania Mirza

*Isha Ambani* on Nita Ambani

*Jaydev Mody* on Zia Mody

*K.V. Kamath* on Nita Ambani and Sudha Murty

# CONTRIBUTORS

*Kalyani Chawla* on Anamika Khanna

*Karan Johar* on Kareena Kapoor Khan

*Karisma Kapoor* on Kareena Kapoor Khan

*Khupreng Kom* on Mary Kom

*Kiran Mazumdar-Shaw* on Sudha Murty, Yasmeen Premji and Indra Nooyi

*Krishen Khanna* on Swati Piramal

*Kumar Mangalam Birla* on Rajashree Birla, Zia Mody and Shobhana Bhartia

*Madhukar Kamath* on Indra Nooyi

*Madhur Bhandarkar* on Priyanka Chopra

*Mahesh Bhupathi* on Sania Mirza

*Mangte Tonpa Kom* on Mary Kom

*Manish Malhotra* on Kareena Kapoor Khan

*Masaba Gupta* on Anamika Khanna

*Mukesh Ambani* on Nita Ambani

*N.R. Narayana Murthy* on Sudha Murty

*Nandan Nilekani* on Kiran Mazumdar-Shaw

*Narayanan Vaghul* on Kiran Mazumdar-Shaw and Swati Piramal

*Neerja Birla* on Rajashree Birla

**Onler Kom** on Mary Kom

**P.V. Sindhu** on Saina Nehwal

**Parineeti Chopra** on Priyanka Chopra

**Parupalli Kashyap** on Saina Nehwal

**Prakash Padukone** on Saina Nehwal

**Prasad Bidapa** on Anamika Khanna

**Priyanka Chopra** on Mary Kom

**Pullela Gopichand** on Saina Nehwal

**R.C. Bhargava** on Shobhana Bhartia

**R.K. Krishna Kumar** on Indra Nooyi

**Raghav Bahl** on Shobhana Bhartia

**Rajeev Sethi** on Indu Jain

**Ranjit Shahani** on Rajashree Birla and Swati Piramal

**Ranveer Singh** on Priyanka Chopra

**Rishad Premji** on Yasmeen Premji

**Rohan Murty** on Sudha Murty

**Rujuta Diwekar** on Kareena Kapoor Khan

**Sachin Tendulkar** on Nita Ambani, Mary Kom and Saina Nehwal

# CONTRIBUTORS

**Saif Ali Khan** *on Kareena Kapoor Khan*

**Samir Jain** *on Indu Jain*

**Sanjiv Goenka** *on Nita Ambani, Anamika Khanna and Shobhana Bhartia*

**Sanjoy Narayan** *on Shobhana Bhartia*

**Shah Rukh Khan** *on Nita Ambani and Saina Nehwal*

**Shakuntala Jain** *on Anamika Khanna*

**Shashi Tharoor** *on Shobhana Bhartia and Indu Jain*

**Shobhana Bhartia** *on Nita Ambani and Rajashree Birla*

**Siddharth Chopra** *on Priyanka Chopra*

**Siddharth Roy Kapur** *on Priyanka Chopra*

**Soli Sorabjee** *on Zia Mody*

**Sonam Kapoor** *on Anamika Khanna*

**Subhash Chandra** *on Shobhana Bhartia*

**Subroto Bagchi** *on Sudha Murty*

**Suhani Pittie** *on Anamika Khanna*

**Sunil Mittal** *on Zia Mody*

**Susmita Bagchi** *on Yasmeen Premji*

**Swati Piramal** *on Nita Ambani and Rajashree Birla*

# CONTRIBUTORS

*Tarun Tahiliani* on Anamika Khanna

*Tina Ambani* on Parmeshwar Godrej

*Trishla Jain* on Indu Jain

*U. Vimal Kumar* on Saina Nehwal

*Vasavdatta Bajaj* on Rajashree Birla

*Vijay Khanna* on Anamika Khanna

*Vijay Mallya* on Kiran Mazumdar-Shaw

*Vineet Jain* on Indu Jain

*Vinita Bali* on Indra Nooyi

*Vishal Sikka* on Sudha Murty

*Yuvraj Singh* on Sania Mirza

*Zahir Chinoy* on Yasmeen Premji

*Zena Soli Sorabjee* on Zia Mody

*Zoya Akhtar* on Priyanka Chopra